Ulaş Sunata

Highly Skilled Labor Migration

Ulaş Sunata

Highly Skilled Labor Migration

The Case of ICT Specialists from Turkey in Germany

LIT

Black Swan Phenomenon
Cover Illustration by Yiğit Unan and Ulaş Sunata

∞

Gedruckt auf alterungsbeständigem Werkdruckpapier entsprechend
ANSI Z3948 DIN ISO 9706

Bibliographic information published by the Deutsche Nationalbibliothek
The Deutsche Nationalbibliothek lists this publication in the Deutsche Nationalbibliografie; detailed bibliographic data are available in the Internet at http://dnb.d-nb.de.

ISBN 978-3-643-11003-9
Zugl.: Osnabrück, Univ., Diss., 2010

A catalogue record for this book is available from the British Library

Fresnostr. 2 D-48159 Münster
Tel. +49 (0) 2 51-620 320 Fax +49 (0) 2 51-922 60 99
e-Mail: lit@lit-verlag.de http://www.lit-verlag.de

Distribution:
In Germany: LIT Verlag Fresnostr. 2, D-48159 Münster
Tel. +49 (0) 2 51-620 32 22, Fax +49 (0) 2 51-922 60 99, e-mail: vertrieb@lit-verlag.de

In Austria: Medienlogistik Pichler-ÖBZ, e-mail: mlo@medien-logistik.at

In Switzerland: B + M Buch- und Medienvertrieb, e-mail: order@buch-medien.ch

In the UK: Global Book Marketing, e-mail: mo@centralbooks.com

In North America by:

Transaction Publishers
New Brunswick (U.S.A.) and London (U.K.)

Transaction Publishers
Rutgers University
35 Berrue Circle
Piscataway, NJ 08854

Phone: +1 (732) 445 - 2280
Fax: + 1 (732) 445 - 3138
for orders (U. S. only):
toll free (888) 999 - 6778
e-mail: orders@transactionpub.com

ACKNOWLEDGEMENTS

Looking back at the time that I have spent for this work, I see countless contributions from many individuals and institutions. Inevitably however, I hereby mention the most invaluable ones due to their crucial role in the development and execution of my work.

First of all my indebted gratitude goes the Hans Böckler Foundation for not only the full scholarship I've received for three years but also for their refreshing dedication to the ideal of another world. The financial support of DAAD in the early period of my study is gratefully acknowledged. I would like to mention the University of Osnabrück for its permission to carry out this thesis and to my colleagues, especially to Sigrid Pusch, at the Institute for Migration Research and Intercultural Studies (IMIS) for many useful hints and practical help. In particular, thoughtful comments of Anna Sosna, Snezana Stojcic, and Bethany Hicks were and still are of great help. Moreover, I would like to express my sincere acknowledgement of Claire Aanes, Sophie Wedin, Cliodhna Quigley, Max Kornhauser, Isak Sexson, and Robert Muil for their excellent editorial work for this thesis. I further extend my gratitude to all committee members, notably Prof. Dr. Andrea Lenschow as my primary supervisor and Prof. Dr. Andreas Pott as my associate supervisor, for having kindly accepted to review this thesis. I use this opportunity to especially thank Prof. Dr. Klaus J. Bade, Prof. Dr. Martin Kohli, Prof. Dr. Dirk Lange, Prof. Dr. Hans Joas, Prof. Dr. Helga Rittersberger-Tılıç, and Tanıl Bora.

I cordially thank all the participants who devoted time and shared their experiences during the conduction of the interviews and the people, who provided lodging in my fieldwork. I would like to express here my deepest gratitude to my beloved family for pouring into me all the good wishes in my life. I am so thankful to Dr. Bülent Anıl, Özgür Baykal, and Ümit Ezerce for all the inspiration they have offered to me over the years and to Barbara Gingele, Sabrina Lutz, Norman Frenzel, Patricia Gozalbez Canto, Phillip Casula, Dr. Bülent Küçük, Ulaş Şener, Tobias Sochocki, Sultan

Dağ, and Feride Kolikan who have supported me with their friendship throughout my stay in Germany. I am deeply grateful to my dear friends, Jochen Guter and Friederike Zigmann, for their constant precious support and chess rivalry during the course of my project. My utmost gratefulness goes to Alper "the speedy Gonzales" Açık for lifting me up when I could not do it on my own. Finally, I thank muscular and nervous systems of my body, which allows the dissertation completion, without a persistent companion.

This thesis is dedicated to Prof. Dr. Michael Bommes, who, perhaps unsurprisingly, had an unmatched contribution. Without his endless sacrifice and care throughout the work, the successful completion of the thesis could not come into question. As my principal advisor, he encouraged me at every stage of the work, from the incipient research proposal in 2005 till the happy end you are staring at now. He also guided me, and let me add, still does guide me with his immense patience through the subtleties of scientific writing. As a friend, he has never left me alone during my struggles with the migrant life in Osnabrück.

TABLE OF CONTENTS

LIST OF TABLES

LIST OF FIGURES

CHAPTER 1. OVERVIEW

1. Introduction

During the 1960s and 1970s migration from Turkey to Germany consisted mainly of labor migrants, the so-called "guest workers" (*Gastarbeiter*). Additionally, a considerable number of asylum seekers and refugees from Turkey have been migrating since the late 1970s. These waves of migration – combined with the second and third generation, marriages, and family unification that are all continuous consequences of the former kinds of migration – provide a fairly differentiated picture of the history of migration from Turkey to Germany. However, highly skilled labor migration (HSLM) as another form of migration, though scarcely researched, has increasingly emerged between these countries. Although contemporary migration from Turkey to Germany does not consist exclusively or even primarily of HSLM, there remains a noteworthy share of "highly skilled" labor (HSL) migrants from Turkey.

Even though labor migration from Turkey initially started to become institutionalized in the 1960s (Gitmez, 1983; Zürcher, 1993), recent years have witnessed a considerable rise in numbers of highly-qualified professionals and university graduates moving to Europe. Since the 1990s, Turkey has become a sending country of HSLM to most receiving countries in Europe, with the same tendency having already been found for the USA, Canada, and Australia, where more than half of the Turkish migrants are highly-qualified.[1] In particular, the geopolitical and historical importance of its migratory relations however long rendered Turkey the strongest origin country of HSLM to Germany. Turkey's political relationship with Europe has remained tense in many respects, including a pronounced fear of increased immigration of low quali-

[1] For the USA in comparison with other destination counties, HSLM from Turkey is well documented. See Oğuzkan, 1971; Kurtuluş, 1999; Akgün, 2000; Kaya; 2002; Sunata; 2002; Işığıçok, 2003; Tansel and Güngör, 2003.

fied persons.[2] In spite of growing HSLM, migration from Turkey remains a highly controversial issue in the discussions surrounding Turkey's future access to the EU (European Union). The fact that a large number of highly qualified Turkish-citizen immigrants move to Europe (in particular to Germany, the United Kingdom, and the Netherlands) supplying the demand of numerous sectors, has been largely ignored so far. Whereas the migrant communities from Turkey in Anglo-American countries were mostly made up of HSL migrants, the newcomers to Germany crucially encountered a rather heterogeneous picture of people from their country of origin, due to the previous migration waves mentioned above. The analysis of HSLM depicts to what extent the migration of highly qualified persons is interrelated with other types of migration in Germany.

Despite the conditions formed by the gradually stricter immigration policies at the national and supranational levels in the last two decades, the demand for HSLM has escalated. The Information and Communication Technology (ICT) sector in general has attracted increased attention since the late 1990s, when skills shortages began to emerge as the European ICT-sector grew and expanded significantly. For this reason, in recent years, many European countries including Germany started a "Green Card" system in order to invite expert labor power related with ICT from outside European Union.[3] As such, Germany explicitly took part in the race to attract HSLM, a competition in which Anglo-American countries have been and still are the central receivers including from Turkey. With only a few exceptions, in Germany, Indian ICT specialists became the paradigmatic group represented in most media and scientific studies on the Green Card program: it went so far as to trigger a controversial debate on the Green Card recruitment scheme in an election campaign, culminating with the CDU's famous catch

---

[22] See Zimmermann and Bauer 1999; İçduygu, 2000; İçduygu, 2002; İçduygu, 2003; Aydin and Keyman, 2004; Derviş et al., 2004; Erzan et al., 2004; Flam, 2004; Gorny and Ruspini, 2004.

[3] The early 1990s in German migration policy were already signals for the demand for HSLM within "*Anwerbestoppausnahmeverordnung*" (ASAV).

phrase "*Kinder statt Inder*" ("Children in place of Indians"). Whilst there is indeed a significant amount of Indian Green Card holders in Germany, there nonetheless remains, since the inception of the program, a large number of ICT specialists that have been, and indeed still are, recruited from other countries, including Turkey. In fact, still before the inception of the program, Turkey – a non-EU member, provided the highest number of foreign ICT specialists to Germany (Dobson and Salt, 2004:132).[4] The eighth biggest entity (3.6 percent) of 'Green Card' holders in Germany is also from Turkey.[5] What is more, in the winter semester of 2003/04, 24,448 Turkish persons (including 6,474: "*Bildungsausländer*") formed the second biggest foreign student population in Germany, as well as a large number of Turkish ICT-graduates from German universities already having found a workplace in the country. Other factors underline this remarkable and widely ignored part of the relationship between Germany and Turkey: Turkish ICT specialists come by means of intra-organizational labor movements to Germany (Kolb et al., 2004:156) and ICT-entrepreneurs from Turkey settle in Germany, encouraged and subsidized by some German federal states prioritizing the ICT sector.

Scientific studies and media analysis have largely ignored this 'divergent' migration strand from Turkey.[6] One can find plenty of literature about HSLM from different sending countries to different receiving countries.[7] There is also an abundance of studies on migration from Turkey to Germany, although literature on the issue of HSLM from Turkey to Germany is not common. As a matter of

[4] According to year 2000 statistics, this is also the second highest number (1,438) in the German ICT sector, behind Austria (1,467).

[5] The total number of 'Green Card' holders from Turkey is 405 in the period between 1.8.2000 and 31.12.2003.

[6] For example, Venema (2004) prepared a case study on Green Card holders in Germany. His sample contains 5.3 percent of ICT specialists from Turkey, being the sixth biggest quantity, followed by those from India, the former Soviet Union, and Romania. However, his study compares "old" labor migrants, differentiated as Turks, ex-Yugoslavians and Greeks, and "new" migrants who are not differentiated in terms of nationality.

[7] See Erickson, 1972; Bhagwati, 1976; Khadria, 1978; Rao, 1978; Hayhoe and Henze, 1984; Rouse, 1991; Sabour, 1997; Iqbal, 2000; Krishnadas, 2001; Murthy, 2003; Zweig, 1997; Khadria, 1999; Hunger, 2003; Barrere et al., 2004; and McKenzie, 2006.

fact, the considerable lack of information does not allow definite judgments on this matter, even though both the above mentioned quantitative importance of HSLM from Turkey to Germany and the indicated qualitative change of the migratory relations between these countries make it worthwhile to investigate this case more thoroughly. This dissertation attempts to address this academic gap by identifying key features of HSLM in the ICT sector for the last two decades.

A core part of this study concentrates on a better understanding "*Dasein*" (being-there, human existence) and "*in-der-Welt-sein*" (being-in-the-world), of migration, in the Heideggerian terminology (1962). In other words, this thesis intends to characterize patterns and specify trends of HSLM from Turkey to Germany by means of highlighting experiences of the *embodied* and *situated* agents: HSL migrants.[8] It aims to focus primarily on the reality of migration careers of these *"invisible migrants"* and their perceptions of themselves.

In my master thesis *"Not a 'Flight' from Home but 'Potential Brain Drain'"*, which forms the basis of this study, I investigated the 'potential brain drain' of ICT specialists from Turkey in the context of globalization. The primary purpose was to reveal motives and intentions causing individual migration projects.[9] One main result of this pre-study is that the perception of 'being in demand' and an abundance of opportunities for employment prove to be important factors for the "choices" of ICT specialists. However, when asked for the main reasons for their potential choices, the respondents usually refer to "vicinity" in terms of culture, language or geographical distance. "Vicinity", conceptualized as a social-

[8] For more information about the embodied agent to reconsider the structure/agent divide, please see Shilling, 1997. For a detailed discussion about the embodiment and situatedness of the agent, see also Shilling, 1993; Shilling and Mellor, 1996; Gallagher, 2005; and Gallagher, 2008.

[9] A sample survey entitled "Migration to Work Abroad Survey" (MWAS) carried out in 2002 among 178 individuals, defined as 'potential brain drainers', by submitting a web-questionnaire. Additionally a number of in-depths interviews with information technology experts in Turkey were conducted.

cultural index, deals both with physical and imaginary concerns.[10] Germany in particular is perceived as a country "close" to Turkey in terms of geographical proximity, military, political[11] and migratory relations, and the growing importance of tourism.

This thesis is intended as a follow-up-study to my master thesis and investigates the empirical situation of ICT specialists who actually migrated. It analyses the scope and dimension of HSLM from Turkey to Germany and investigates the motives and intentions of migrants, as well as their course of migration and related individual careers. The aim of the analysis is to develop typology of HSLM from Turkey to Germany based empirically on the conduction of biographical interviews with HSL migrants from Turkey.

2. Review of HSLM

I

After long years of religious wars in Europe, the Peace of Westphalia initiated a new order based on the concept of state sovereignty.[12] Max Weber, influentially defines this concept in his two major works *Politik als Beruf* and *Wirtschaft und Gesellschaft*. According to the Weberian definition, a sovereign state exists if and insofar as its administrative staff has the monopoly on the legitimate use of physical force in the enforcement of its order in a given

---

[10] The physical concerns contain geographical proximity and climate similarity. The imaginary concerns deal with historical emigration experiences from Turkey and with cultural connections and ties articulated in education, advertisement, television, music, cinema, and sports.

[11] Especially the history of German refugees from Nazi Germany to Turkey, many of them academicians and intellectuals taking a leading role in the early formation of the Republic of Turkey.

[12] The Peace of Westphalia refers to the two treaties, which were signed in 1648 in Osnabrück and Münster. They drew political boundaries by exposing the principle of *Cuius regio, eius religio*. In spite of the emergence of the nation-state in the sixteenth and seventeenth centuries of Europe with the ideal of state sovereignty, its distinguishing features covering the institutions of nationality and citizenship were mostly developed in the nineteenth and twentieth centuries by the ruling elite claiming nationalism, belonging to a nation and a state, emerged within the necessity of conscription for the warfare and taxation for the welfare. The periods of conquest, colonization, two world wars, and post-colonization witness the expansion of sovereignty over territory beyond boundaries. With these notable exceptions, the form of the nation-state fully spread over the globe.

territory. That is, a state is a political association with effective sovereignty over a geographic area and representing a population. As a principle of international law, the nation-state, therefore has the right to control the entry and exit of persons across its political boundaries against "unwanted migration".[13] That leads to the detection of migratory patterns.

Human beings had migrated before for centuries under the hegemony of space and time. As the breaking point of the migratory cosmos, the detection of migration, however, loses its universality. Migration has hence been evinced as a more complicated social phenomenon. After its detection, the second milestone comes in the second half of 20th century, with the novelties in the fields of transportation and communication. The innovations are fast moving in the direction of vaporizing the hegemony of space and time, which, at the time Marx uttered the words "All that solid melts into air", still remained solid as a rock. The last half-century, known as the migration era by Castles and Miller (1993), witnessed a significant increase of individual, mass, and small scale migrations and their changing forms. In 2000, there were more than 150 million registered international migrants. What is important here is the quantitative increase and the qualitative diversity in migrations that are still not isolated from detection. But, it is generally claimed that as capitalism and nationalism are updated under the conditions of globalization, that labor migration is today intrinsic to the processes of global capitalism.[14] Within this second milestone of human history, migration has hence been conveyed as a more divaricated and prolific social phenomenon. It is not any more an indifferent subject but rather an issue of continuously increased relevance to social

---

[13] Passport and visa regulations first develop in the nineteenth and twentieth centuries. While the exit visa being almost out of date after the end of the cold war, the entry visa has gradually come into prominence for some countries. It is argued that the reason of boundary control is closely related to welfare rather than warfare, and to internal affairs rather than foreign affairs.

[14] Assuming globalization of labor, Khadria (1999:37,42) however discusses the existence of the world market of labor power through international migration of workers across countries for ages. Still, Hannerz (1996:92) claims that globalization is a new phenomenon because of its accelerations.

sciences. Examining the causes and consequences of migrations provides tools for seeing social, cultural, economic, and political transformations of respective societies and regions through a specific frame.

According to the *neoclassical economics theory*, people migrate from a low-wage country (labor supply-rich, capital-poor country) to a high-wage country (labor supply-poor, capital-rich country) in accordance with rational choice/action. Based on this theory, migration happens as a result of isolated individual cost-benefit calculation of human capital, and it is seen as purely economic, voluntary, and free choice of the agent. The *new economics theory* breaks new ground for migration studies: larger social units, rather than individuals, initiate migration not simply to maximize income, but also to reduce or diversify risks. Massey et al. (1993:438) summarized this challenge to the oldest migration theory as the following: "households send workers abroad not only to improve income in absolute terms, but also to increase income relative to other households, and, hence, to reduce their relative deprivation compared with some reference group". These two migration theories are agency-oriented and clearly ignore structural determination concerning market and policy.

The *Dual labor market theory*, however, argues that workers move due to the labor demands of industrial countries. This argument is associated with the state sovereignty in the context of migration as mentioned above. It is generally known that labor migration, as long as it takes place under the control of the nation-states, is seen as relatively desirable compared to the other types of migration throughout the world. There is no doubt that the markets enforce governments in the direction of relaxing immigration controls to meet labor demands. The reason of capitalism is simply to find cheap labor or hold down wages, while maintaining high rates of profit. As a matter of fact, Scott (1968:2-3), in due time, announced the point that migrations adapt themselves to economic fluctuations and nationalistic demands of the receiving countries. As opposed to these three migration theories, the *world systems theory* stresses the political-economic determination on migration at the macro level, and independently from both migrants as the decision-makers and parameters of the sending country and the receiving country. That is why countries do not have independent economies but are part of the world economy as well as states having never been societies but instead, the political units of modern society's interstate system. Like the dual labor market theory, this theory confirms the existence of cheap labor demands of the "core nations". It also argues that the world-system redistributes skilled professional labor as resources through migration from the periphery to the core. Thus, the core of the world system, industrialized countries attempt to create flexible migratory conditions in order to attract highly qualified persons during the last decades. A clear competition in invitations to highly skilled people among the "core" states has been noticeable. In fact, the European Commission explains:

> "The Commission proposes, therefore, that the Union recognizes the realities of the situation of today: that on the one hand migratory pressure will continue and that on the other hand in a context of economic growth and a declining and aging population, Europe needs immigrants. In this context our objective is not the quantitative increase in migratory flows but better management in qualitative terms so as to realize more fully the potential of immigrants' admitted (Migration News, 2002)."

Thus, like the USA, Canada, and Australia, in recent years, other European countries have started several new systems to attract HSL from the developing countries in their peripheries.

The main stress point in the previously discussed structure-oriented theories concerns the role of the nation-state with regard to migrant labor power. Key figures of the globalization thesis argue that nation-states partly lose or transfer their immigration regulatory role to local authorities, private organizations, and most notably to other supranational institutions like the EU. As a matter of fact, Soysal (1994) heralds the end of state sovereignty in the context of the relationship between nation-state and migration. Nevertheless, Joppke (1999) objects this and proposes that the nation-states have "self-limited sovereignty," because in the end it is still states which decide over entry though migrants push the functional de-ethnicization of nations. Importantly, Ong (1999) argues that states have fashioned creative responses to global capitalism, and that the idea that the nation-state necessarily loses power because of these changes needs to be interrogated. What is more to the point is that she explains the changing role of nation-state as "graduated sovereignty" referring to ways of regulating various approaches to global markets and to controlling special production zones.[15]

Migration can be clearly evaluated as one of the main challenges to the nation-state. However, the above-described theoretical discussions in migration research have not fully answered the questions related with the mutual relationship between nation-states and migration. By investigating HSLM, this thesis aims at a contribution to the current debate concerning the changing or even shrinking role of nation-states within the course and the dynamics of international migration.

II

HSLM became the focus of serious studies and scientific debates after the 1960s in the academic literature. The term "brain drain" was invented by the British in the 1960s to describe their losses of professional people – mainly scientists, engineers, and physicians – through emigration. Indeed, brain migration and brain drain terms are used synonymously in literature. Besides brain migration and brain drain, there is a huge terminology about HSLM: mobility of highly skilled workers, mobility of highly skilled persons, expats, optimal brain drain, brain waste, brain circulation, brain gain, brain exchange, brain globalization, brain export, and brain over flow. The terms "brain", "highly skilled labor", and "highly qualified labor" are often interpreted in literature in terms of educational attainment. HSLM is thus conceptualized as the migration of highly educated individuals to a foreign country with the intention to work professionally. These people have been defined as professionals, specialists, experts, knowledge workers, the creative class, creative professionals, craftsmen, journeymen, or golden-collar workers.

[15] See also Ong, 2000.

HSLM experienced an incremental rise in the growth rate since the 1960s. In the recent preferences of immigration politics since the 1990s, there has been an explicit shift of the selected migrant profile from the unskilled to the highly skilled laborer, from uneducated peasants or working class individuals to well-educated and reasonably affluent middle class or new petty bourgeoisie, and from blue-collar workers to professionals.[16] It is definitively observable in the case of the Federal Republic of Germany, which was conservative in immigration politics, and applied "*Anwerbestopp*" (ban on recruitment) in the context of labor migration since 1974. Bommes (2006:156) argues that the German labor market has provided the ground of new forms of immigration concerning HSLM, like student migration and contract migrant labor power, since the 1990s by the so-called "*Anwerbestoppausnahmeverordnung*" (an ordinance on exceptional regulations concerning the recruitment ban). Therefore, HSLM has never been in the limelight as much as today. Although one can confidently predict an incrementally oriented HSLM, the corpus of studies that would forecast with accuracy the specific patterns of this migration and its impacts is still lacking.

The widespread utilization of HSLM is, in part due to the availability of easier integration opportunities, to meet the demands for highly valued skills that are in shortage and therefore necessitated by the global labor market. Some point out, HSL migrants are much wanted, welcomed, and quickly naturalized in the immediate country.[17] Findlay (1995) further emphasizes that this is also valid for countries which share a growing antagonism to immigration of manual labor. Its reason is seen as their contribution not only to its economy but also to the receiving society; or rather it is not their skills but their economic benefits without creating social burdens on the destination country. Moreover, some argue that the new migrants are educated, job-skilled, English speakers, and so they quickly adapt themselves to where they are. Sassen (2000:147) thus

[16] See also Vaknin, 2002; Piore, 1979; Khadria, 1999; Sunata, 2002.
[17] For instance, see Findlay, 1995:519-20 and Khadria, 1999:35.

announces the emergence of a new immigrant workforce, i.e. "new transnational professional class" (Sassen, 1998).

The term "transnationality" has become a prominent catchword in migration research over the last years.[18] In this respect, it is argued:

> "[Transmigrants] become incorporated in the economy and political institutions, localities and patterns of daily life of the country in which they reside. However, at the very same time, they are engaged elsewhere [and] maintain connections, build institutions and influence local and national events in the countries from which they emigrated." (Glick-Schiller et al., 1997:121)

Transmigrants are assumed to be multilingual, multicultural and able to act in two or more different societies. On the one hand, this approach is supported with migration systems, of "countries that have close historical, cultural or economic ties" (Kritz and Zlotnik, 1992:1).[19] The Turkish-German context is seen as one of the main migration systems. On the other hand, HSL migrants count as role models in the context of the debate on "transnationality". In any case, the rough sketches of this approach however illustrate that HSLM is related to "transnationality" in a number of different ways: HSL migrants have *presumably flexible* working conditions and accordingly they are *highly mobile* persons. In this manner, Düvell (2004:18) states that the new immigrant workforce, i.e. "globally mobile economic actors", are not members of a particular community. Rather, they live within a network of like-minded people who commonly share a "hybrid cosmopolitan identity", that is, they are territorially, socially, and culturally uprooted (Rouse, 1991; Papastergiadis, 2000). It is generally argued that they neither belong to a network consisting of members from the same national background, nor are they rooted in an ethnic community. The general basis of their network is built upon a profession that implicates not a shared ethnic but a "shared economic identity" (Düvell, 2004:18). As a consequence, the new migrants do not link together

[18] Also referred to in literature as transmigration, transnational communities, and transnational migration space. See also Goeke, 2004; Pries, 1997; Pries, 1999; and Sklair, 2002.
[19] To Mabogunje (1970), migration systems distinguish migration movements. Networks are the cores of migration systems (Düvell, 2004:19).

countries or communities but markets (Zlotnik, 1992; Findlay, 1990). These arguments slightly differ from Erickson's empirical study on English and Scottish immigrants in professional, commercial, and clerical occupations in the 19th century America. In his study, Erickson (1972:396) concluded "because of the highly individualistic motives for emigration, and the fact that many had already loosened their family and community associations [...], these individuals did not move within a social network of distribution either of family or of a trade".

With respect to the effects of international migration on social processes of identity formation and the importance of social networks for a successful migratory project; the current assumptions on HSLM are problematic in two respects: on the one side, they fail to integrate the findings of sociological theories; on the other, they are not yet empirically supported.[20] One of the general tasks of this thesis is therefore to evaluate these two issues regarding HSLM from Turkey to Germany.

3. Chapter Structure

The current research relies methodologically on a combination of quantitative descriptions and qualitative procedures. Chapter 2 will begin with describing HSLM from Turkey to Germany in the relevant terms quantitatively. Afterwards, the qualitative research procedures will be explained. In this context, I will portray the purposive sampling techniques used to choose the sample from the invisible population of HSL migrants under consideration. After the selection process based on the defined standards, I will explain why and how I used a semi-structured interview protocol in this study. Moreover, I will deal with analysis methods that utilize typology construction. Let me here underline the fact that this dissertation uses grounded theory with hermeneutic reading as the main methodological approach in order to construct a typology. Even though the grounded theory remains theoretically sensitive, it does

[20] See Granovetter, 1973; Choldin, 1973; Granovetter, 1974; Granovetter, 1978; Burt, 1982; Haug, 2004; and Haug, 2005.

not start with theoretical discussions. That is why it permits, even privileges, knowledge that is derived from empirical data through hermeneutic reading, rather than knowledge which is shaped with existing literature. In other words, it does not force understanding the data in the frame of the existing arguments. Instead, it allows the emergence of theses and concepts from the data in order to discuss the arguments under this light. As a consequence, this work contributes to the theoretical literature in multiple ways after comprehending the data collected in the fieldwork.

Chapter 3 will introduce a preliminary and brief assessment of my fieldwork practice. In the field, 66 interviews were conducted with HSL migrants from Turkey who have working experience in the German ICT sector. By the end of the fieldwork period, half of them were however excluded either due to voice-recording errors or for reasons that will be specified in Chapter 3. In that chapter, the selection process of interviews and the personal profile of the 33 participants will be introduced. Subsequently, I will touch upon how, during the descriptive analyses, 15 participants are preferred over the rest in order to generate a theoretical sample. In addition to the method of composing the theoretical sample for interpretative analyses, the determination of the five crucial dimensions –family background, education background, migration story, labor relations, and social relations – will be presented in this chapter.

I will review interpretations of the interviews in Chapter 4. The interpretive analysis as the basis of the current thesis addresses several aspects, namely at a 'subjective level': individual migration dispositions as an effect of family background, education, and occupational training; the factual courses of migration processes; reliance on resources like social networks based on relatives, ethnic or regional bonds; the relevance of professional links; actual and future expectations linked with the individual migration projects; social aspirations and political attitudes; and self-perceptions regarding migration. At an 'objective level', the analysis concentrates on the economic and political conditions relevant for the realization of migration as perceived by the migrants. This focuses especially on labor market conditions, the role of companies in influencing national openness to migration and, finally, the relevance of political and legal regulatory structures of nation states and the EU.

The interpretative analyses of the interviews are additionally supported with the contextualization of factual information in biographies and observations. Contextualization for the purpose of typology will be presented in Chapter 5. HSLM in itself carries three principal components as social contexts: education, work, and migration. Therefore, biographical information embodied in the description is contextualized with information about the relevant social circumstances under these three components. In the end, contextualization reveals pragmatic strands for understanding the related phenomenon.

After the interpretation of the interviews and their contextualization, Chapter 6 will focus on the typology construction through the five dimensions mentioned above. The relevant emerged attributes and concepts under every dimension will be debated.

Chapter 7 will conclude the typology of the actors who are situated and embodied in HSLM from Turkey to Germany. Besides these primary results of the study, the Black Swan Phenomenon as a secondary finding will be conceptualized. Finally, the implications of the thesis to migration studies will be discussed.

CHAPTER 2. METHODOLOGY

1. Quantitative Description

The available statistics on HSLM in general cannot count as reliable and present a distorted picture. As this is also the case for the data on HSLM from Turkey to Germany, it is only possible to present some general trends and a rough sketch about its scope and its rate of growth.[1]

TABLE 1. EMPLOYEES FROM TURKEY IN GERMANY, BY OCCUPATIONAL GROUPS*

Occupational Group	2000	2005
ISCO-1	1,893	2,279
ISCO-2	5,150	4,968
Engineers	1,476	1,709
ISCO-3	17,994	16,661
Total (Occupational Groups ISCO 1-3)	25,037	23,098
Total (All Occupational Groups)	556,498	458,243
Share of ISCO 1-3 in All Occupational Groups (%)	4.5	5.2

* I deduced this table based on the data from *Bundesamt für Migration und Flüchtlinge*. The data includes the numbers of employees from Turkey subject to social insurance contributions in Germany.

Currently, between 2000 and 2005, Turkey has remained the largest origin among the third countries, in every category of the stock statistics of HSLM for Germany, with more than 20 percent (about 25,000 persons). That is, at least one of every five educated labor migrants including skilled workers (technicians) in Germany comes

[1] Indeed, reliable data are only available from the Federal Office of Labor, but its sources have limitations. There is also little empirical research about HSLM from Turkey to Germany, either statistical modeling or case studies, which employs comparable methods.

from Turkey. HSL is divided into three categories according to ISCO by Hess and Sauer (2007). ISCO-1 covers legislators, senior officials, and managers. ISCO-2 covers professionals such as engineers, medical doctors, scientists, pharmacists, lawyers, and teachers. ISCO-3 covers technicians and associate professionals. My study focuses on the occupation group of ISCO-2, notably engineers. As seen in TABLE 1, the amount of the professionals from Turkey in Germany in the first half of 2000s is about 5,000, which is the highest number of all sending countries. Taking the engineering expert into consideration, Turkey still provides the largest amount of labor migrants for Germany. Another indicator about HSLM in Germany is the quantity of permanent residency permit based on HSL (*Niederlassungserlaubnisse nach § 19*).[2] In the end

[2] Permanent residency permit is given for the purpose of the consolidation of the stay of a foreigner in the Federal Republic of Germany territory and is unlimited. It provides opportunity to being employee and to the practice of a self-employed. The fundamental conditions for the issue of a permanent residency permit are in accordance with § 9 Abs. 2 S. 1 AufenthG: the five-year Conglomerate of a residence permit (No. 1), the safety of living costs (No. 2), the proof of at least 60 months compulsory contributions for legal old age pension insurance (No. 3), the fundamental exemption from punishment (No. 4), permission for the occupation as an employee (No. 5), the possession of the knowledge for the practice of the self-employed (No. 6), sufficient knowledge of the German language (No. 7), basic knowledge on the law and social order and the living conditions in Germany (No. 8), and sufficient dwelling (No. 9). In addition to these individual conditions, there are in each case exceptions and supplementing regulations. Apart from the fundamental regulation of § 9 the residence law for the issue of a permanent residency permit, there still some special regulations are, after which (under relieved conditions) permanent residency can be likewise given: highly-qualified one (§ 19 AufenthG), self-employed one (§ 21 Abs. 4 AufenthG), humanitarian reasons (§ 26 Abs. 3 and 4 AufenthG), family partnerships with Germans (§ 28 Abs. 2 S. 1 AufenthG), and former Germans (§ 38 Abs. 1 S. 1 NR. 1 AufenthG). The fee for the issue of a permanent residency permit is determined according to the residence regulation (AufenthV) and as an amount of between 85 Euro and 200 Euro (§ 44 AufenthV), whereby also releases and reductions are possible (§ 52 AufenthV). Article 19 in the relevant act, AufenthG (Aufenhaltgesetz), under the Migration Law, ZuwG (Zuwanderungsgesetz) states:
§ 19 Niederlassungserlaubnis für Hochqualifizierte
(1) Einem hoch qualifizierten Ausländer kann in besonderen Fällen eine Niederlassungserlaubnis erteilt werden, wenn die Bundesagentur für Arbeit nach § 39 zugestimmt hat oder durch Rechtsverordnung nach § 42 oder zwischenstaatliche Vereinbarung bestimmt ist, dass die Niederlassungserlaubnis ohne Zustimmung der Bundesagentur für Arbeit nach § 39 erteilt werden kann und die Annahme gerechtfertigt ist, dass die Integration in die Lebensverhältnisse der Bundesrepublik Deutschland und die Sicherung des Lebensunterhalts ohne staatliche Hilfe gewährleistet sind. Die Landesregierung kann bestimmen,

of July 2006, Turkey was located the third place with nine percent in this term, behind the USA and Russian Federation.[3]

The size of ICT specialists from Turkey in Germany in the early 2000s can roughly be estimated as between 2,000 and 2,500 in the light of above-mentioned statistics. This quantitative description of HSLM in this occupational context provides the empirical starting ground for the subsequent steps of analysis.

2. Qualitative Research Design

My interest in why and how migrants live their migration career led me to the use of qualitative research methods. The current study does therefore not primarily rely on the collection of official quantitative data, but rather it attempts to gather and analyze qualitative data. In order to achieve an investigation on the social phenomenon of HSLM from Turkey to Germany, the researcher must be empathetic toward the researched group in her/his attempts to understand their positions, experiences, perceptions, and expectations. The need for empathy is found in the qualitative research doctrine of *Verstehen*.

Indeed, I have been encouraged and inspired by the notion of research that might serve as a mutually beneficial endeavor for both the researcher and the researched. I prefer the "researcher as instrument" approach, which uses human capacities to limit bias and subjectivity while capitalizing on intellectual responsiveness to let the study emerge. With this approach, the intent is to learn from the participants and interpret their experience and perceptions central to the study. For the sake of the ethically responsible research, *a priori* conditions – mainly intellectually mediated, ethically sound, and socially responsible – are also taken into account in my study.

---

dass die Erteilung der Niederlassungserlaubnis nach Satz 1 der Zustimmung der obersten Landesbehörde oder einer von ihr bestimmten Stelle bedarf.
(2) Hoch qualifiziert nach Absatz 1 sind insbesondere 1. Wissenschaftler mit besonderen fachlichen Kenntnissen, 2. Lehrpersonen in herausgehobener Funktion oder wissenschaftliche Mitarbeiter in herausgehobener Funktion oder 3. Spezialisten und leitende Angestellte mit besonderer Berufserfahrung, die ein Gehalt in Höhe von mindestens dem Doppelten der Beitragsbemessungsgrenze der gesetzlichen Krankenversicherung erhalten.

[3] See Hess and Sauer, 2007.

2.1. Sampling and Limits of the Study

This thesis is dealing with phenomenological interpretation of *Dasein* and being-in-the world of HSLM from Turkey to Germany. On purpose, I concentrated on the HSL migrants as the embodied and situated actors. A case study of ICT specialists was organized and carried out on them for one year during November 2005 to November 2006. The target population of the research was selected according to three pre-defined criteria:

(i) They should be university graduates with the ability to work in the numerous industries of the ICT sector.
(ii) They should have worked for a period of at least one year in Germany during the last ten years.
(iii) They should be from Turkey.

The last criterion, being from Turkey, is a bit open to interpretation, but taking into consideration the migration history between Turkey and Germany, a restriction of being born in Turkey may exclude some interesting cases with migration background such as people born in Germany but brought up in Turkey or contra verse.

Collecting exploratory data was accomplished by a combination of two sub-types of *purposive sampling*: snowball sampling *and* heterogeneity sampling. According to purposive sampling, the researcher uses her judgments about which sample best meets the aims of the survey to choose (Bailey, 1987:94). On the one hand, snowball sampling is an especially useful technique when trying to reach populations that are hard to find. As mentioned, the HSL migrants from Turkey are a hidden population in Germany. Snowball sampling removed barriers to access them and provided practical benefits. This technique implies that after identifying people who meet the criteria for an inclusion in the study, they then became "chain referrals" of the study. That is, they were asked to recommend relevant acquaintances and then the relevant candidates were evaluated according to the criteria of participation or identification of cases of interest. Its handicap is its ignorance of "isolated" cases. On the other hand, heterogeneity sampling provides maximum variation and identifies important common patterns that cut across variations. A heterogeneity sample includes all related opinions or views and serves the intention of revealing different typologies. Still, the purposive sampling methods do not allow probabilistic conclusions, and limit generalizations of the results.

2.2. Semi-Structured Interview Protocol and Confidentiality

After identifying potential cases, *in-depth personal interviews* were conducted with a semi-structured guideline. Methodologically, the interviews were realized with the help of the *general interview guide approach*. In order to apply this type of interview approach, a basic checklist was prepared to ensure that all relevant topics are covered. This checklist includes ten segments: personal profile; family and social background; occupational career; current occupation and work conditions; migration career; understanding and interpretation of the migration project; lifestyle preferences; future expectations; social networks; and social aspirations and political attitudes. During the interview, the interviewee was however free to explore, probe, and ask questions deemed interesting to the researcher. As a matter of fact, the logic of the interview protocol required that the interviewer, I, "maintain a delicate balance between providing enough openness for the participants to tell their stories and enough focus to allow the interview structure to work" (Seidman, 1998: 13).

I tried to provide an atmosphere of open conversation for the interview. At first I introduced myself and then explained about the study's content. I purposely underlined that the study's main aim was to collect different stories from new labor migrants of Turkey in Germany. Afterwards, I asked for the interviewee's own story. As a result, the main and first question is "Can you explain your migration story?" I used the afore-described checklist, if needed. When the interviewee could not think of more to say and she/he stopped her/his own expression, I asked one question according to the predefined draft topics, like "I wonder what you think about working conditions in Germany." Also, I sometimes used a way of connecting with the previous theme the interviewee had mentioned; that is I did not have a strictly direct way of asking, but rather a flexible and indirect way with incompletely determined questions. Although I attempted to shift the topic when the interviewee began to speak about very specific issues out of the study's concern too much, I always tried to protect an interactive dialog during the interview.

The main goal of these interviews was the reconstruction of the participants' migration experiences. Therefore, the interviews would try to obtain information on their social backgrounds, professional goals, occupational and migrational careers, family relations, political points of view, expectations for the future, lifestyles, social networks, and understanding and interpretation of their migration project. None of them showed any reluctance to voice recording, and all interviews were digitally voice-recorded.

All interviews in this study were carried out in Turkish. Turkish is the mother tongue of most interviewees. There are some cases whose mother tongue is Kurdish, but they learned Turkish at the latest in the first class of the primary education. That is, their knowledge of Turkish is advanced.

The digital voice-recorder allowed the research to capture the interview in a detailed manner. Participants were assured of confidentiality regarding the information they disclosed. All interviews were recorded with the permission of interviewees. Recordings were then transcribed into Turkish. Unfortunately, transcription as a transformation process from the spoken to the written language would kill the authenticity of the conversation at particular times and places, but in this way it became preserved. Transcription in itself was both an assassination and mummification of the interview.

Killing and eternalizing the interviews, I changed all names of interviewees to tree names in Latin to ensure anonymity. It can also ironically be read as an abstract transformation from "migrants" to "tree-people". For instance Rhus, meaning sumac, is a pseudonym. Moreover, different pseudonyms were used to keep specific information mentioned in the interviews. Company names were replaced with bird names. Virtual community names were also changed.

In order to write obituaries in lieu of serial murder, transcribed interviews were, at first, translated from Turkish to English. Moreover, I worked with a collaborative native English speaker to improve translation and control apprehensibility of notices. Afterwards, reductions of translated texts from the dialogue format into descriptive pillars were provided to describe the interview. Concurrently, ignoring the original sequence during the interview span but still taking every part of the interview into consideration, the interview as a whole was descriptively categorized and organized. In doing so, all selected interviews adhered to a standard outline. To confess my sins under the eyes of sociology, interpretation reviews are presented in Chapter 4.

2.3. Grounded Theory with Hermeneutic Reading

I

Grounded theory as a systematic qualitative research methodology in the social sciences was selected for the current thesis in order to generate theory from data. It is worthy mentioning the analysis does not use theoretical knowledge with the purpose of "emerging" instead of "forcing" of empirical data.[4] In accordance with the grounded theory, I however preferred not to abandon theoretical sensitivity.

One theoretical sensitivity of the current thesis is related to the capital forms, especially Bourdieu's concepts of *cultural capital* and *symbolic capital*.[5] Cultural capital refers to forms of knowledge, skills and education and leads to a persons (dis-) advantages with respect to their status in society. Symbolic capital comprises of the amount of honor and prestige possessed by a person with regard to acting structures. Following the Bourdieuen approach,

[4] There has been a debate about this issue in the grounded theory. See Glaser (1978; 1992), Strauss (1970; 1987; 1990).

[5] See Bourdieu, 1983; Bourdieu, 1984; Bourdieu, 1986; Bourdieu, 1990, and Bourdieu, 1999. The below-mentioned research questions on social networks explain Bourdieu's concept of social capital.

Nohl et al. (2006:12) argued that the labor market integration of HSL migrants is structured by a multi-dimensional process of the utilization of these capitals. I assume that individuals' cultural and symbolic capital underlies major changes and modifications during a migration process. The patterns of devaluation and revaluation of these capitals through migration were read by means of the biographical information set (Weiss, 2006). For instance, "[i]nstitutionalized cultural capital is usually applied in national contexts, and its value or relevance diminishes through migration" (Nohl et al., 2006:5). In the case of ICT specialists, specific expertise functions as a "passport" (Iredale, 2001). Not only institutionalized and incorporated cultural capital but also symbolic capital decreases through migration, since their accumulation is valid within the socialization process. Taking all into consideration, I investigate not only the relevant forms of cultural and symbolic capital but also the self-perception of the migrants with regard to their capitals' validity and recognition in different related social environments. This provides the appropriate empirical basis to account for the effects of migration on social processes of identity formation.

Another theoretical sensitivity is dealing with social networks of the migrants. This study intended to investigate which of the social networks are relevant with regard to the migratory project, their importance with respect to (i) their function as migration channels; and (ii) their ability to provide access to the necessary knowledge and resources for a successful migration. The former parameter is related to the information hypothesis: with the aid of social networks, the tendency to migrate increases.[6] Also, migration to places where the living and working conditions are known becomes more attractive.[7] The more social relations one has at the place of destination, the more migration channels these relationships provide. The latter is related to the facilitating hypothesis: the social networks facilitate adjustment to the place of destination.[8] Accord-

[6] See also Boyd, 1989; Faist, 1997; Haug, 2000.

[7] See also Choldin, 1973; Coombs, 1978; Jedlicka, 1978; Tilly and Brown, 1967

[8] See also Choldin, 1973; Tilly and Brown, 1967; Massey, 1988; McKenzie, 2006.

ing to the information and facilitating hypotheses, social networks work as a kind of pull-factor (Haug, 2005:7).

II

After transcribing interviews and their descriptive analyses, I applied a *hermeneutic* reading method to interpret the interviews by composing a theoretical sample. The hermeneutic method covers repetitive and reconstructive investigation, and provides a reevaluation of all parts of the interview within their full context. Theoretical sampling is used in order to decide whom to interpret next according to the state of theory generation. Comparative interpretations composed building stones for conceptualization and construction of typology.

For the interpretative analysis, the guideline is to use the so-called "interpretevist paradigm" in "phenomenography" that investigates the qualitatively different ways in which people experience something or think about something (Marton, 1981; 1986).[9] It is concerned with the relationships that people have with the world around them. Thus, phenomenography is a description of appearances (Hassselgren and Beach, 1997). Phenomenographic research involves identifying the conceptions and looking for their underlying meanings and the relationship between them (Entwistle, 1997). In other words, this analysis aims at the conceptualization of observation to understand appearance of phenomena, observation of reality, as well as observation of observation.

The analyses are both to inform through knowledge and understanding of pertinent social circumstances and to carry out contextualization of the biographical information in the interview. In other words, it provides contextual exploration and reevaluation of factual information derived from the interview data within social circumstances by means of sources other than the interview data in order "not to treat it as a unique case, self-contained in its own solipsistic bubble" (Crouch and McKenzie, 2006:490). Clearly, to understand any personal experience it is necessary to comprehend it

---

[9] It is derived from the words *phainonmenon* (appearance) and *graphein* (description).

in social conditions. In other words, this intention lets "paradigm shift" which is like a round trip between the individual and the structure. Comparison between the personal experience and the social context facilitates understanding the HSLM phenomena and makes the theory strong.

2.4. Typology Construction Process

The final target of the thesis is to develop a typology of the embodied and embedded agents of HSLM to explain the patterns and trends of HSLM. The patterns of HSLM were determined based on who the HSL migrants are and its trends were comprehended based on what their dispositions, motivations, and justifications are in their life course.

Every typology is the outcome of a grouping process by means of some selected attributes.[10] As a consequence, typology construction is based on an attribute space, which is represented with the help of multidimensional tables. This space is a result of all possible combinations of the selected attributes relevant for the research question and their theoretically conceivable dimensions. Between single properties, not only empirical correlations have to exist (*Kausaladaequanz*), but also meaningful relationships (*Sinnadaequanz*) (Weber, 1972/1921:5; Kluge, 1999). This being said, the elements within a type (a particular constructed subgroup with common attributes) are required to be as similar as possible (internal heterogeneity on the "level of the type") and the differences between the types have to be as strong as possible (external heterogeneity on the "level of the typology") (Kluge, 1999:26).

As Kluge (1999) explained, there are four main stages in *the process of typology construction* for obtaining an empirically-grounded type construction; the following rules are employed: *development of relevant analyzing dimensions* (thematic coding of the interviews, dimensionalization, construction of variables ("quantification") with thematic case analysis and case contrasts), *grouping the cases and analysis of empirical regularities* (contrast of cases,

---

[10] See Bailey, 1994:1; Friedrichs, 1983:90; Haupert, 1991:240; and Sodeur, 1974:1

computer-assisted grouping procedures (cluster analysis), concept of attribute space (construction of the entire attribute space (cross tabulation), assignment of the research elements, analysis of empirical regularities and – where appropriate – reduction of the attribute space), *analysis of meaningful relationships and type construction* (consideration of further attributes, systematization by computer-aided coding, search for "contradicting" and "deviating" cases, reduction of the attribute space to types, confrontation (of the individual cases with their ideal type)), and *characterization of the constructed types* (relevant analyzing dimensions and further attributes, meaningful relationships, describing the typical through prototypes, ideal types, extreme types etc.).

These typologies allow showing differences in certain dimensions in HSLM from Turkey to Germany; comparing these dimensions allows finding out significant correlations that are determining factors for a certain kind of migration career. This study presents types according to every dimension and at the end the whole picture of the HSLM typology.

CHAPTER 3. REPORT ON FIELDWORK

1. Selection of Interviews

For the purposes of the current thesis, I accessed 123 ICT specialists who are originally from Turkey and have working experience in Germany. They were selected in accordance with the pre-defined three criteria: (i) being a university graduate with the ability to work in the ICT sector; (ii) having at least one year working experience in Germany during the last ten years; and (iii) being from Turkey.[1] In the fieldwork, I conducted semi-structured interviews with 66 people in total. 55 of the interviews took place in eleven cities of Germany and the remaining 11 were conducted in the two biggest cities of Turkey. These interviews took place between November 2005 and November 2006.

Before the interpretation phase started, I however purposely filtered them depending upon five types of consideration: (i) being not labor power but entrepreneur; (ii) not having enough uninterrupted working experience in Germany due to short-period intra-company movement; (iii) being a return migrant, not an active labor migrant, (iv) being not essentially a labor migrant but a refugee; and (v) holding a Bachelor of Science degree not from a university in Turkey, but a university in Germany, the USA, the UK, or Kyrgyzstan. Furthermore, if the interview voice recording was corrupted due to the device failure, no attempt was made to reconstruct the interview from memory. That eliminated two more cases. As a result, 33 interviews with ICT specialists from Turkey in nine different cities of Germany composed the empirical data framework of the current thesis.

[1] For details, see Methodology and Research Design.

2. Brief Profile of Participants

The personal profile in TABLE 2 provides information on the interviewees' age, gender, marital status, current city of residence, and Germany residence period based on years. The median age is 30 with a range from 26 to 47. The age interval 27-33 covers more than two thirds of interviewees. The median of their residence time in Germany is four years; their average is about five years. In my case, almost all ICT specialists from Turkey came to Germany in the last decade. Hence, this study is influenced by the German Green Card Program, which was regulated in 2000 in order to attract specifically ICT specialists from the third countries outside the EU. Except for six of them, all took part in this program. A clear majority began their migration career as a single in the late twenties. Taking this stage in life into account, an overlap between migration experiences and changes in the marital status is not unexpected. All their partners, spouses or ex-spouses are highly educated like themselves. As my fieldwork shows, the number of men is higher, whereas there are an increasing proportion of highly educated urbanite migrant women. In my fieldwork, I have not found any female ICT specialist migrant from the rural areas of Turkey. This shows that women of rural origins have few opportunities to become HSL migrants.[2] West Germany is remarkable as the destination of HSLM. The most popular residence is found along the Frankfurt-Stuttgart-Munich line, where most industrial companies are located in Germany.

[2] See Contextualization for Typology, the section of Education System for details.

TABLE 2. PERSONAL PROFILE OF THE PARTICIPANTS

Interviewee	Age	Gender	Marital Status	Child	Current Residence	Germany Residence (>years)
Prunus **(10)**	27	Male	Engaged	X	Dortmund	5
Buxus	34	Male	Married	0	Wiesbaden	2
Magnolia **(11)**	31	Female	Single	X	Wiesbaden	3
Juglans **(8)**	44	Female	Married	0	Frankfurt	12
Sorbus **(9)**	26	Male	Single	X	Frankfurt	4
Salix	38	Male	Divorced	0	Frankfurt	4
Rhus **(1)**	30	Male	Single	X	Frankfurt	4
Castanea	31	Male	Single	X	Frankfurt	4
Acer **(6)**	29	Male	Single	X	Frankfurt	1
Populus	26	Male	Single	X	Munich	4
Tilia	30	Male	Married	1	Stuttgart	4
Cercis	26	Male	Single	X	Stuttgart	3
Fraxinus **(3)**	39	Male	Single	X	Stuttgart	4
Abies	28	Male	Single	X	Stuttgart	6
Fagus	30	Male	Single	X	Stuttgart	3
Ailanthus **(7)**	29	Male	Married	0	Munich	4
Laburnum **(13)**	31	Female	Single	X	Munich	3
Sambucus **(14)**	29	Male	Married	0	Berlin	2
Juniperus	35	Male	Single	X	Hamburg	3
Rhamnus **(15)**	31	Male	Div.soon*	0	Hamburg	4
Syringa **(4)**	30	Male	Divorced	0	Stuttgart	3
Hippophae	31	Male	Married	0	Stuttgart	9
Quercus **(12)**	47	Male	Married	0	Stuttgart	14
Mespilus **(5)**	31	Female	Divorced	0	Munich	5
Picea	30	Male	Single	X	Munich	5
Euonymus **(2)**	30	Female	Single	X	Munich	6

Betula	29	Male	Married	Exp**	Heidelberg	5
Morus	38	Female	Married	1	Frankfurt	8
Platanus	28	Female	Single	X	Frankfurt	3
Robinia	28	Male	Married		Frankfurt	5
Celtis	33	Male	Single	X	Frankfurt	5
Pinus	32	Female	Single	X	Frankfurt	5
Carpinus	31	Male	Single	X	Cologne	4

* He is going to be divorced soon.

** He is expecting a child.

3. Composing Theoretical Sample and Dimensions

By using the above-presented empirical data framework, I began to determine cases *consecutively* by theoretical sampling in order to cover all comparable divergent and related convergent points in the stories. The primary interest of my research question is not to identify the "average" or "model" highly qualified migrant, but to obtain a broad spectrum of divergent cases. It was systematically organized by the effort for securing both heterogeneous and redundant features among cases. This effort was not only limited with my repeated reading all interview transcripts but also guided by continuously renewed attributes which emerged from the already-analyzed interview data by open coding. That is, the properties under scrutiny were compared and enriched with the next case of the theoretical sample. The methodology, in fact, gives priority to comparisons based on the interviews by contextualization and conceptualization. In the end, I intentionally selected 15 rich-informant interviewees for my theoretical sample. They were signed in TABLE 2 according to the interpretation sequence.

Based on the above-described personal profiles, my theoretical sample hence provides the same age interval despite covering the experiences of the outliers and its median is still 30. One third of them are female so as to look into gender-specific conditions. Based on the time of the interviews, about half are single, one is engaged, four are married, one will soon be divorced, and two are already divorced. But, all of them migrated to Germany as single, except for Mespilus who came with her ex-spouse, as well as Juglans and Sambucus who prefer Germany in order to be with their spouses of German citizenship.

These 15 interviews were comparatively and cumulatively interpreted in order to focus on the typology of HSLM from Turkey to Germany, while the rest, 18 cases, stood ready to enrich the developed typology via theoretical sampling. The interpretative analyses from full interview transcriptions to grounded theory brought further details to light and highlighted relevant contexts and concepts. By the same token, five dimensions of the typology were clarified: (i) family background; (ii) educational background; (iii) migration story; (iv) labor relations; and (v) social relations. Now, I will introduce interpretation reviews, which are summaries of the interpretative analyses with reduced and combined attributes. Afterwards, the typology will be developed by way of examining the determined attributes under five dimensions.

CHAPTER 4. INTERPRETATION REVIEWS

1. Rhus, 30, single, male

Rhus, born in Istanbul, comes from a conservative middle class family. Here the term conservative is not employed in order to awaken a religious connotation, but as a descriptor of the values that can be identified in the construction of Rhus' and his family's lives. Such choices include he and his two sisters (pharmacists) choosing professions that are suitable for their genders, given the corresponding stereotypes, and the selection of a private high school for Rhus that furthermore has a nationalistic, Kemalist orientation. Even though his parents are junior high school graduates their investment in the education of their children – all university graduates – displays once more their middle-class status, which upwardly lives on with their members' artisan experiences, notably the father's small-scale enterprise. Apart from the educational paths I have just cited, the absence of social relations between Rhus and his distant relatives in Germany after his migration there can be even read out as a sign of the elitist stance encountered in such conservative middle class circles.

His educational history is a common "success story" that is a direct consequence of the above-mentioned family stance. Secondary education at a private high school, followed by a Computer Engineering degree at the prestigious Middle East Technical University (METU), and entering a post-graduate program at the similarly prominent Bosporus University is one of the best routes to take in Turkey before the start of a professional life. But the post-graduate study, which was later quit without having obtained a degree, is suggestive of the fact that this was a maneuver to postpone the compulsory military service. During those two years, Rhus was working for a small-scale ICT firm on a part-time basis, and as soon as he found a job abroad, he did not hesitate to leave school, since he now had a better escape from the army. But overall, this education career still contains all elements for preparing the potential migrant for take-off.

While still studying and working part-time, he encountered an advertisement in a Turkish newspaper by a large-scale, US-based international firm, Falcon, regarding job openings in Germany directed towards ICT specialist in Turkey. When asked, he was very clear about the reasons behind this choice: First, this was to get rid of the military service problem, since men working abroad for at least three years have the opportunity to fulfill this requirement by means of a payment and three-week long light training. Second, he wanted a taste of the experience of living abroad, since he saw this as an important addition to his skills, which could later prove crucial when he wanted to work in Turkey again. This latter attitude towards working abroad is underlined by his observation that the job he has in Germany does not let him earn more money than he would have in Turkey. But, importantly, he explains that this equality only holds if one wants to keep – as he did – the living standards one is used to. He accepts that the people, who sacrifice the establishment of a social life in Germany, have the chance to save money for later use. Actually this situation, together with his generalized temporariness towards his presence in Germany, is responsible for him not being able to make any long-term plans in his life. Thus, the motivation behind his migration is, on the one hand, finding a solution to the military service, and, on the other, the accumulation of a life abroad and work experience, which I regard as advanced cultural capital.

Although the USA was at that time the first country in his mind in the context working abroad, he rejected a job offer from the USA since it was only at a small-scale company. He was then hired and moved to Germany in 2001 when Falcon Frankfurt recruited more than 100 ICT specialists from Turkey by the facilities of Green Card program to lease them to other firms according to projects.[1] But the end of this year coincided with the global financial crisis; it caused a significant reduction in the projects and so gathered the unemployment wave. Falcon working through the "up or out model" had fired about 80 of the employees from Turkey until

[1] The term "project" almost all interviewees often use to describe their work seems a prominent catchword and indicates the new flexible labor relations.

2004. Rhus believes that he has shown effort to break this wave and the subsequent ones; in fact, he came up in Falcon, not out. Although he experienced anxiety about losing his job during periods of the crisis, his anxiety has partly disappeared since his promotion.

Rhus noticed the absence of the prestige in Germany related with his educational career in Turkey, devaluation of status, but that does not disturb him much. Also, he evaluates "cultural plurality" in his work atmosphere as a major contribution in his professional life. Meeting unbelief in his profession due to his nationality at the first glance is however worth considering for him. He in fact said, "Certainly, there is an image of Turks in Germany. [...] when we are being acquainted with Germans, they immediately ask if we are *really* computer engineers. As a matter of fact, a person working in the same company is surprised." Moreover, he mentioned, after saying his age, loneliness for single migrants as one of important disadvantages of being here, even though it feeds to his maturity. Loneliness in migration, which can be considered as solitude at some degree, leads to individuation such as having time to listen to himself and make something for himself. Ever since fulfillment of his military service by payment in the vacation time last year, he had already decided to go back Turkey. Still, he applied for permanent alien residency and he planned to work in Germany for another one or two years.

Eventually, the rather professional attitude towards and the cold description of the migration experience further resonate when we hear Rhus say that he prefers a secure life, both in the domestic and professional sphere. He has very limited knowledge about labor unions in Germany, since he finds the rights provided by the existence of a social state in Germany enough. Such 'rights' include vacation or monetary payment for overtime hours and compensation for being laid-off. The presence of the social state in Germany appears as an intervening factor for him, since he has before and actually still interpreted these rights as natural consequences of working for the old-established large-scale company. Furthermore, he upon his planned return to Turkey wants to work for an international, large-scale company, instead of starting his own company, which he find risky due to the bad experiences his friends had. Indeed, his path on a secure and linear professional career resembles his educational background, which, as argued here, bears the same qualities. All these together with his effort to promotion by showing his work performance expose his unitary perspective in labor relations.

While listening to the social relations Rhus has established as a HSL migrant, the echo of selectivity fills the ears. His connections are mostly limited to highly educated people from Turkey, with whom he becomes the "we" in most of his sentences. There are two main interests behind this "we", the professional ethnic network. The former is solidarity for adaptation to Germany: "We learned from ourselves for ourselves." According to Rhus, when there was such a quantity of Green-Card-Holders in Falcon from Turkey before the resignation and dismissing waves, they had closer relations among them. Yet more, he formulated that their previous size and their intimacy brought about dissociation from Turkey. In this context, internet communication platforms still play a significant role to share simultaneous migration experiences. As the second meaning of this network for him, this "we" is trying to "correct" the "wrong" image of Turkey and its people, which has its roots in the first generation of labor migrants from Turkey to Germany in the 1960s and 1970s.

> "[…] When 'we' meet with German friends, 'we' try to explain about life in Turkey; for example, how 'we' live, that 'we' are quite modern one can, either have a headscarf or not it does not matter, drinking alcohol is possible, swimming with a bikini or swimsuit in public, etc… Certainly all these kinds of prejudices constitute the image in Germany concerning Turks and Turkey. They look only at Turks living here. These Turks living here really live like they are living in a village in Turkey, and also they live introverted and have separated (different) quarters that have high crime rates, there are even women in a religious black dressing (*karaçarşaflı*) walking the streets in these quarters. When I see them, I acknowledge the public opinion of Germans to be right, because 'we' are the minority here, the rate of the Green-Card-Holders in the whole Turkish community in Germany is about one-two percent. As a consequence, Germans mostly get in touch

> with these Turks, non-Green-Card-Holders; even there are some Germans who study at the same college with second- or third-generation Turks. For instance; these Germans have also some experience with Turkish girl friends, they can complain about the absence of walking hand-in-hand and kissing in public. […]"

Due to this now-isolated and introverted crowd, which is characterized by a rural origin and a lack of education, most "Germans" have a rather distorted idea about Turkey and its people that translates into adjectives such as primitive and macho. That is, while Rhus is trying to convince the locals, non-migrants, that his own profile like the other highly educated people from Turkey in Germany is the 'real Turkish person', he becomes a victim of clichés regarding prejudices within the influence of the crowding phenomenon. Furthermore, it can be determined that Rhus, from some of his sentences in this context, indicates his Atatürkist (Republician) perspective, which refers to believe in nationalist, modernist, and laicist Turkey and its people.

> "When I talk with Germans, I noticed they have some prejudices and I try to destroy them, for example about the Armenian genocide. Germans still think that Turks come from Arabian roots. This thought bothers me. I always tried to break down this kind of prejudice... They ask some very absurd questions, such as if we speak Arabic in Turkey, if we go swimming with our clothes on… […] As a Turkish man, I confront with some extra absurd questions, like the issue of polygamy; the procedure of marriage; for example, whether there is polygamy in general or in your family, and whether your family chooses your wife; and having a macho character; for example, whether you do not to think much of women".

As opposed to show his appreciation to the cultural plurality in work, he talked about cultural difference in leisure, especially regarding German colleagues and the old migrants from Turkey. He has a little contact with the second and third generations of the migrants, who are mostly presented as "people born and brought up in Germany" by the new highly educated labor migrants. According to his observation, they are "neither German nor Turkish" and the highly educated ones among them did "becoming Germanized".

2. Euonymus, 30, single, female

Euonymus was born and raised in Balıkesir, a city in northwest Anatolia. Her father, a doctor, came to Balıkesir in his childhood age with his family who were members of the Turkish minority in Bulgaria. Her pharmacist mother, on the other hand, was originally from Antalya, a city in southwest Anatolia. The pharmacist wife and doctor husband combination is considered prestigious especially in relatively small-cities. Thus, Euonymus, our first female migrant, had highly educated parents with migration backgrounds themselves.

She went to the Balıkesir Anatolian High School, a well-above-average state high school. Given her educated parents, this instance can be considered a reproduction of cultural capital, in contrast to the economic-to-cultural capital transformation encountered in the case of Rhus. Upon graduation, she passed the national tertiary education entrance exam and earned the right to study Computer Engineering at the Bosporus University, a very remarkable achievement in Turkey. Like Rhus, she later noticed the prestige devaluation of her university in her HSLM career in comparison with in Turkey but it does not annoy her either. Once during university, and once short upon prior to obtaining her degree, she had been to Germany twice for the purpose of an internship, which established her sole work experience prior to migration. Due to following extracurricular courses and internship experiences, her German competence is now close to perfect like her English, which she learned as a first foreign language and has actively used in her education life since primary education. That is, after a very high-quality education in her homeland, she entered the HSLM path.

Euonymus has a relatively close relative, an uncle, and some distant relatives in Germany. She did not know before her arrival to Germany about this kinship network excluding her uncle. Like Rhus, she has abstained from this kin network in Germany in spite of partly using its functionality in her first internship period.

Where her second internship was completed at is one of the largest ICT corporations in the world and she also received her first offer from them. As an ICT consultant, she worked in and around Stuttgart for more than three years. After that, she moved to Munich to take up a project managerial position at a regional (Bavarian) but large-scale media company. While she started working for the media company, she was a Green Card holder for about four years, but at the time of the interview, she already had a permanent alien residency. Like Rhus, she is working on a project-by-project basis, and staff-differences between projects are common.

With her own words, even though it had been only six years, Germany is the country where she is feeling at home. Eventually, she described my question of where she is feeling at home as appropriate in her case. Please note that Rhus was finding it hard to feel at home in Germany. Euonymus attributed her feeling to the fact that she did not own a house in Turkey. Interestingly she added that while her home is here in Germany, her homeland is there in Turkey. Furthermore she likes in Germany the absence of a negative societal influence upon her, meaning at least the limiting, less-than-free social environment – which might or might not be gender related - she had perceived. As for advantages of living in Germany, Euonymus said, "nobody interferes with one another" while determining the existence of "societal pressure" as the disadvantage of living in Turkey. In other words, she put forward a dichotomy of the absence of social intervention in Germany versus its presence in Turkey.[2] In this concern, she found that "nobody was interested in one another to a definite extent in Germany" positive. She negatively evaluated Turkey in the context, because every action in your life should be restricted in a frame of certain rules of society. That is, every movement should be expected to fit in the frame of definite rules. As a matter of fact, she said, "Your life should be expected in certain limits (boundaries). Positively about here, because of an absence of societal pressure." It can be argued that you feel more societal pressure in your homeland, whereas in a host country

[2] As above determined, she used "*toplum baskısı*" in Turkish whose direct translation is "societal pressure." Actually the common term "social influence" in English covers similar meaning; however the term "societal pressure" carries itself negativity, therefore I preferred to use its direct translation "societal pressure".

you can live freer from it. You probably have an easier time setting up a home, far from societal pressure, outside of your homeland.

On the other side of the coin she saw a more intense prejudice towards the women ICT specialists in Germany, compared to Turkey, where Euonymus could recall more female ICT specialists. The *amazement* that appeared upon seeing a female ICT specialist was further multiplied when her country of origin was revealed. More generally, the prejudice against people from Turkey was given as one of the reasons for not wanting to have children in Germany. Another reason was the potential identity crisis the child would experience, if the partner were German. In addition to her claim "being a foreigner in Germany generally means encountering prejudice", she finds being a single migrant difficult like Rhus. Before giving advice to potential migrants ("should think again, and consider [your] own future"), she argued that migrants regardless of their genders had always trouble assembling a family in a host country. Given both the pros and cons of living in Germany and her migration experiences, Euonymus was undecided between going back to Turkey and staying in Germany. She associated it with the "ball-rolling": back and forth, to and fro. Furthermore, there was no consideration of a yet another country, since it would be another blank page.

Since Euonymus works on a project-by-project basis, the people working with her were changing, and as such, her social relation with her colleagues was most of the time temporary. But still, she was satisfied with her degree of social contact. In Germany, she found the presence of many vacation days in Germany (more than double as much as in Turkey) as a very important advantage. Furthermore she was filling part of her leisure time with activities such as learning languages and light sports.

It is important to note that Euonymus opened up the topic of prejudice towards people from Turkey multiple times. After the initial discussion in the context of her long-term plans in Germany, Euonymus returned to the topic while describing her social relations. She had observed that the prejudice and its amount depended on with whom she was interacting with, and the city in which the interaction takes place. Even though prejudice was felt rather often in Stuttgart, she had mostly no problems in her current city Munich, suggesting a negative correlation between discrimination and city size. But when it comes to more intense, personal relationships, she stressed that problems of communication and understanding that occurred between inhabitants of Germany and people like her were limiting factors. Moreover a partner from Germany was now seen undesirable due to "cultural differences", which was partly experience-based. Even though she had once came to the point where they considered marriage with a boyfriend from a country neighboring Germany, due to the felt influence of his family, the result was negative. Like self-development courses, this love affair remarks the process of individualization against societal pressures and biological imperatives. Nevertheless, her experience with ex-partner as the individualized other brings out collective descriptions like cultural belongings. To sum up, even though Euonymus, still single, had satisfactory social relations in her daily life, based on prejudice and cultural differences, she was describing more personal relations as difficult.

Unlike Rhus, Euonymus first took a distance from the professional ethnic network. During her first years in Germany, she has completely had contact with Germans and people from other countries. Over time, she established some contacts with people come from Turkey in Germany following a similar pattern, in order to deal with similar problems and common interests. She follows internet communication platforms of the professional ethnic network as a passive member. Like Rhus, she has hardly been in contact with the old migrants from Turkey and their descendents, "people who were born and raised here" in Germany in her words. Still, she allows an open door for some of them, probably those highly educated.

3. Fraxinus, 39, single, male

Fraxinus was born in Kapadokya, Nevşehir, a touristic town due to its famous "fairy chimney" rock formations. Unlike the two previous examples, his family displays lower middle class characteristics. His mother is a primary school graduate and a housewife. His father, on the other hand, had received vocational tertiary education and was a retired electrical technician. Both parents were born and raised in Kapadokya, and were still living there apart from the two winter months each year, which they have spent in Ankara, since they did not have a central heating system in their house. Similar to two previously examined interviews, the family of Fraxinus seems to attach importance to the education of the children, given that both of Fraxinus' siblings are university graduates working as teachers. A small detail regarding his childhood memories is interesting in relation to his migration career. "*Alamancıs*", the so-called guest workers from Turkey to Germany, impressed him. As Fraxinus suggested, nearly everybody in Turkey knows one or more such workers in Germany personally. He said that their wealth, as displayed by all the presents and goods they were bringing from Germany during their holidays, was obvious. This had convinced him that the life abroad is better, or at least more prosperous. Thus, his lower middle class family that valued education and his observations of the Turkish migrants working in Germany had established the early factors for his later migration experiences.

When he was only twelve years old, he left his hometown for Balıkesir, in order to attend the Vocational and Technical High School. These state-boarding high schools, encountered in many cities in Turkey, can be considered a source of above-average secondary education especially for the children of lower middle and working class children, since they are free. Albeit limited in content, the first language he started learning there was German, corresponding to the single formal German education in his life. His movement to west from mid-Anatolia for the purpose of high school education was followed by a move to Istanbul, where he attended the Electric and Electronics Engineering Department of Istanbul Technical University (ITU). In engineering sciences, ITU is considered the most prestigious state-university in Istanbul and teaching is done partly in English. After obtaining his Bachelor's of Science degree he gained job experience working at one of the largest steel companies in Turkey. After that, another phase of state initiative began in his educational career. Due to the high points he scored in the relevant exam, he was selected for a difficult-to-obtain state grant, and left for England where he took up Master's degree. These state-grants for graduate studies come with a condition. The receiver of the grant, upon the completion of his/her studies abroad, must come back to Turkey and work for a year at a state-related institution, which usually also channels the money for the grant. In order to fulfill the condition of the obligatory service, he worked at Etibank, which was founded as a state-run company in order to supply the natural and financial resources to the economy. Then, like many other computer and electronics/electrical engineers, he completed his compulsory military service as a reserve officer, teaching English and Electronics at the Naval War Academy. In Turkey, the university graduates are drafted as either common soldiers and finish the service after around six months, or as reserve officers and finish in one year. The reserve officers have the advantage of not having to endure difficult conditions the common soldiers face and furthermore, they receive a monthly payment. Since it is the army that decides who will be drafted as what on the basis of needs, it is much more common that engineers become reserve officers, compared to, for instance, the graduates of social science branches.

During his Master's years, Fraxinus was impressed by the UK. The government offices functioning logically, the extended freedom, the respect for human rights, all relative to the conditions in Turkey, made him decide already there that he should live abroad. Actually, this role of education abroad as a preparatory factor for later HSLM was already observed in the case of Euonymus, for whom her internships had a similar influence. This in mind, after the end of the military service, he applied for and received permanent alien residency in Canada. At this point, the special role of Canada as a receiving country of HSLM is worth a closer inspection. 18 percent of the population of Canada is foreign-born. Canada's immigration policy differs significantly from that of Germany, since it is a *permanent* immigration program, meaning that most of the people who move to there in order to join the labor force are granted permanent alien residencies. Annually about more than 200,000 people start to live in Canada as a permanent resident. In 2005, 82 percent of the migrants from Turkey moving to Canada were professionals or skilled workers under the category of economic migrants, with the vast majority of them in possession of a permanent alien residency. The contrast between Germany's and Canada's migration policies is further exemplified in the case of Fraxinus, who was granted the Canadian citizenship after four and a half years of work experience there, whereas in Germany he would need seven years. He was working in Toronto for a large-scale global Canadian company in the domain of semiconductors of the ICT sector. Further adding to his multifaceted international migration career, he had spent six months at the USA office of the company. After working in Canada, he decided to add yet another country to his HSLM experience, namely Germany.

The reasons behind Fraxinus' choice of leaving Canada for Germany, despite his freshly acquired dual-citizenship, can be understood under his practical approach. Geographically he wanted to be closer to Turkey, since he wanted to be able to visit his family at will, which actually was given as the sole reason for going to Turkey. Furthermore, he wanted to use the advantages of the Ankara agreement for labor migrants from Turkey and was immediately granted his Green Card. Furthermore, Fraxinus was not registered at the Turkish consulate in Germany, but at the Canadian consulate, suggesting that Canada would be more helpful than Turkey if he had any problems where his state could intervene. As such, using the Turkish passport for working in Germany, but his registration at the Canadian embassy displays another aspect of his practical concern and the care he took in order to make the process of moving to and living in Germany as smooth as possible.

Fraxinus' ways of describing himself, his country of origin and the country of residence complete the picture concerning the migratory path he took in his life. As a person calling himself a humanist liberal, he was sick and tired of the rights violations, disrespect for individual freedom and other inconveniencies that disturbed him during daily life in Turkey. Moreover he argues that he never had any adaptation problems abroad. As will be described later, he had experienced prejudice as a person coming from Turkey to Germany like other migrants, but according to him this did not have an influence on his adaptation process. After these parameters legitimizing the migration, selection of Germany as the final destination after several tries is mostly based on the fact the annual vacation time here is very favorable for Fraxinus'. Please note that this was also the case for both Rhus and Euonymus. Furthermore the way Fraxinus spent his leisure time after work was also more satisfactory in Germany. Living in the center, compared to his flat in the outskirts of Toronto, and the amount of other migrants from Turkey in Germany were cited as other advantages of life in Germany for him. As a person who separates his leisure from work time, he mentioned the special importance of leisure time for any migrant worker to integration into the new country. He still underlines that he has never any problem adapting, although he generally feels nowhere at home.

In the context of his labor-related experiences Fraxinus named social security (*sosyal güvenlik*) as the main advantage of working abroad in general. That is, the security provided by compensation in case of job-loss and state support for the unemployed were seen as the sole work-related advantages of his life abroad, which for him were not as important as other pros of the migration experience. Eventually, after that remark he went on to say that the best advantage of working abroad is living abroad itself. According to him the work environment in Turkey is not worse than in Germany, but the panorama, which is characterized above in relation to basic rights and freedoms, you encounter after work is. That is to say that the main pulling factor for Fraxinus was not the work conditions *per se*, but the absence of the issues derived from the presence of the social state that bothered him while in Turkey, which is not unrelated to his liberal and individualistic character.

In Germany, he had been working at a large-scale, international company based in the USA. He displayed neither interest nor knowledge when it came to labor unions. Actually, he had never been a member of any such union, despite his work experience in

Turkey, Canada, the USA, and Germany. It seems, most highly skilled employees, especially engineers, are not prone to be affiliated with a labor union, since they are satisfied enough with their basic rights provided by the social state directly. In addition to this, Fraxinus was working on a short-term contract basis, but this temporariness of his job did not bother him, and he grounded that in his relatively young age. He argued that this situation was his choice, and he could have behaved differently if he'd been 45 or older, preferring a more stable work life. Indeed, Fraxinus prefers the temporary nature of his current job due to the associated flexibility, arguing that, thanks to his age, the probability of insecurity is irrelevant before the threshold age of 45.

Fraxinus observes a two-way prejudice between the inhabitants of Germany and migrants from Turkey. In his own experience, since most migrants from Turkey are unqualified or semi-qualified employees, like the cleaning staff at his company, the locals are surprised by the fact that there is now a highly qualified person from Turkey among them. As such, he has to show that he is different by displaying his intellectual repertoire, in addition to his professional skills. That is, he has to actively oppose the belief that somebody from Turkey cannot be a highly educated, intellectual person. On the other hand, Fraxinus observes that the migrants from Turkey are prejudiced towards Germans, and as such, he further has to prove that this is not the case for him.

It seems one strategy Fraxinus has discovered, in order to oppose the above-mentioned prejudice towards Turkish migrants, is to show his English skills. He argues that for most people, being able to speak very good English is seen in stark contrast to being from Turkey, and as such, leads to a change in how the people evaluate and/or categorize him. He even declared that the inhabitants did then say, "you cannot be a Turk" to him. That is, with his English competence and other similar abilities; he ceases to exist as a member of the "Turks" category. This process can be described as follows. When the locals in Germany meet a HSL migrant from Turkey for the first time, they notice that the attributes of that person do not fit the "Turks" category. Figuratively, this is like a first-time encounter with a "black swan", after having seen thousands of "white swans". The conflict that creates for the definition of the category can be resolved by ascribing distinction and difference to the "black swan" such that, he/she will be kept separate from the general "swans" category, that still has the "whiteness" property (basic or average education and no intellectual accumulation). But accepting "black swans" as "swans" is an action that deconstructs the predefined categorization system.

During the course of the interview, Fraxinus touched differently upon a gender-related issue that had attracted his attention like Rhus'. The sexist and patriarchal system in Turkey produces an illusion regarding how German women view Turkish men. According to this illusion that is reproduced in the media, German women are fond of macho Turkish men due to their masculinity and "sexual" powers. The truth according to Fraxinus, on the other hand, could not be more incorrect, which he formulates, in its all bareness, as "German women actually hate Turkish men". Furthermore Fraxinus seems to take sides with the German women, giving the example of the so-called honor killings associated with Turkey and Turkish men in Germany. Later it will be discussed whether this taking sides attitude observed in the case of highly skilled male labor migrants from Turkey connotes to a kind of feminization.

Fraxinus' description of and approach to the older migrants from Turkey, who came to Germany as the so-called guest workers, reveal the dilemmas and antinomies of the HSLM phenomenon in the context of social relations and identity. Fraxinus accuses the old migrants with indifference to "life in Germany" and ignorance concerning the developments in Turkey in the last decades. He calls them explicitly "very underdeveloped". One example is, the migrants emptying the instant coffee shelves in markets before their trips to Turkey, since they still believe that this product is not available in Turkey. According to him, old generation migrants from "underdeveloped" Turkey of the 1960s in Germany are more conservative, while new ones from "developed" Turkey of the 2000s are more liberal. They have no idea about the progress observed in the cities of Turkey, and this is due to the fact that all they see while in Turkey is their small villages. He attempts at strengthening his argument by referring to Turkish TV series shown in Germany, which display only the rural village life with a special emphasis on the feudal lords. As such, the integration problem in Germany is explained by the negative characteristics of the Turkish community only, without any need to question the insufficient integration policies of the German state and the reaction of the society towards these migrants. The antinomy appears when the current developmental status of Turkey is addressed with an emphasis on regional differences. Fraxinus argues that cities are developed, which is indeed true, but Turkey is known to have a great divide between its rural and urban parts. As such, the migrants, many of whom come from rural, underdeveloped areas, still find the resembling situation upon their arrival in their village. Fueling this are the serials mentioned by Fraxinus which are however produced mainly for an audience in Turkey, and not to fulfill the "wrong" fantasies of the migrants in Germany. Such preconceptions on his side further explain why he has only limited contact with such migrants. His interactions with them are restricted to small talk at work and in Turkish coffeehouses, where he watches the Turkish football league matches. To sum up, Fraxinus views himself as a representative of the current, developed Turkey and sees a contrast between himself and old migrants, who, according to him, live in a frozen Turkey of the 1960s.

Fraxinus does not have any membership to any association in Germany, because he thinks that there are enough relevant associations here in Germany. Even though he had initiated the foundation of certain institutions while in Turkey and Canada, he thinks there are enough such platforms in Germany. That is, without a founder role, he does not seem to display interest in such platforms. But he is following many virtual communication platforms, both for Green Card holders in general and for the HSL migrants from Turkey only. According to him, the function of the latter virtual communities is to learn possibilities about living and working in other countries, to discuss various issues, and to be informed about news and social activities related to the homeland. That is, his wider social network is limited to virtual relations with an absence of any organizational commitment.

4. Syringa, 30, divorced, male

The family history of Syringa, who was born in Germany, differs from the three examples that were studied before. At the beginning of the 1970s, his primary-school graduate parents from Malatya, a city in east Anatolia, had moved to Germany and joined the guest workers here. That is, his parents belonged to the working class. In 1977, when he was one year old, he went back to Turkey with his mother who remained as a housewife. His father stayed in Germany, but in 1980. He helped out some other guest workers from Turkey to visit their homeland. He rented a bus and took the migrants who wanted to go to Turkey. At the border he was arrested due to a large amount of foreign cash in the bus, which was illegal. The military coup at the time had put the justice system in Turkey on hold, and he spent six months under house arrest while waiting for a court date. After his acquittal, he could not go back and work in Germany anymore, since his permit had expired. He worked in Turkey as blue-collar employee, and at the time of the interview was already retired. Syringa has an older, university graduate brother who migrated to Germany in the 1990s and at the time of the interview he was working as medical doctor and living here with his family. The working-class background together with the migration history of the family has an important influence on the HSLM career of Syringa, unlike the previous interviewees'.

The education history in the case of Syringa is less shiny compared to the previous examples. He attended a General High School in Malatya, where he probably learned only introductory English. After that he entered the Department of Mathematics of Hacettepe University in Ankara. It was there he had his German courses, and the courses were partly taught in German. This might have been an intentional choice, suggesting that the history of the family of Syringa had already biased him towards a life in Germany. Actually, right after the university, he attended a five-week language course in Germany, while staying with his brother. After approximately four years of work experience in Ankara and Istanbul at companies with commercial relations to Germany, he was able to profit from his job connections and migrated to Germany. Thus, his whole educational and occupational choices prior to migration seem to indicate a will to migrate to Germany.

His came first to Germany in order to start working on a project with another ICT specialist friend who was already in Germany. Upon the cancellation of the project before the take-off, he briefly thought about going back to Turkey but he then looked for a job and was successful. For a year he worked at a company that needed an ICT specialist with good Turkish skills. At the time of the interview he was working for a branch of a Dutch company, where he was the single foreigner, and as such, the single Green Card holding employee. He had been living in Stuttgart for three years at the time.

Syringa had two reasons two migrate and he recited those multiple times with the same following order: escaping military service and the absence of work ethic in Turkey. Indeed he came to Germany when he had only 20 days left before being drafted. But these are not the only advantages of Germany for him. The rising nationalism in Turkey was disturbing him, and the unjust distribution of wealth there was yet another factor. As such, Syringa was not only concerned about his own career, but he was sensitive to the overall socioeconomic and political conditions that were affecting Turkey, like Fraxinus. For instance, he said, "[…] Money is not the main reason for my immigration to Germany, perhaps the last reason. However, the economic division in Turkey played a large role." As such, the presence of the social state in Germany was very favorable. Concretely speaking, the fact that in Turkey he was earning fifteen times as much as the minimum wage there, was a reason to leave, and not a reason to stay.

One of the milestones of Syringa' migration experience was his divorce. Between his two jobs in Germany, he had visited Turkey for a project related to his previous work. He married there his long-term girlfriend who is an ICT specialist as well. They came to

Germany together and after a year they had a divorce. Syringa's reflections upon the factors that contributed to the divorce are important. Here the terminology of orders of migration seems suitable. First order migrations are the spouses who first migrate. The second order migrant joins the first in the host country. But the first order migrants generally come with a prearranged job, and more than often, they have prior experience regarding this country, and hence are more likely to have the required language skills. These differences hit the second order migrant from two sides. On the one hand, finding a job upon arrival is not so easy. And repeated attempts that end failure have an obviously detrimental effect on self-confidence. On the other hand, insufficient language skills prevent the second order migrant from establishing a social circle, highlighting the importance of leisure time together with the working time. To sum up, Syringa's partner had adaptation problems in Germany, their marriage ended after a year and she returned to Turkey.

"Where do you feel at home?" question was no stranger to Syringa. He had been asking himself the same question all the time. He was not sure whether he had a satisfactory answer yet. Even though he said he did not feel at home anywhere, he added that he felt at home in his flat, suggesting that only the material connotation of the word home was fulfilled. Furthermore, he said that he was feeling uneasy about feeling at home in Germany, which was granted by the "regular life" here; and as such, he actively avoided the thought.

Syringa's description of his work life shows that even though the second order migrants might be seen to have qualitatively more problems during the adaptation process, the first order experience is not free from difficulties either. Even though he defined his work atmosphere as quite good, he did not have relations with his co-workers outside the office. In Turkey he was spending his leisure time with his colleagues from the office, such as going out at night for a drink or making trips to other cities on the weekend. He said that he was not a very social person and admitted that outside the work hours, he was often bored, and was still trying to find more useful ways to spend his time. That is, the reorganization of leisure time creates problems for both first and second order migrants. Syringa, who is not a member of any social or political organization, was that of a loner character after his divorce, which was intensified with his rather limited social life, to which I will return later.

Again in the context of work, Syringa compared the pros and cons of professional life in Germany and Turkey. Paradoxically, even though he had more leisure time in Germany, due the absence of a satisfactory social atmosphere, the life in Germany was reduced to work and money for him. The only concrete thing he had was his secure job. In Turkey on the other, he had friends, he loved Istanbul, but work covered most of his life since there were no effective work ethic and regulations there. That is, the dilemma experienced by Syringa can be described as a double dissociation: A work-oriented life in Germany, despite more leisure time and vacations, versus a leisure-time oriented life in Turkey, even though there is no real leisure time, since the working conditions are employee consuming.

With the exception of his brother, Syringa's social relations in Germany are mostly restricted to other HSL migrants from Turkey, with whom he communicates via virtual, e-mail-based platforms. But during his interactions in the largest of these platforms, he came across nationalist expressions, which he has openly criticized. This had the consequence of him being unsubscribed from the group by an administrator. Such developments turned him into a person, who would select people on the basis of certain criteria, and this selectivity was new and confusing for him. On the one hand, most of the older migrants in Germany do not have a good education; hence he distances himself from them. Accordingly his 'we' becomes in his sentences the highly skilled migrant population from Turkey. But a second criterion arises as a reaction to discriminatory Turkish nationalism, which is most probably just natural, given his Kurdish background. To sum up, seeking education and non-nationalistic disposition in communication partners reduces the amount of people he has contact with.

Syringa's self-described elitism, i.e. selectivity, leads to the employment of the term "different" quite often, while referring both to himself and others. After the end of his membership to the largest HSLM virtual platform for Turkish people, he noticed that there was smaller group that consisted of different and like-minded people. He established good connection with some of those people and had even met one of them in person. Similarly, according to Syringa, his father was an atypical migrant. Unlike others he learned German and tried to help out other migrants who wanted to visit their homeland, revealing his interest in self-development and social sensitivity. Long story short, in the example of Syringa it is obvious how difficult the migration experience becomes during resocialization in the host country, while one tries to find like-minded people on the basis of criteria such as education, non-nationalist disposition, and a similar migration history.

5. Mespilus, 31, divorced, female

Mespilus comes from an urban middle class family that lived during most of her lifetime in Istanbul. Her high school graduate father was a retired branch director of a bank. Her mother, on the other hand, had arts education at the level of senior high school; the fact that she did not work probably reflects the financially advantageous status of the family. Mespilus stressed the fact that that they have *no village*, meaning that unlike most people who migrated to Istanbul later, they are a relatively old Istanbul family, with no functional roots anywhere else in Turkey. Actually, she explained her lack of any relatives in Germany by this factor, which is a reminder that it was rural Turkey that sent the first generations of worker migrants to Germany. Conversely, Istanbul seems to be the important locale in the context of HSLM, considering that all the interviewees so far were either directly from Istanbul (Rhus and Mespilus) or they have spent a certain portion of their educational and/or professional career there (Euonymus, Fraxinus, and Syringa).

Mespilus attended a prestigious General High School for girls. Such prestigious and old General High Schools are an exception to the rule that General High Schools offer relatively low-quality education. After that, she studied Mathematical Engineering at ITU and graduated from there.

Mespilus had come to Germany with the Green Card program more than five years before the interview. Adding to the effects of economic crisis in Turkey, her husband, also an ICT specialist was going to be drafted, and he wanted to avoid military service. It shows indirect influence of military service obligation as a pushing factor on female HSL migrants. Via internet in the light of information taken from a friend from METU, she found a position in Germany and they migrated together. Her husband found a job one and a half months after their migration. When they first arrived, neither of them had German skills, but both spoke good English. They divorced after living together for about three years in Germany. Before coming to Germany, they had been married for around two years, which was preceded by a four-year relationship. Moreover, at the time, she had a permanent residency permit for one month.

Mespilus and her husband's decision to come to Germany instead of another country seems at first sight coincidental. But she explicitly said that getting a visa for Germany would be easier than getting one for the UK, for instance. This suggests that the Green Card Program Federal Republic of Germany function well in terms of pulling HSL migrants from Turkey. Indeed, for them, two weeks were enough to make-up their mind and start making arrangements. She had found the job, and the company had even helped them find a flat in Frankfurt. Even though they were first shocked after they found out that Frankfurt was so small in comparison to Istanbul, they got used to it. To sum up, even if the migrants themselves are not completely aware of it, Germany as a HSLM receiving country has certain advantages relative to other countries and these advantages play a definite role in the migration decision and during the migration career.

Overall, Mespilus seemed to be happy with her migration decision and experience. The reasons she provided included the orderly life in Germany, the advantages of the social state, "secure streets"– which is especially important for women, she said, long leisure hours and more vacation. She added, "Everything is open here. You can *be* as much as you *want*. In addition, I am thinking about doing an MBA." It was such that she could not find any reason to go back to Turkey apart from her family. Just like Rhus she argued that the amount she earned in Germany was comparable to before. She ruled economical advantage out as a reason to prefer the life in Germany. Regarding her yearning for her family, she was visiting Turkey, and her parents were coming to Germany both twice a year. Accordingly, Mespilus, while enjoying the benefits of her work and life in Germany, was able to overcome the distance from her family with frequent visits of both parties.

Similar to Syringa's experience, Mespilus had a divorce after the migration. I told her that divorce following migration is rather common among ICT specialists from Turkey, and asked what the reasons could be. Mespilus described both the reasons leading to the decision and the factors that help avoid the negative consequences of divorce. Like Rhus and Euonymus as becoming migrant as single, Mespilus thinks that people, who come to Germany as couples have an easier time to start a life in Germany. But if the adaptation processes of the two partners differ, that is, if the coping mechanisms they employ in the face of distance to family or their novel habitat are different, then the marriage starts to shake. Mespilus talked about it with the following sentences:

> "[…] In the end you are not with your family anymore […]. You leave your habitat and come to a very different one, and you get isolated, you don't have any friends. You ought to create a new environment for yourself. During this process people start changing. People's likes and dislikes might diverge. For instance you have more time here than in Turkey, and one is supposed to do something with that. Because of that one might get depressed, or you can do something else with it."

At this point, it is important to remember that most interviewees so far have admitted having more leisure time in Germany, and that this leisure time plays a significant role in the re-socialization and adaptation process. Hence, the diverging adaptation processes of the two partners can correspond to distinct activities they prefer to fill their leisure time with. Moreover, according to Mespilus, for partners, who are both financially independent and who have no children – which is a consequence of working hard – divorce is not a difficult decision to take. This answer entails that some of the unwanted or difficult-to-solve consequences of a typical marriage do not hold for couples of this type. As such, for partners with diverging adaptation-to-migration processes, the divorce becomes a natural choice if they do not have financial and parental interdependencies.

Considering the short amount of time Mespilus had spent in Frankfurt, the amount of her regular social activities was remarkable. Apart from painting at home, she had been active in theater, and at the time of the interview she was singing in two choirs. She was singing Requiem for a philharmonic orchestra and Turkish Art Music in the other choir. In addition, even though she was not active inside, she was a member of *Atatürkçü Düşünce Derneği* (ADD, Association for Atatürkist Thought). ADD is a Kemalist NGO in Turkey, with offices in Germany, including in Frankfurt and Munich. She said that the increase in her leisure time as a result of migration allowed her to be this socially active.

Mespilus described her German skills as insufficient. While in Germany, between two jobs, she had attended a course for three months, and after that she had followed an evening course for a while. Even though she accepted that her German was better than many of her friends from Turkey, she still saw room for improvement. But unlike Fraxinus, who was using English as means to show he is "different", Mespilus preferred to speak German even at work, even though her co-workers were more eager to speak English, in order to practice their language skills. Actually, her German skill was the first thing that came to Mespilus' mind, when she was asked about her initial adaptation.

Before her migration, Mespilus had worked as an ICT specialist for a total of four years at two companies in Turkey. Both companies were international and large-scale. How she found her first job in Germany in one of the largest banking corporations has an interesting story. A friend, who probably knew of Mespilus' and her husband's intention to migrate abroad for work, informed them about a position at that banking corporation, where he/she was working too. Even though it was her husband who applied for the position, during his job interview, it was understood that he was married to an equally qualified ICT specialist. The company, who probably wanted to hire women, in line with the positive discrimination policies in Germany, gave the job to Mespilus. That is, in the example of Mespilus, the priority of HSLM-employment becomes visible.

Mespilus started working for the banking corporation in Frankfurt, but four years before the interview, that corporation became a wholly owned subsidiary of an insurance corporation. Even though she did not lose her job, during commercial discussions between her company and its subsidiary firm, she was unemployed for three months. After that she continued working there, but this time in Munich. She mentioned that during that process around 5,000 people have lost their jobs. Some had to resign since they did not want to move with their families to Munich. The company is a Germany-based country with offices worldwide, but according to Mespilus, 99 percent of the employees were from Germany. At the time of the interview she held a project leader position, which was intermediary between a common employee and a project manager. She argued that the positions she held in Germany were comparable to those in Turkey, suggesting an uninterrupted occupational career in spite of the migration experience.

At the time of the interview, Mespilus was recently granted the permanent alien residency. Being able to work now as a free-lancer or launch her own start-up were regarded as a source of relief, but she made clear that since she always possessed a Green Card and so a five-year permit, the practical change for her was minor. This suggests that the privileges of ICT specialist migrants, and the relatively positive working conditions and rights in Germany decrease the significance of a permanent permit on top of them.

Mespilus' direct comparison of the working conditions in Turkey and Germany bring out to light themes already familiar from the previous interviews. Like all other ICT specialists covered, Mespilus is very critical of working rights and conditions in Turkey. The hierarchical structure at work, overtime without extra-pay, and job insecurity are some of the particular reasons. Other differences are in the social domain. The now familiar difference between the German colleague and the Turkish colleague, the former being less personal (colleague is colleague), and the latter more like a friend had been spotted by Mespilus too. Remarkably, Mespilus shared Euonymus' observation that female ICT specialists are more common in Turkey than in Germany. But unlike Euonymus, who complained about "prejudice" towards women in the sector, Mespilus enjoyed working with men only, probably due to the privilege provided by her high-level in the company, even though her position is classically a man's position. Mespilus clearly preferred working in Germany and had no intention to return under given circumstances.

Mespilus has a relatively big social network mostly consisting of "Turks" even though she complains about insufficient solidarity in the professional ethnic network. She reproachfully said "Well, *orientation* (Original is English),,, everybody made his/her own orientation. Nobody,,, helped really. […]" It is worth mentioning that she has contacts with not only other new HSL migrants from Turkey but also with second and third generations of the old migrants. Interestingly, partly due to her own experiences, she thinks that the solidarity among newcomers is weak, especially if compared to the solidarity displayed by the first generation migrants from Turkey. It was clear that she did have expected more help from other HSL migrants from Turkey than from other people. She was criticizing especially the virtual networks, which, she argued, could be used more efficiently. The absence of other highly educated migrants from Turkey working at the same company explains why she has turned to virtual platforms for help.

Her social relations with second and third generations of the old migrants from Turkey distinguish Mespilus from many other interviewees. She explains that most of the newcomers from Turkey are not interested in active involvement in activities such as Turkish theater and choir. The participants were mostly older migrants or their descendant. Actually, such experiences had convinced her that especially the educated individuals from the second generation are not so different from people like her. She had a second-generation highly educated boyfriend who had come to Germany when he was one year old. But Mespilus also admitted that she had very limited contact with friends in Turkey, suggesting that her remarkably large social network in Germany was replacing her previous circle of friends.

6. Acer, 29, single, male

Acer's family bears the marks of a (lower) middle class family. Both parents are high school graduates, his father is retired as low-level civil servant, and his mother is a housewife. Acer has an educated housewife mother in common with Mespilus' and Rhus'. The presence of the educated housewife mother figure in the family is conspicuous. In addition, Acer does not have any relatives in the destination countries of his migrations like Fraxinus and Mespilus.

Acer spent all his educational life in Ankara, where he was born and brought up too. He is a graduate of an Anatolian Technique High School and Ankara University, where he studied Electric and Electronic Engineering.

After his university graduation, Acer worked in Istanbul for six months at a prominent Conglomerate known for their telecom branch. In 2000, because of a project at a company related with the Conglomerate, he came to Darmstadt, Germany for six months. But due to the economic downturn in Turkey, the project was cancelled. He went back to Turkey and continued working at the same Conglomerate. After two years of preparation, he took an Internetwork expert exam in 2002, and received the prestigious international certificate, which at the time was possessed by only 7,000 people in the whole world. Afterwards he went to the UK, sent his CV to headhunters, and he waited for job offers. But since he did not have a work-permit, it was not possible to find a regular job. In that period he had part-time ICT jobs and took business classes.

Upon an invitation from the single telecom company of Saudi Arabia, he moved there and worked as an ICT consultant for four months. This work phase was followed by another migration to Istanbul, where he worked at a telecom company, which was owned by another very prominent Conglomerate in Turkey. But according to his own words, Acer was bored with this adventure after eight months. Thanks to the headhunters in the UK, who still had his CV, he was offered an ICT-consultant position in European State Agent in Darmstadt, Germany. He received his Green Card as soon as he started working there. Since he was again bored, he voluntarily cancelled his contract at the end of the six months long probation period and left for Istanbul. Inside the framework of a project, he again started at the last Conglomerate he worked for. After a year, due to the fact that this project's headquarters, a telecommunications company, were in Frankfurt, he had come back as a senior board engineer to Germany two weeks prior to the interview.

At the time of the interview, he was a manager of an ICT team consisting of four people from Germany. But the overall atmosphere of the company was international, with migrants from, for example, Bulgaria and Kyrgyzstan.

Acer is a very career-oriented person. His answer to the "where do you feel at home?" question is remarkable: "where I make money". He was extremely sure of himself and described his whole professional career as a series of his well-calculated decisions. He was working abroad, since this meant gaining a global perspective and knowledge about the world for him. He was always reading technical books, since in the ICT domain, being up-to-date and mastering the state-of-art technologies was essential: "Investment in our job is knowledge". He argued that job security could become a problem only for people who are not good at what they are doing. Since he was always aware of the latest advances in the field, he was never afraid of losing his job. With his "surfboard" made of knowledge and experience, he said he was ready for the second wave of telecommunication, which he expected to arrive in the near future. Being away from his family and home city was not an issue to him, since with technological advances such as internet, physical distance had lost its meaning. In the context, Acer so argued that either working in Istanbul or in another country makes no difference for him. He also said that if he had found the right person, he would marry her, only after having realized his plans such as starting his own small but international company.

Acer did have observations regarding the internationalization of the ICT-labor market. Internet is extremely important, since 99 percent of the time one can find a job there. He explained that headhunters in London were trying to close the staff gap in Europe and Middle East, and certainly Europe is run from the center of London. Even though the ICT market in the UK is still the largest one, the market was still bigger in Germany than in Turkey. Also, he spontaneously mentioned that the brain drain was a benefit for receiving countries such as Germany, and Turkey, after investing a lot in the education of people like Acer, was not doing enough to keep the workforce inland. “The market and the people won’t let me work in Turkey”, that is, the work conditions and ethics in Turkey were to blame for the outflow of the highly educated. In the descriptions he provided, HSLM was a phenomenon completely explained and defined by the market, without a need to make a reference to any agent.

Regarding prejudice towards people from Turkey, Acer said it was worse in Germany than in the UK and Saudi Arabia, explaining that only here he had to talk to people for some time in order to prove that he is indeed an educated person.

> “I think that social relations depend on the person, whereas a person should break some certain prejudices. [...] In Germany, you need fifteen minutes in order to explain being educated. They look at your manner of speaking and your attitude, and then they decide to talk with you. However, when they see me as a Turk, a typecasting Turk, from a distance, there is always a prejudice.”

He had further observed the prejudice against the Turkish men, now familiar from the previously covered interviewees Rhus and Fraxinus. Actually, against that prejudice, he had developed the tactic of waiting for the woman to act. He said one should wait for her to get in touch with you, since otherwise the prejudice would set it. The disbelief in that a person from Turkey can be highly educated and the negative image of the Turkish men are commonly encountered by the migrant sample of the present thesis.

Acer's approach to other migrants from Turkey can be understood under his individualism. First of all, underlining that it is established with experience rather than a bias, he argues that the old migrants in Germany from Turkey live in another world that resembles the 1970s. That is, average or below-average education level of the old migrants led him to put a distance in between, by minimizing his social interactions with those people. Furthermore, even though he was a member of virtual platforms for HSL migrants from Turkey, his interest was not in finding other people from Turkey, but "people like him". Eventually, he added that if the HSL migrants from Turkey would establish their own community, this would be similar to the isolated ghettos of the old migrants. He has a clear fear of resembling the old generation migrant community in terms of social network. His evaluation of this issue with the context of "adaptation to the society you live in" together indicates some traces related with de/re-ethnicization. To sum up, Acer was not interested in neither the old nor the new migrants from Turkey, he wanted to have limited relations with only people who are similar to him.

How Acer fills his leisure time is in harmony with his limited social contacts. He loves Yoga, since it is his means of becoming one with the nature. He reads books on progress in business life together with criminal and adventure novels. He watches Science-Fiction films, and displays a clear dislike for "books dealing with social issues". In conclusion, Acer is a career-oriented HSL migrant, displaying all signs of individualism.

7. Ailanthus, 29, married, male

Ailanthus was, like his parents and grandparents, born in Istanbul. But on one side of the family, the great grandparents had come to Istanbul from Thessalonica in the 1920s, during the forced migration of the Greek Turks. Even though his mother with a high school degree had a higher level of education than his junior high school graduate father, she was a housewife. The educated housewife mother figure encountered in the elite family appears again in the case of Ailanthus. His father was the owner of midsize printing house. Ailanthus admitted their social status was above a certain level. Eventually, similar to Rhus, Ailanthus had went to a typical private high school owned by a Turkish foundation. Furthermore upon his father's death in 2001, he immediately started looking for a job abroad, so that he, replacing his father's role, could support his brother's study at a private university. This explicitly reflects once again the transformation of economic capital to cultural capital in the family unit as practices by both Ailanthus' parents and himself. To sum up, Ailanthus from Istanbul has an upper-middle class family that values the education of its members to a large degree, similar to the rest of the interviews seen before.

After the graduation from the private high school, Ailanthus was not successful at his first attempt at the tertiary education exam. At that time, he had prepared for math and science, but since he did not enjoy science topics, the second year he prepared for Turkish and math and gained the right to study Informatics at the Marmara University in Istanbul. This department is of particular interest for the purposes of the current study, since the classroom language is German and the content of the study makes it special given the Green Card program of Germany, which is designed especially for ICT specialists. After one year of German preparatory class, the students take for two years the same classes as the Department of Management, where the classroom language is again German. The last two years they focus on computer engineering related themes, and Ailanthus actually argued that the name of their department should be translated as management informatics. He explained that, upon arrival in Germany, it was very easy for him to get a Green Card, since he has an informatics diploma. Germany was trying to fill informatics positions, and as such, whereas graduates of departments such as management had to answer questions about what their relation to ICT was, Ailanthus had no such problem. In 2000, as a third-year student, he attended a summer school in Bremen, Germany with a DAAD (*Deutscher Akademischer Austauschdienst*, German Academic Exchange Service) scholarship. This summer course, given at the University of Applied Sciences, was about management. Immediately after that, he completed a two-month internship at the ICT department of an international company based in Munich. With his own words: “During my internship I had liked Munich. It was around then when I started contemplating working in Germany”. As in the cases of Euonymus and Fraxinus, the role of phases of education and internship had made Ailanthus more eager to move to the same country in order to work there. Indeed, at the university they were always informed about such summer schools, student exchanges, and internships in Germany. Furthermore some of his schoolmates were already in Germany at the time he migrated, making his migration experience less complicated. With the death of his father, which meant he should find a job in order to support his brother’s study at a private university, the decision to migrate became easier. It can be said he completed a full-preparation for Germany in educational background before his migration. All points under his education background (private high school, tertiary education of Informatics in German language in Istanbul, a summer school for two months and an internship in Germany) appear as parts of a causal chain of events that led to a migration to Germany.

According to the terminology that was introduced with Syringa, Ailanthus is a first order migrant, who got married in Turkey and started living with his wife in Germany. When he came to Germany for the first time, leaving his girlfriend – who now is his wife -, his family and Istanbul was difficult for him. Regarding migration, he said he wanted to “try it at least”, thinking that in case it would not work he could always go back to Turkey. The support of his girlfriend was important too. He was feeling at home in Turkey, but added that his physical home was in Germany. This reveals the discrepancy between the physical and social/emotional home, which is a result of the migration experience that was discussed previously also by Euonymus.

Being a married migrant, Ailanthus was overall very happy, and the main difference with Syringa’s marriage experience seemed to be the way he handled his leisure time. His highly educated wife, who could not speak any German before, had come with a family unification visa, and still had no work permit. Even though the visa process itself was easy, the emotional component of the migration experience was felt heavily since his wife was very much attached to her family. But he added that she turned out to be even stronger than him. She had been learning German for eleven months with good progress and, more importantly, Ailanthus had re-arranged his leisure time around her. The frequency of his visits to Turkey had dropped; he was not seeing his friends in Germany as often. They were going to the European cup away matches of their team from Turkey, visiting the lakes in Bavaria, and even though they were not very socially active, Ailanthus was completely satisfied with his married migrant life.

Ailanthus' usage of the "we" was always referring to him with his wife. And in his future plans, they were playing interchangeable roles. For instance, he said that he wanted to try to establish his own business. In order to be secure, his idea was that one of them would still have regular job, and the other would take care of business. It is clear that his new family unit (Ailanthus and his well-educated wife) tries to develop a future plan to use the whole unit's capacity while minimizing risks around it. But since they did not know whether they were staying in Germany for a long time or not, such plans were on a hold. Ailanthus said they would have to make that decision if they would have a baby, or at the latest before the child's school age. He explained that they wanted to raise the child without a big change in his/her environment, especially not after the start of formal education. He had observed that children who had to change countries in the early years of life had adaptation problems. Ailanthus was very careful regarding each transition in his migrant career; with the first transition being the migration itself, the second becoming a married-migrant, and the third is the potential addition of a father role. By considering, for instance, the differences in insurance systems between Germany and Turkey, Ailanthus was trying to establish the best atmosphere for a possible nuclear family in the future.

Due to his educational background, Ailanthus had a perspective about life and work in Germany, and this positive perspective prove to be correct. He wanted to run away from the economic downturn in Turkey, and believed that both the monetary and work-ethical conditions are better in Germany. Unlike the rest of the interviewees, Ailanthus was convinced that he was earning more money than he would be earning in Turkey. But his lack of work experience in Turkey might be contributing to this conclusion. Furthermore, he thinks the migration had other educational contributions to his personality as well. While he learned to live alone and stand on his feet, he had progressed socially too. He went on to say that having work experience in different countries was an advantage in the business life, and he was now considering himself successful in that respect. He preferred the work mentality in Germany over that in Turkey. He defined the mentality in Germany as refined and clean, suggesting regularity, honesty, and employee-friendliness of the work environment. He argues that this is in stark contrast to the mentality in Turkey, where people think only of themselves and do not respect the other people. That is, even though Ailanthus believes he earns more money in Germany, the work ethic seem to play a crucial role, as was heard from the rest of the previous interviewees.

To sum up, Ailanthus wanted to go abroad for work so that his could provide money for his brother's study, and the monetary opportunities, living standards, work conditions, and the regularity of life in Germany had attracted him. The uncontrolled growth of Istanbul, the unethical work practices in Turkey, and the normalized rudeness of people were the pushing factors. Ailanthus, while being completely satisfied with his decision in those respects, was even viewing the discrimination in Germany towards foreigners as part of the game.

Similar to Mespilus and Acer, Ailanthus had found his job in Munich via internet. After the largest engineering company of Europe approached him, he was invited to Munich for a face-to-face interview. He defined his company as "state-like", that is, they have very clear and straightforward regulations that apply to all candidates and employees. As such, he even had been able to guess his salary before their offer. Furthermore the company paid the costs of his move to Germany and took care that his Green Card was ready within one week after coming to Germany with a temporary visa. He had been working there for four-and-a-half years and was at the sales department of the mobile-network section. Their project involved the online charging of cell phone cards. He described his functions at work as gathering information provided by several technical departments, combining that information into a whole, and presenting it to the client with an easy-to-understand language. The ratio of migrant workers at their department was close to 50 percent, with people from Arab countries, Belgium, Turkey, and so on. This also meant that both German and English were used at work. He was happy to be working in Munich and for his company.

He was satisfied with his working conditions. During the week, he had to work a total of 35 hours that he could distribute among the days as he wished. Furthermore, he had already used the advantages of the social state when the company was considering to lay people off. He explained that when this comes into question, the company and the state have to agree. On the one hand there is a system of how to decide which employees can be laid off. With age, years at company, martial status and number of children, employees gather points, and the ones with few points are chosen. That is, the older employees who are married with children are generally not considered. Since he was the newest and the youngest at the department, it was considered that he was moved to the "*Betriebsorganisatorisch Eigenständige Einheit*". This unit, which can be translated as management-organizationally independent unit, establishes an alternative to unemployment. People moved to that unit receive 66 percent and 19 percent of their previous salary from the state and their company, respectively. This means that they are still paid 85 percent of their previous salary. Moreover, the company provides assistance in finding a new job and preparing their applications. This prevents these people from being listed as unemployed, and helps them to find a job as soon as possible. But in his case, it later emerged that he could work at the mobile-phones department, and after spending some years there, he was now back at the network in the same company again. Such experiences wiped off his fear of losing his job to a degree, since it showed the effectiveness of the social job security system.

Ailanthus further explained the different recruitment processes at the company. He was employed directly by the company, that is, without an intermediary contractor firm. The companies hire around 90 percent of work force directly, and the remaining part comes from the contractor firms. The recruitment of the former group costs less for the company, but the regulations about ceasing their employment are stricter, as seen in the case of Ailanthus. The workers hired via a contractor firm cost more to the company, but these people can be laid off if something goes wrong, without encountering any difficulties. This shows the interplay of the company, state and the contractor firm in order to regulate the work force in the market.

Even though Ailanthus was not well informed about labor unions and the unit at his company responsible for worker rights (*Betriebsrat*), he had already benefited from their existence. After he started working at the company, he received a phone call from the unit at the company and was asked about his starting salary. After he told the amount, they said that everything is all right. They added that during the preparation of the salary offer, the company was considering a smaller figure, but the union intervened arguing that it was too low for a university graduate, and as such, against the law.

There is one main difference, which Ailanthus has observed in the working practices between Germany and Turkey. He argues that the people in Germany are more completing/finishing oriented. He explained that, whereas he was working on many different things interchangeably during the day, his German colleagues were focusing on one job at a time, and they were not moving on to something else before finishing the current job. Even though he admitted both strategies had their merits, he was still finding his own method the less efficient of the latter. In a partially similar manner, Rhus' following words in the context of cultural plurality pros in the work atmosphere bring to mind: "[…] German people are much disciplined and perfectionists. For example, Turks say 'it can be done either this way or that way' but Germans say 'it should be done this way'. Due to working together 'we' are now however much more disciplined." It can be said that both approached about the interaction of working practices in the end.

Ailanthus had not many social contacts. Reminiscent of Euonymus and Acer, he was avoiding social contacts with other highly educated migrants from Turkey. He was not even a member of the largest virtual platform for HSL migrants from Turkey in Germany. He has some contact to the graduates of his department living in Germany. Moreover, he said that they have dinner cross-visits with some of their German colleagues at work. But similar to almost all previous interviewees, more apparently in the cases of Rhus, Euonymus, Syringa, and Mespilus, he added that the relations with German colleagues are not very intimate. In summary, he has not much contact with other HSL migrants from Turkey in Germany but partly with close classmates from the university and some of his German colleagues.

In the adaptation process of Ailanthus, the concept of "tolerance" has a special place. He was finding the dominant culture in Germany as tolerating towards foreigners, and the prejudices he had experienced and observed were normal to him. For instance, he had learned and understood that speaking one's native language with other foreigners in public was annoying and disrespectful. When migrants speak their language, others would think that the foreigners do so in order to prevent them from understanding. As a person who had to tolerate the behavior of "rude" people while even in Turkey, Ailanthus could totally understand why the Germans are at times critical of the behavior of the people with migration background from Turkey in Germany.

> "[…] You can expect from these people directly to be more distant towards foreigners, or to have prejudices against foreigners. Because, think of it the other way around… You are in Istanbul, you are in Turkey, you are in Istanbul; and you can't even take the be-

> havior of your fellow countrymen,,, you can be prejudiced even against them. […] They are citizens of the Republic of Turkey,,, and you can be prejudiced even against them. Because, here these are people who come from outside, and their effects on your order, on your country,,, I mean, one can think they damage these. And I think the Germans got over these issues quite well. In this respect the Germans are a tolerating nation. For instance if somebody made a mistake, if somebody did something bad, 'Oh it must be a Turk', that I hear often, frankly."

According to him, the foreigners come to a new country and the inhabitants see that their established order is affected, which leads them to disprove the behavior of the foreigners. He shows an empathy towards the leading culture in Germany as he is used to be part of the leading culture in Turkey. Clearly, he hesitated talking on his Turkey or his Istanbul. It is meaningful because he knows Istanbul more than Turkey, and people of Istanbul are known as the bearers of the leading culture for centuries even though the city has received many internal migrants from rural Turkey in the last five decades. For him, "the people being tolerated" (migrants/foreigners /minorities) should not expect for much more tolerance from "the people showing tolerance". Similarly, he argues that it is normal that a foreigner at a company in Germany cannot advance in the job as high as German citizens. It can be said that he accepted the circumstances of discrimination against foreigners in Germany, in particular against people from Turkey in the German labor market. He approves this tolerance limit, i.e. the "indirect discrimination" with his own words, and it is perfectly normal that the inhabitants go like: "you come and work, and I direct/manage".

Ailanthus displayed a certain amount of contempt towards the old migrants from Turkey. This shapes his understanding and justification of the prejudice towards the migrants from Turkey. He draws a line between the "Turks in Turkey" and "Turks in Germany". Similar to the previous interviewees, he views the old population from Turkey as less educated, conservative, and culturally-isolated. He argues that the people from Germany understand the difference when they go to Turkey or meet counterexamples like him. He said that even though most of the Germans have prejudice against people from Turkey, but since they are tolerant, they do not speak this out most of the time. But if they meet a counterexample, that is, a "black swan", they say, "you are different". Eventually, he displayed displeasure at isolated districts and lives of the Turkish minority in Germany, and held them responsible for the negative views on Turkish people held in Europe. He and his wife knew only one Turkish-German highly educated friend with older migration-background, and that was the wife of a friend among Ailanthus' alma mater network, who had met her in the USA. In a very similar way with Fraxinus, Ailanthus, who differentiates himself from "Turks in Germany" on the basis of education and culture, enjoys that the same distinction is noticed by the Germans upon meeting him.

Ailanthus' words on man-woman relations at the meeting point of people from Germany and Turkey display on the one hand the affirmation of prejudice, and on the other, he again holds the migrants responsible for the prejudice. He knows from friends that many German families try hard to prevent their children having serious relationships with people from Turkey. But in the context of the negative view on the Turkish men in general, he argues that the behavior of the Turkish people who are new in Germany produces that view. These people, who come from a more conservative country, think that they can have more sexual interactions in Germany. And their self-confidence and selfishness that bear the marks of the relatively patriarchal society in Turkey determines their expectancies in Germany. Once again, Ailanthus views the migrants as the only agents contributing to the emergence of prejudice and bias, attaching no value to the role of the host society and state in the adaptation process.

8. Juglans, 44, married, female

Juglans was born in Istanbul and then brought up in Ankara due to her father's appointment. Her father is a retired army sergeant (noncommissioned officer). Her mother graduated from primary school and is a housewife. Her parents currently spend the warm months in Antalya, and the cold months in Ankara. Like Mespilus,

Juglans graduated from a well-known established general high school, in Ankara. After that she studied Industrial Engineering at METU, Ankara, and correspondingly she has very good English skills.

The conditions and the timing of her migration to Germany differ from the rest of the interviewees, which is crucial in order to demonstrate both the variant and generalized aspects of the migration experience. After university she had eight years of working experience, and prior to her migration she was working as a senior programmer. She met her future-husband from Germany "without migration background" in Turkey, and after the marriage they first tried living in Istanbul. But in the early 1990s they decided to move to Germany together. Accordingly, at the time of her arrival, the Green Card program had not yet started. Otherwise Juglans had neither clear intention nor wish to work abroad, but like nearly all highly educated experts, she had considered the USA as an option. Even though the main reason for her migration was, like in the case of Mespilus, her husband; she was nevertheless no second-order migrant, given that her husband did not migrate to Germany. The pre-Green Card arrival in Germany after marriage with German citizen "without migration background" distinguishes Juglans from other interviewees.

Juglans explains that before the Green Card program, it was impossible to find a job at the ICT sector without speaking German, with the exception of contractors. Furthermore, neither her work experience in Turkey nor her prestigious METU diploma was of any worth in Germany. After her arrival in Germany, she first started learning German at home. Due to the heterogeneity of the educational background of the participants, she did not want to go to the German classes of the local adult education center. Hence she got enrolled in the five-month German course of the local university. Only after that she could start looking for a job. German became the spoken language both at home and at work, for her. Unlike the Green Card holder migrants such as Fraxinus, who is using English in order to show that he is a different Turkish migrant, or Mespilus, who preferred German, even though her co-workers wanted to practice their English, for Juglans it was a must to have very good German skills.

As noticed from TABLE 2, a highly educated person from Turkey becomes migrant labor typically in the late twenties. However Juglans came to Germany at 32 of age in order to be with her German husband in addition to continuing her work life. The devaluation of an educational and professional career from Turkey to Germany disturbed Juglans, who became a labor migrant ten years earlier in comparison with the previous interviewees, more than the others. They notice this devaluation especially in the context of extremely reducing in university prestiges but they find it negligible. Unlike the previous examples, Juglans said as follows:

> "My arrival in Germany is a rather personal thing, that is, neither something I contemplated much about, nor something I really wanted. […] I was 32 when I first came, I did not speak any German. Moreover, I was working in Turkey. Furthermore, I was a graduate of the Middle East Technical University, METU. As a consequence, I had a certain status. Let's say: having a status. Okay? Then, you had to set that status to zero and to go somewhere else to start over… ["And Germany", I added.] Yes, you are a Turk in Germany; you are a woman and 33 years old. Three things. Something like 'triple trouble' (she said this in English)."

Juglans described her situation at the start as a "triple trouble": She was a woman, a migrant from Turkey and in her thirties. That is; age, gender, and ethnicity were factors making her adaptation in Germany difficult. And as mentioned, her occupational and educational capital from Turkey was worthless in Germany. After the language course, she started at a bank at the wage level of a new graduate. Obviously, in the absence of a program such as Green Card, the business life in Germany is hard to enter for someone in her position. With all these in mind, it comes as no surprise to hear that after ten years of staying in Germany, she was still feeling at home in Antalya or Ankara.

The above-cited factors influencing her migration experience negatively are most apparent in the work context. At the bank and the department where she works, the English skills of her co-workers are limited. Moreover, she wants to be able to express herself as clearly as possible, and when writing German texts, she asks the help of her colleagues, who do not really understand why she is acting as a perfectionist. Juglans argues that with English, her first foreign language, it would be much more convenient. Significantly, Juglans is the author of two literary books in Turkish. She states that, until reaching a level, where she can express herself as capably as with English or Turkish, her relatively limited German will be a bother to her.

Despite her eight year of working experience in Istanbul, she had started working in Germany with the lowest wage possible for university graduates. Furthermore, the future she envisioned for her career was similarly limited. She argued that the main reason was the multi-faceted conservatism of the finance sector. After ten years of work at the bank, she is now holding a senior position, but she argues that a promotion to a managerial position for a female migrant from Turkey would be unheard of. She described the ICT sector of a couple of years ago as the leading sector in terms of hatred towards foreigners. Juglans had observed discrimination in terms of nationality, gender, and sexual orientation in the labor market of Germany, especially in the conservative sectors such as finance and banking. According to her, the typical manager profile wanted in this sector is, or was at least, a German male with a family. Although she thinks the structure of the labor market has positively altered according to the new kinds of management models and requirements for labor power, discrimination towards migrants and women in the context of upward mobility in some sectors is still present.

Being an earlier migrant than the Green Card generation, Juglans had more interest in and knowledge about the institutional aspects of the labor market. For instance, she had no fear of losing her job, since she was convinced that most ICT positions are relatively secure. At her bank, 13,000 people were fired a couple of years ago, but she always knew that she was going to stay. Furthermore, unlike most the rest of the interviewees, she was well informed about labor unions and related structures at work. She was following the trends in the structure of the councils that represented the employees. She argued that at the time of the economic downturn, many independent candidates, instead of big labor union candidates, such as from ver.di (*Vereinte Dienstleistungsgewerkschaft*, United Service Union of Germany, a well-known labor union in Germany), were selected for posts at the council. But after the crisis, with the start of the stabilization, the major labor unions started getting their seats back. It can be argued that Juglans' lack of fear of losing her job stems, at least partly, from her knowledge about the dynamics of the labor market including the functioning of the worker-representative organs.

In Germany, Juglans observes that the rights of employees were better in the 1990s compared to the present. She argued that before the economic downturn, it was possible to drop some shifts in addition to the 30 days of holidays. Their working hours were fixed, and they would not work more than eight hours. This had all changed for worse, and only recently, with the intervention of labor unions the situation regarding the work hours was returning to before. Interestingly, she mentioned that young unemployed people are more eager to work without extra pay, which was resulting in a struggle between the old and young generations inside the labor market. Significantly, she mentioned that the companies were still keeping the regulations that were put in effect during crisis. For instance the companies were trying to keep the wages at the same amount, even years after the crisis. Another practice shortly before the downturn was to hire a lot of contractors, and when the company decided to lay off people, those were the first to go. According to her, such practices were part of what is going on in a global scale, like in the case of Turkey, where she knew of people who were not paid for months. It can be argued that the companies use the economic downturn era as an opportunity to renew their work force and to take away certain advantages of the employees not temporarily but for good.

Juglans, while explaining the advantages of working in Germany, touched upon the reasons that brought the highly educated people from Turkey to Germany. From her point of view, the employee rights were better protected in Germany. Losing the job was more unlikely, and in case this had happen, with policies such as social income, being unemployed for some years was not a big problem. More vacation days is yet another advantage. But she said that job security at large firms in Turkey was comparable to Germany. As such, she concluded that the main reason behind HSLM is not money. According to her the highly educated were coming to Germany for the sake of working abroad itself, and the social state related advantages had a small but visible role too.

In stark contrast to Acer, Juglans argues that she does not have an "organic relation to work". That is, unlike the career-oriented migrants, she does not define herself in relation to her profession. Even though she thinks she does not have a real hobby, literature has an important place in her life. She is writer herself, and accepts she reads a lot at home. She explicitly states that her work stays only at work, and her leisure time at home is spent with different things. It can be observed that Acer and Juglans establish the two extremes regarding the role of job in their existential stance, with other interviewees falling somewhere in between.

Identical to Mespilus and Euonymus, Juglans was convinced that the woman to man ratio in the ICT sector was higher in Turkey. She explicitly stated that unlike the conservative finance sector in Germany, there the women were not disadvantaged. She added that the dimension along which the education level changes both in Germany and in Turkey is the class issue. Just like in Turkey, she was aware that there were big differences between the university entrance rates of children that came from working class families and highly educated families. But in Germany there was also a gender dimension, with girls being directed towards gender-stereotypical occupations such as nursing. Please note that Juglans' observation regarding educational equality for men and women is based on middle and upper middle classes of Turkey. That is, a gender gap in education can still hold for lower middle and working classes in Turkey. To sum up, the gender differences present in certain sectors in Germany do not hold for the economically advantaged urban families in Turkey.

Juglans' social relations were to a large degree restricted to her old friends from Turkey most of whom were also working abroad. Similar to the other interviewees, she said that the relations with her co-workers were limited to the office, with no meetings during leisure time. Interestingly, despite her husband being German and her ten years of experience in Germany, she said that she did not have any relations to other Germans either. Eventually she argued that in Germany one learns not to be so close to people. Her two good friends were also highly educated migrants from Turkey, who probably came around the same time as she did. This, together with limited interaction with the Green Card generation from Turkey shows the importance of the synchronicity of the migration experiences for the establishment of social bonds.

Her relation to older working class migrant families from Turkey was next to nothing. She complained that her METU diploma had no meaning for the people from Turkey in Germany, and she views this as a lack of support from their side. Indeed, as the exact opposite of Mespilus, Juglans further argued that there is no real solidarity among them either; according to her, it was more like a competition. She described the problematic stance of older migrants from Turkey in Germany in terms of norms and the modernization experience. That is, they were holding onto both the norms they have brought from Turkey and the norms of the German society. But since the people in Germany judge migrants only with the local norms, their existence in relation to Turkey had no relevance here. Moreover, on the one hand, since they live in Germany, the modernization in Turkey, which is felt in the lives of the people here, is something that they experience indirectly. On the other hand, the modernization in Germany is a top-down process; it is the German society dictating how they should change, and they display a reaction towards this. Unlike Mespilus, Juglans perceives the later generations of the old migrants similarly. According to her, even the educated individuals of the second generation have old-fashioned and conservative values, and they always establish their exclusive social groups. Furthermore the families neither were concerned with nor valued the education of their children. Apart from greeting each other, she has contact with the second-generation people working at the same bank, markedly with female ones. Juglans read the old migrants and their descendents as if they constitute or belong to a different kind of society that is neither Turkey nor Germany.

Juglans stated that she does not think that the Germans will ever stop being hypocritical regarding their approach to Turks. She does not believe that the hidden racism in Germany will ever go away. She added that what they call tolerating is actually ignoring, which is the exact opposite of the view held by Ailanthus. Interestingly she draws an analogy between "Alevis in Turkey" and "Turks in Germany". To her, both groups are "the others". They are objects of social exclusion and also objects of curiosity in these countries. They are ignored, but there is a mystery surrounding them. People are actually curious about their lives, and it is more than common that one hears urban legends about them. As such term "parallel societies" is not enough to the whole process of otherization, since it covers one part of this process: exclusion. The other part that is fed by fantasies can be explained as an "imaginary secret society".

The main wish of Juglans was being perceived as an individual in the society. She complains that typically people view her with her social identity: A woman from Turkey in her thirties, who is an ICT specialist. She generalized this to the rest of the new HSL migrants from Turkey as well. They were all puzzled by being conceived in the image that was established by the older migrants from Turkey. At the same time, they experienced return of the repressed for individuation through migration. She explained this complex picture with the following sentences:

> "[…] If the Kurds come to Germany due to political reasons, they would be of course together, since they have to identify themselves here. Just like the Turks who come as workers. I see such things as neutral, not as positive or negative. There might be a cynical part to it, but if they can identify themselves as Alevis for the first time here, of course they will establish the Alevi Confederation, or of course they distribute an Alevi newspaper. If a person wouldn't live as a Kurd in Turkey, that person can directly identify himself/herself as a Kurd right after arrival in Germany,

> and that this has nothing to do with practicing freedom. [...] Somebody who studied in Ankara, going to the university there, this person comes here for a PhD, looks for a scholarship, and than suddenly says 'I am a Kurd'. [...] They say one understands that he/she is a Turk only after going abroad. I see for instance in the mailing lists of METU, a student doing an internship was asked by a woman from work, whether she will have to have a headscarf in case she goes back to Turkey. Then you ask, why did she say this now, why do they see us like this, Turkey is such a country on the other hand. [...] Here you are identified with your social state of belonging. But you want to know people individually. You ask yourself, why they do not perceive you individually. This is something very sad actually. Rejecting the social state of belonging, on the one hand, and suffering from not being perceived individually. Lately, the people who come here from Turkey have such a conflict. Well, even though I never wore a headscarf, I don't have the right to say 'Turkey is a modern country, it is not like what you think', because this is not what Turkey is. It is just easy to perceive people with their social identity; it is some kind of laziness."

She argued that their new generation was rejecting the social state of belonging, and wanted to be accepted as an individual.

9. Sorbus, 26, single, male

Sorbus was born in Eskişehir, a big city in mid-west Anatolia, but his parents later moved due to their appointments with the following order to Siverek (in Şanlıurfa), Inegol (in Bursa), Iznik (also in Bursa) and finally to Büyükada, Istanbul. Whereas his mother is originally Albanian, his father comes from the Black Sea region of Turkey. His high school graduate father was an electric technician turned tradesman, that is, he was self-employed. His mother was a graduate of Occupational High School for Teaching, and at the time of the interview, she was already a retired primary school teacher. Sorbus had no relatives in Germany, and his migration decision was more accepted than supported by his family.

After the junior high school, he passed the entrance exam for Science High Schools and went to Eskişehir Science High School as a state-boarding student. These high schools give math and science centered education and their graduates are very successful at the university entrance exam. Sorbus argues that at the high school he came across the common ideological and political groups in Turkey for the first time in his life. The school administration was nationalistic and the dormitory chief was very religious. Among the students, there were Nurcus (a religious, sectarian community with known relations to Fethullah Gülen) and leftists/communists. Sorbus did not belong to a group and did not like such formations. After the high school he moved to Istanbul to study Mechanical Engineering at ITU.

Sorbus initially wanted to go to the USA to attend a Master's degree program and took the TOEFL and GRE. Only later his professors informed him that his cumulative grade point average would not be enough for a scholarship and he could not afford to pay for his studies there. From one of his professors, he learned about an English Master's program in automotive engineering in Göttingen, Germany. His application was accepted in 2001. He had taken basic German classes before moving to Germany, and since he wanted to improve his German during his Master's years, he tried to speak German in every possible occasion and even wrote his thesis in German. Obviously, Sorbus' migration was to a degree a result of his Master's study in Germany.

Sorbus wanted to avoid the military service, and this was the main reason that he wanted to continue his education and work abroad. He described military service as unnecessary. To him, it was simply loss of time, independent of how old one is. As argued in the cases of Rhus, Syringa and Mespilus – whose husband wanted to avoid being drafted – compulsory military service in Turkey is one of the strongest pushing factors of HSLM. Indeed, at the time of the interview, Sorbus was planning to fulfill his duty in the form of the fee-paying short period (three weeks) military service. Gaining the right for short-period military service is why Sorbus will complete the required time of working abroad for it in the next three months.

Sorbus does not work as an ICT specialist even though his position satisfies the pre-determined criteria of the current thesis, and as such, an outlier in the sample. At the end of his studies, he wrote his Master's thesis at a large-scale, international company with headquarters in Frankfurt, Germany. After that, the company wanted to hire him as a research engineer and they decided that he would get a Green Card, which was not available for people who came from a non-ICT background. While he was filling the application form in the federal employment office, he first wrote "mechanical engineer" and then they said that he should erase it and write instead "electronic engineer". He added that certain programming languages, which he has neither used nor known before, were written in his job application form. Moreover, the staff department of the company had direct connection with the employment office and he believed that without their help his employment would be difficult. He said that another large-scale company, which was also interested in him, could not get over this process. Furthermore, the people with non-ICT degrees can be only employed if they are going to have a salary of at least 35,000 Euro annually, and Sorbus had started with salary around 40,000. The importance of the Green Card program for ICT specialists and the advantageous conditions it creates for migrant become apparent in the case of this odd-one-out of the sample.

Sorbus argued that he was very happy with his life in Germany. He was totally satisfied with his both social and professional life here. But he added that he would certainly go back to Turkey some time after the military service. His plan was to have a home in Turkey, get married, and establish his "settled life". That is, he knew that he was going to leave the "active life" behind. Whereas active life was characterized by typical bachelor characteristics such as going to bars or discos and drinking with friends, settled life corresponds to having a home and family in Turkey. Actually, he had already started making plans about what he was going to the do in Turkey. This included, first working for a German company in Turkey and then at a certain point start up his own work. Currently, Sorbus chooses to feel homeless, which is for him the active bachelor life he currently has. Accordingly, even though he is completely satisfied with his life in Germany, he will feel at home only when he has a family and work in Turkey.

Sorbus was holding a Road Support Management position at the advertisement and communication department and the work he was doing was about electronic brake systems for cars. Their research and development center was in Japan and they had clients all over the Europe. He described his function as managing the information flow between Japan and Europe establishing a bridge in between. Sorbus was aware that his prestigious ITU diploma had no special value or meaning in Germany, but this had not hindered him from moving fast in his career. He also believes in the critical role of his additional Master's degree from a German university provides for him in the German labor market. After only two years of working experience he was promoted to this managerial position from a lower-level data analyzer position. He is having frequent business trips to the USA and Japan. To conclude, Sorbus is having a very successful career in Germany.

Upon a question about his relations with the colleagues at work, Sorbus prompted a discussion on work ethic and said that since he had not worked in Turkey, he did not know about the work ethic there. But due to the international character of their company, he had worked with people from several nationalities. Like Rhus and Ailanthus, he argued that people with different national backgrounds had different working habits, such as Japanese working fast and flexibly but being prone to mistakes or the Spanish, who are disorganized and slow but very entertaining outside the work context. Actually, all interviewees seem to be particularly interested in work ethic and prefer to make comparisons among people from different countries. In that context, Sorbus added that the Germans are too disciplined, that is, they are not flexible and cannot leave the frame that was established at the start when conditions later change. Although he supposes they think highly of themselves in work, it can be considered in *Sicherheitsdenken* of the employee in German work ethic. He gave the example of their sales department. One of their clients urgently needed some parts for the construction of cars and since he knew they had the parts at the factory, he contacted the sales department and told them to send the parts. But without seeing an official document stating the request, the sales department would not send the parts, which had made Sorbus very angry. Sorbus argued that even though he was having hot arguments and quarrels about such disagreements before, he was now taking it easier, sometimes saying no to the clients and sometimes to the sales department. This is a consequence of interaction of different working practices, as we met in the work experiences of Rhus and Ailanthus.

Sorbus argued that this work discipline and strictness was only one aspect of the general attitude towards work in Germany. He explained that the Germans do not take work personally and their concern is more their family and free time, adding that, in comparison to Turks, the Germans were spending more time with their loved ones. He stated that at the work, Germans have clear responsibilities and they are concerned only with what they are supposed to do, nothing more and nothing less. It is not trying to do your best or acting creatively and flexibly, such that the company will be even more successful. Sorbus said that the stance of Japanese, Americans and Turks (he used the word "we") were the words, "work work work". But with time he had changed his attitude. He said he internalized that this is not his or "his father's company", and was happy doing only that what is expected. Sorbus had adapted to the work ethic in Germany after some time, and was no longer expecting more from people than what they are supposed to do.

Sorbus' opinion on the advantages of working and living in Germany is in close agreement with the views of the previous interviewees. In the work environment, one has more leisure/vacation time, the working hours are flexible, and the working experience is overall stress-free and satisfactory. With his coming to Germany, he wanted to avoid military service, develop his vision, obtain new experiences, get to know different people, and learn a new culture. Only later he added that he had also thought that perhaps he would make money. Once again, the pulling factors in Germany are often more cultural/social than economic. Also, his words on migration as follows are striking:

> "[…] I am obtaining a certain life experience. Afterwards, I want to transfer all these to Turkey. I think of here as (like) a step. For example, if I stayed in Turkey, I would be a different person. But, I came here. I have been here for four years. A lot of things in my self are changed. If a person who knew me four years ago and had not seen me for four years would see me now, he/she would notice this difference in me. […]"

This sense making pattern of appreciating the advanced cultural capital emerged within individualization process through migration experience is similar to all previous interviewees. But, the intention for the advanced cultural capital transportation to Turkey is restricted with Rhus and Acer, besides Sorbus.

Sorbus had no fear of losing his job, since he could not find any reason for why this should happen. He added that there was no sign suggesting he could lose his job, and if he had noticed such a sign, he would just start looking for a new job and was convinced that this would not be difficult. Interestingly, even though Sorbus argued that having a secure job is important, he was not indifferent to the option of taking a risk for a gain that would be impossible with a normal, secure job. In that context, he said it is more the ignorant, the less educated people, who have the courage to take such risks and reach their ambitious goals. He explained that people like himself have an educational investment, and taking a big risk could mean that you drop that investment. That is, Sorbus argues that the educated people are closer to security at work, since they employ their educational investment in a linear manner. The non-educated, on the other hand, take risks and accordingly, at least some of them reach very high stages in their career.

The leisure time of Sorbus was rather active in comparison to many of the previous interviewees. Since he was in central Europe, making weekend trips to other cities and countries, either by car or plane, was easy and he was using this opportunity often. In Frankfurt, he was going to cinema, doing sports, and meeting friends to go bowling, dancing or drinking. His circle of friends was international, with friends from Mexico, Turkey, and Spain. He made clear he was meeting the German friends very rarely outside of work. Actually he used the term "acquaintance" for Germans, reserving the word "friend" for the rest. That is, like nearly all other interviewees, Sorbus has no social contact to his German colleagues during his free time.

In his relations with older migrants, Sorbus is similar to Mespilus, and differs completely from Rhus, Fraxinus, Acer, Ailanthus, and Juglans, who showed a clear contempt towards them. Among the Turkish friends of Sorbus, there are second and/or third generation migrants, and he thinks there is nothing odd about them, they are just born in Germany and have a different culture, that's all. He argued that for a newer migrant to say something like "they can't even speak Turkish" was also pointless, and he found it normal that he had to speak German with some of his friends with migration background.

Sorbus was one of the founding members of the largest virtual platform for the newer highly educated labor migrants from Turkey in Germany, especially the Green Card owners. He explained that first they were four or five people, who met in different cities. One of those others had the idea to start the virtual platform, and Sorbus was excited and contributed with his ideas. He further mentioned that the president of the German-Turkish Chamber of Commerce and Industry (*Almanya-Türk Ticaret ve Sanayi Odası*), who was also a member of TUSIAD, was very active in terms of establishing this network. Sorbus both benefited from this virtual platform and helped people there on several occasions. He stated that there were unnecessary disputes on topics such as the Kurdish issue in Turkey, or unwanted e-mails from migrant candidates in Turkey asking questions, the answers of which can be found in Internet. But overall, it was fulfilling its information sharing platform role quite effectively. He further mentioned that some of his friends established other smaller virtual networks that served more narrowly defined purposes. But due the circulation of the founding members between different countries, such small networks were not as successful and long-lived. But due to its size, the large virtual network seems to be very stable, and it is still a precious source of information for the highly educated migrants from Turkey.

10. Prunus, 27, engaged, male

Prunus comes from the Samandağ province of Hatay, in south Anatolia, where his parents still live. He identifies himself as an Arabic-Alevi and regarding his socio-political stance; he uses the words "laic" (secularist) and "*Türkiyeli*", that is, a person from Turkey. His parents are primary school graduates, and whereas his mother is a housewife, his father is a fisherman, but he was not working anymore. As such, they used to belong to the 400 fishing families of Samandağ, suggesting a rural, lower-middle class nature.

As the border city neighboring Syria, Hatay is a one of the most multi-ethnic and multi-religious cities in Turkey. Even though their numbers decreased over years, members of many different religious denominations such as Assyrians, Alevis, and the Greek Orthodox, and various ethnic groups such as Armenians, Arabs, and Kurds still live there. Following Sunnis, Alevis constitute the second largest religious community in Turkey, and their number is estimated between 15 and 25 percent (10 million-15 million) of the total population. Nusayris who live in the cities of Hatay, Adana, and Mersin present themselves as Arabic-Alevis due to similarities in doctrine and practice to Alevis, and their number is estimated at two millions. Alevi philosophy, customs, and rituals differ largely from both the Sunni and Shia traditions. They have a Sufi doctrine of the "Perfect Man" (*İnsan-i Kamil*) and salvation lies partly in emulating perfect symbolic figures. Their tradition is commonly seen as humanistic. In brief, the characteristics of the ideal Alevi include (i) love and respect for all people ("The important thing is not religion, but being a human being"); (ii) tolerance towards other religions and ethnic groups ("If you hurt another person, your prayers will prove worthless"); and (iii) respect for working people ("The greatest act of worship is to work"). It is natural to assume that the Alevi/Nusayri minority culture, especially the emphasis on education and work, had a certain influence on the life course of Prunus.

Reminiscent of Sorbus, after junior high school Prunus earned the entrance exam for science high schools and left for Trabzon (a big city in northeast Anatolia) as a state-boarding student. After his graduation, he studied Computer Engineering at Ege University, Izmir and received his degree in 1999.

Like Rhus, Syringa, and Sorbus; Prunus' main motivation to go abroad was avoiding the military service, or rather gaining the right for the short-term draft by payment. According to Prunus, he was the first applicant and receiver of the Green Card from Turkey. He received it in October 2000. Like many other previous interviewees, he had first thought about migrating to the USA, but after hearing about the Green Card program, he chose Germany due to its relative proximity to Turkey.

Even though Prunus was happy to be living and working in Germany, the place where he felt at home was clearly Turkey, which is different than all the examples encountered so far. During the five years he had spent in Germany, he had been visiting Turkey four times a year and had online and telephone contact with friends and family. Conversely, he was going to receive his permanent alien residency in some months, and he was soon going to marry his fiancé, who was going to join him in Germany. One explanation for his preference for Turkey as a home, despite his mid-term plans in Germany, can stem from the prejudice towards the people from Turkey that was disturbing Prunus. He argued that unlike the USA, which he described as an immigration country, in Germany the migrants such as him were feeling that they are "second-class citizens". Independent of the level of their German, their accent was enough for receiving prejudiced looks from the people. That is, the prejudice that is mentioned by every single interviewee so far is identified by Prunus as the main disadvantage of living in Germany.

Prunus had working experience at an internet service provider in Izmir, Turkey. He had started there already during his university years and continued for another year after his graduation. After that in October 2000 he migrated to Dortmund, Germany and started working at a US-based international large-scale company. His work was related to networks and servers. Similar to many other interviewees, they were working on a project basis. When he first started, due to the internationality of the projects, English was enough at work. But over years, they started getting more projects from national firms, and as such, German was used as well. Before coming to Germany he had only very basic German skills, but upon migration he took German courses, which were paid by his company. Prunus, who now has proficient German skills, was interested, similar to some of the other interviewees, in learning German. But it is obvious that German is not a must in the work context.

Prunus' answer to the question about the advantages of working in Germany is in line with the responses of the previous interviewees. He had flexible working hours, as such, he could determine when he would go to or leave the office. The working environment was peaceful and quite, and the hierarchical work relations that he knew from Turkey did not hold here. Moreover, Prunus argued that while he had to know at least a bit about every aspect of their work while working in Turkey, in Germany he had to "know one thing very well", a remark that was made by Sorbus too. Furthermore, identical to Rhus, since Prunus had worked at a single company, where he was at the labor council board without being labor union member, he was not sure whether it was the social state in Germany, or the large-scale international company that was responsible for the advantages.

Interestingly and contrary to the prior examples apart from Fraxinus to some degree, Prunus clearly argued that they had limited leisure time, and attributed this to the nature of the ICT sector. In his leisure time, he was doing team sports with friends, going hiking, and visiting nearby cities where his friends from the state-boarding high school were living. But he stressed the fact that he had only his weekends for such recreational activities.

Similar to Acer, Prunus sees a bright future for the ICT sector. He thinks that it will enter the lives of the mankind from every aspect.

Regarding regional differences, he argues that even though the USA is still leading the sector, the difference now is becoming gradually smaller. Germany is progressing especially fast, most notably in the software development field. But regarding internet service, he complained about the monopoly in Turkey, and argued due to the absence of the monopoly in Germany, service quality here is better than in Turkey.

Prunus' social relations displayed certain differences to the HSL migrants discussed before. He acknowledged that in the ICT sector the average age is lower in comparison to other sectors, which he viewed as an advantage for him. He was getting along well with his colleagues, and they were meeting and spending time together outside work too. These co-worker friends were mostly Germans and some people from the UK as well. He knew people with migration background of Turkey, and some of those were recent migrants, but the rest were the descendants of the old migrants, that is, they were born and/or raised in Germany. Regarding the old migrants from Turkey in Germany, he had no generalized viewpoint, and he argued that there are persons, with whom he could get along, but there were also others with whom he could not even speak with. He still added that the descendants of the old migrants were experiencing a "cultural fracture", but this was more a sociological statement than a biased, negative one, which was encountered in the examples of Rhus, Fraxinus, Acer, Ailanthus, and Juglans. Furthermore, he was a member of the largest virtual platform for Green Card owners from Turkey and he had attended some of their real-life meetings. He mentioned that inside that network, there are not only people living in Germany, but return migrants as well, revealing the interesting bridge role of these networks. Even though Prunus' close relationships with his German co-workers distinguish him, the rest of his social relations follow already familiar patterns.

11. Magnolia, 31, single, female

Magnolia was born and raised in Kayseri, the hometown of her father. Her mother had migrated to Kayseri upon marriage from Muğla, a city in south-west Anatolia. Her mother, who was a nurse, had quit her job after marriage; her father, on the other hand, used to be a civil engineer, and at the time, he was accepting jobs as a contractor. Kayseri is a rather wealthy and modern city in central Anatolia, especially known for the entrepreneurship traits of their inhabitants, which goes parallel to the city's conservatism as reflected with 54 percent and 57 percent of the general election votes from the city going to AKP in 2002 and in 2007, respectively. But with both parents being educated, the schools Magnolia has attended and the later decision of the family of Magnolia to migrate to Ankara after she started studying there; suggest that her upper-middle class family belonged to the more liberal and/or Kemalist minority in the town.

Magnolia went to Kayseri TED High School, which is a private, modern high school offering an education in English. The families in Kayseri who appear as "social democrat" or "liberal" in the context of Turkey prefer their children to attend this decent school in order to complete a secular and national (Kemalist) education. After the tertiary education entrance exam, Magnolia gained the right to study at the prestigious Department of Management at METU. The closed communities and the snobby looks of the upper class, mostly urban students characterize the management and economy departments of METU. Magnolia explained that those people were living in their own world, and she had only limited contact with them. After some work experience in Turkey, she found about the international Master's degree programs in the English language in Germany at a DAAD conference at METU. She argued that the reason to choose Germany for continuing her education was the absence of high study fees in Germany, like Sorbus. She came to a very small city around Freiburg, and took up her studies related to cognitive science, SAP ERP, and other ICT related themes in an international setting with English as the teaching language. Once while writing her Master thesis and once after obtaining her degree, she completed two paid internships for companies based in Germany, and the former of those was at the Antalya (Turkey) office of the company. The education pattern observed here is common for the children middle and upper-middle class families, as was discussed in the context of previous interviews. Obviously, as in the cases of Ailanthus, Sorbus, and Euonymus; graduate study and/or internship in Germany is the crucial factor in the HSLM path of Magnolia.

Like nearly all of the interviewees, Magnolia said that before moving to Germany, even though she had thought about working in the USA, obtaining an American Green Card was not possible. Multiple instances have Magnolia describing the migration decision as an investment for her career. Actually, after she had applied for the Master's of Science program in Germany, she quit her job in Turkey, and she argued that she would not come to Germany if she had found another job there in Turkey. Furthermore the ease provided by the German Green Card program is obvious in her case too. When she first started working in Duisburg, she was immediately granted a Green Card for Germany. She said she worked there for only three months before joining another international company's Wiesbaden office; accordingly the company name on her visa was changed. But she did not know much about the formalities and regulations surrounding the Green Card, since everything was taken care of by the companies and the local foreigners office, without a need for her to get involved in the process. That is, both the educational background and the advantages of the Green Card program count as pulling factors of Germany as an HSLM receiving country.

Even though Magnolia regards migration itself an investment for her career, the uncertainty of her future and the temporariness associated with the migration experience were bothering her. She had not save much money. On the one hand, just like all the previous interviewees, she was convinced she making more or less the same amount of money in Germany as she would in Turkey, which made saving money difficult. On the other hand, since she did not know whether she would stay longer in Germany, or she would go back to Turkey, or even to yet another country, making investments was perceived untimely. In that context she added, jokingly, even though she could understand neither the people trying to migrate to Germany, nor the migrants such as the old worker generations making investments in Germany, the migrants already in Germany, just like her, were not leaving Germany so easily.

The temporariness was readily observable in her accommodation practices and her feeling that she was at home nowhere like Fraxinus. During her postgraduate study in Germany, Magnolia had stayed in a furnished dormitory room. Thereafter all the flats she had lived in were furnished too. All the flats but the last one she had lived in were one room only, and she had changed that only after everybody reminded her that she was no longer a student. She actually was agreeing with a friend, who had told her that by renting furnished flats she was avoiding putting any weight on her shoulders. This suggests that to live on as migrant labor power, one does not need more than suitcases, as if some personal luggage is enough. But she did not sound happy about this situation. She said that it is a very bad to feel at home nowhere, unlike Fraxinus who appears being glad at this feeling. Even though she was sometimes getting close to feeling at home at her “mothers’ place”, she added that it is still her mothers’ and not hers. Moreover, for her to be able to feel at home, she should be present at a given location with her daily routine such as work and a flat to live. Regarding where she could live in the future, she named Istanbul and Izmir. Even though while she had worked in Istanbul she did not like the city to due to traffic and disorder, after her later visits, she had come to the conclusion that Istanbul, as the most real return destination for her, is the most beautiful city in the world. It is important to note that while she worked there, she was staying at a hotel. But she went on to say that if she were to buy a house, that it would be in Izmir. That is, the felt temporariness of her experience was coupled with different types of uncertainties regarding her mid-term future.

Another dimension of temporariness stems from Magnolia’s difficulty to organize her leisure. She explicitly states that she is bored and has to find some social and recreational activities. Furthermore, recently she had a couple of business trips, which left her tired. These trips obviously introduced gaps in the continuity of her life in her city. Apart from attending driving lessons, she sounded to be mostly passive. She added that while in Turkey she was at least meeting some of her friends, but in Germany she just did not know what she could do. But she had heard and met some members of an amateur theater group by other highly educated migrants from Turkey, and she was considering joining that. And without having a car, she argued that she did have not access to sport facilities. To sum up, Magnolia's leisure time was frequently interrupted by business trips, and this resulted in a relatively passive life outside work.

Like seven of the ten previous interviewees, Magnolia has working experience in Turkey. After receiving her Management degree, she started working in the export-import department of a large construction company. There she held a consulting position, but she was constantly ordered to do different tasks. As such, identical to all interviewees with work background in Turkey, she criticized the system in Turkey in the context of work ethic, complaining in general about the hierarchy, the approach to employee rights, etc. In the newspaper, she saw an advertisement about an ICT-related position at a digital media company based in Turkey. While an employee there she worked first in Istanbul, and then in Mersin (a city in south-west Anatolia), where she stayed longer, for a total of 19 months. This was followed by another period in Bursa (a city in west Anatolia). Her company changed names and owners over the years, which brought a considerable instability to the work environment. In 2001, around the time of economic crisis, the company started laying people off. She asked to be laid off, and left the company with a monetary compensation. After six months, she was in Germany, in order to take up her Master's degree study. In other words, after three and a half years of working experience in Turkey, she continued her educational career. She said: "every university graduate dreams of master abroad". But still, she admitted that if she had found a job in Turkey before the start of the semester, she would have stayed in Turkey, suggesting a certain degree of compulsion in the migration.

Similar to her experience in Turkey, her first job in Germany bored her. For three months, she held position directed at upper managing, and as such, she worked under a director like a regular employee. She saw there was no chance of progress in her career, which was the main reason for her decision to apply at another firm. The saliency of this career related factor is increased by the fact that she loved her flat and social life there. While working there, she received a call regarding a position at an international large-scale company of Swedish origin. Actually she had applied there via contractor agents, which she designated as headhunters, already during her Master's study. Even though she was not accepted at the time, since they now needed someone urgently, they had contacted her. She accepted the offer and moved to Wiesbaden, where she had been at the time of the interview, little over a year. After staying three months at a guesthouse arranged by the company, she found a flat for herself.

At the time of her arrival, Magnolia did not have any relatives or acquaintances in Germany, and she could not speak any German. She had started learning German at the beginning of the Master's program, but this was only very basic. She continued learning German after starting to work. Even though she said she was able to understand what is being said and watching German TV, she described her German as very bad. She added she did not need German either, though. She underlined that all of her friends are other highly educated foreigners and at work, she was never supposed to need German. As such, Magnolia's limited German skills match the properties of her international work and social environments.

As discussed before, Magnolia is displaying a considerable amount of uncertainty regarding her mid-term plans, and this is visible in the work context too. On the one hand, she had asked to be repositioned at the Sweden office, since she had good social experiences while working there on a project. But now, she has ambivalent feelings, since re-migration was going to be very tough, which is familiar from Euonymus' hesitations.

She argued that what she is doing at work is more difficult than working in the framework of a project. She is finding FTP solutions to problems that occur while the developed projects are finally applied to the real world. As such, she had to have knowledge of many diverse topics. She argued that even though she was learning a lot like this, it was not possible to become an expert in a single area, since there was no specialization. That is, her situation was the opposite of the "know one thing very well" norm in Germany, observed by Prunus and Sorbus.

The comments of Magnolia on the work environment in Germany are very similar the rest of the interviewees. For instance, she thinks the German co-workers are very straight; they have rules, and do not bring anything personal to their work life. Even though Magnolia found this conformism of her German co-workers boring, she found nothing bad about it in the end.

When asked about the importance of a regular job, Magnolia answered from a job security point of view, and made comparisons between Turkey and Germany in terms of work ethic. While she was working in Manisa (a city in west Anatolia), they all had a constant worry of not getting anymore projects, but in Germany, even though things could happen here too, she has no fear of losing her job. Moreover, in Turkey they were spending half of their lives at work, and they never felt they were important as employees or even as humans. In Germany, on the other hand, the private life of the employee is recognized, and one can feel that he/she is trusted. Like all other interviewees, she says working hours in Germany are considerably less and describes this as one of the most important advantages of working in Germany. In contrast to 12 days in Turkey, in Germany she has 30 vacation days, which she was using to go to Turkey as often as possible, which seemed a necessity for her. She accepts that the amount that is earned is not different in Germany, and adds: "But the stress and aggression you get when you work with people in Turkey doesn't exist here. On the other hand, I also changed a lot as a person, perhaps if I go now, may be nothing like that wouldn't happen".

Magnolia emphasized the mobility of the employees in the ICT sector. This holds for both Turkey and Germany. In Turkey, she had worked in at least three different cities, while working at the same company. She had spent, in one instance, nearly two years without renting a flat. As mentioned before, in Germany, she was already making numerous business trips to countries as far as Argentina.

As described earlier, most of the social environment of Magnolia consisted of other highly skilled foreigners in Germany. Most of those friends, who came from several countries such as Peru and Uzbekistan, were graduates of the same Master's degree program as her and they were now working in Germany too. Meaning that part of the international student network was transformed into a professional migrant network.

Even though Magnolia described both the old migrants from Turkey in Germany and their newer generations as very strange, she still argued that she gets along with them quite well. She was especially annoyed by their fixations hailing from conservatism, regarding issues such as eating pork meat or male-female relationships. According to her, the newer generations were stuck between two societies. That is, agreeing with most of the sample covered so far, Magnolia finds the older migrants from Turkey strange and distant to her. But Magnolia's views on newer, highly skilled migrations from Turkey were not positive either. She criticized their asymmetry regarding their views on the older migrants. She argued that while the new migrants accuse the older ones of living in the distant past, they were themselves not adapting to the life in Germany either. Furthermore, they are complaining all the time, especially about the Germans, who are disliked after some time by most of them, but still stay in Germany. She argued that the discrimination against people from Turkey was not as bad as those new generation migrants were suggesting. She still accepted that it might be possible that the discrimination encountered by those people could have been worse compared to her experience. Unlike most of the interviewees, she never used the term prejudice to describe the discrimination. But she was a member of virtual platforms for highly educated migrants from Turkey, and was attending some of their meetings. To sum up, Magnolia is critical of both old and new migrant populations from Turkey due to their conservatism and inadaptability, respectively and restricts her social environment to other highly educated migrants in Germany. Her point of view in this context is very similar to Ailanthus who empathizes with the people without migration background, "people tolerating the other". Like Fraxinus, Acer, and Ailanthus, she asks for individual acceptance from the locals by differing herself from "the other".

12. Quercus, 47, married, male

Quercus, 47 years-old and as such the oldest migrant in the sample, was born in Babaeski, Kırklareli. Especially after the Lausanne Treaty of 1923, this border city received migration from Thessaloniki, as a result of the exchange of minorities between Turkey and Greece. Still, most of the inhabitants of the city are the descendants of "Turks" who formerly lived in Thessaloniki until the First Balkan War of 1912. The city is one of the most Kemalist cities in Turkey. In the last general election (2007), CHP received 40 percent of the votes in the city, whereas nationwide they could only secure 21 percent of the votes. As will be seen later, the nationalist tendencies of Quercus are in accordance with his hometown's Kemalist stance. The education of Quercus' mother is limited to primary school and his father is a graduate of an Agricultural Vocational high school. At first sight, their education level can be seen low, but given they attended the Turkish education system, especially his father's high school qualifies as a prestigious education institute. The family's old petty bourgeois character appears even stronger when the education levels of their children are considered. Both Quercus and his elder brother are engineers, and their sister is a graduate of Pharmaceutics Department of Hacettepe University, Ankara, which furthermore reveals the now familiar gender stereotypes in occupations. His brother is a director at a multinational telecommunications equipment manufacturer. It can be said that the old petty bourgeois family background in rural Turkey gives birth to new petty bourgeoise. Quercus argued that his parents supported his migration decision. He especially mentioned in that respect his mother, who was despite being a practicing Muslim was more open-minded than his sister, or even Tansu Çiller, the first and only female prime minister of Turkey so far. In summary, Quercus comes from a nationalist border city, and his family displays the characteristics of middle class and/or bourgeois characteristics with a special emphasis on education of the children.

Quercus' first migration is for the purpose of education, and corresponds to a move from Kırklareli in order to study at Edirne High School, Edirne (a big city in north-west Turkey). Albeit a public high school, it has a long history going back to mid 19th century, and since then the quality of its education has been always above average. Furthermore it currently has Anatolian High School status, and offers education in English and German languages. This early educational migration of Quercus underlines once more the old petty bourgeois background of the family.

Identical to his brother, Quercus continued his education at the Electronics and Communications Department of METU, Ankara. He started there in the second half of the 1970s, which were politically and socially active times for Turkey, and this was followed by the most destructive military coup of Turkey on 12th September 1980. During the interview, Quercus displayed a very clear contempt towards the leftist formations and people that indeed characterized METU at the time. He mentioned that the leftists would organize lecture boycotts, and he was arguing that if the students did attend the classes and learn their craft, the dependency of Turkey on imperialist forces, the USA being his primary example, would not increase. As such, he had approached such protest acts very negatively. He defined himself as a person against imperialism in the same context, which again exemplifies his nationalistic stance. This is also supported by the fact that he is against private education. He had further observations regarding the leftist generation of his times. He stated that most of those people had made a 180-degree turn, and they were now either exploiting the Turkish state, or were business people employing workers with the minimum wage. To him, the leftism of most of those people had ended when they entered the private sector. His dislike for the leftism of his times was such that, he later opened up the same thing after a question about whether he is a labor union member. He stressed the fact that, during his university years he never lost a year, and graduated with good grades and an Honors degree. Quercus, who is never politically active, is against private education and imperialism, and as such close to the conservative nation-state approach. His negative approach to his leftist schoolmates and his focus on the university as an educational institute only complement his nationalist and Kemalist attitudes.

After graduation he stayed at METU and while doing his Master's degree, he also worked as researh assistant. He argued that the salary of research assistants in the 1980s was considerably higher than many other state institutions. After receiving his Master's degree, he started his PhD at the Computer Control section of department. During his postgraduate years, he further worked as a visiting academic at the Electronics Engineering Department of Erciyes University, Kayseri, (a big city before mentined located at east of Ankara). At the time, such small-scale universities had a shortage of staff especially in such technical fields. Quercus argued that he had taken all the courses of the PhD program in 1985, but he did not finish his thesis, since he preferred to migrate abroad. Given his postgraduate efforts and his academic career that started already during his Master's years, Quercus can be considered as one of the most competent electronics and communications engineers of Turkey in the 1980s.

As in the cases of Rhus, Syringa, Sorbus, and Prunus military service avoidance is the main force behind Quercus' migration decision. In line with the nationalist attitude, Quercus said that even though military service would not be a complete loss of time, it would still be using the time suboptimally. Additionally, he said that at the time, going abroad had the additional economic advantage. He explicitly said that back then, working abroad had a monetary advantage too. At the time, one year of work experience background was enough to obtain the right for military service by payment which took two months, not three weeks, but he preferred to work two more years abroad before being drafted. He argues that at the end of those years, even if the military service payment is considered, he had made still more money than he would have in Turkey. But he explicitly added that the monetary advantage had disappeared over the years. He gave examples of the new generation Green Card holder migrants in Germany, who were not earning more money than in Turkey, a fact discussed by all of the previous interviewees. This suggests that even though the role of military service as the primary pushing factor of HSLM has remained unchanged over decades, the monetary advantage it has provided in the 1980s diminished with time.

Quercus left Turkey in 1985 in order to avoid military service and worked in Denmark at a large-scale international company. Even though he earned the opportunity for performing three-month military service in Turkey after a year, he worked there in Denmark two more years. He said that around that time the future of the project they were working on was unclear, and it was possible that their contracts were not going to be extended. A big company from Germany, which was in desperate need of computer engineers, held interviews with them in Copenhagen in order to convince them to move to Germany. He asked for time and went to Turkey. After his military service he started up a computer firm in Edirne, which was the first computer firm outside Istanbul. But after a year, when the company was not as successful as he wanted, he accepted the offer of the German company, since he otherwise did not see a clear future for ICT in Turkey.

Quercus' wife was present during the interview. According to the terminology introduced before, she is a second-order migrant, since migrated to Germany in trace of her husband, like Syringa' ex-wife and Ailanthus' wife. She is a graduate of the Department of Mechanical Engineering of Trakya University (University of Thrace), in Edirne, which can be considered an average university in Turkey. They had met in Turkey and were engaged for three years before their marriage. At the time, Quercus was visiting Turkey as much as six times a year. In order to take advantage of the family reunion visa scheme she had to wait for a year. As such she decided to come to Germany with a student visa, for which she waited two-three months. She was first enrolled at the University of Stuttgart, where she first had to take German courses before being eligible for a Master's degree program. But after she passed the

German proficiency exam, she found out that not all the credits she had gathered during her study were counted valid. This meant that she had to start from the third year of the Bachelor's degree program. Probably, this was partly because of the university she was a graduate of. But at the University for Applied Sciences her university education was accepted fully and as such she was able to attend their Master-equivalent program on Machine-Computer. But soon after she completed the program, a job crisis broke out in Germany, and hence, despite being invited to several job interviews, she was unable to find work. After that she preferred to focus on folklore studies, especially folklore dances, together with her husband and stopped looking for a job. In summary, Quercus' wife, now mainly involved in folklore dances, came to Germany as a second-order migrant and after completing postgraduate studies she remained unemployed, for which the job crisis was to blame too.

Quercus and his wife hold different views on where they feel at home. Quercus was satisfied with their life, which was now partly divided between Germany and Turkey. They had been in Turkey recently for three months and they were soon going to spend another four. Quercus was at the time unemployed and explained that his ideal new job would be a counseling position at the communications office of a Turkish company, which would allow him to spend three-four months a year in Turkey. He argued that the fate of the migrant was having one foot in the sending country and one in the receiving country. He went on to say that neither a person nor a place could be perfect. He summarized his preference as "instead of staying here completely or going back to Turkey for good, but being on both sides". That is, the indecision between staying and returning, which was heard from all interviewees was solved by Quercus as a steady state covering both countries at once.

His wife, on the other hand, did not like being divided between two countries. She argued that spending a long time in one place meant getting used to the local customs, and after being back to the other country, she was yearning for those customs. This held for Turkey and Germany. She said that the reason for the sensitivity on this issue might be because of being a woman.[3] Furthermore she argued that in Turkey, her social environment was limited to her family. In contrast, in Germany they both had a remarkable social surrounding due to the folklore activities, for which they had a professional interest. Even though she accepted that both living in Turkey and in Germany had different advantages over each other, she would prefer living at one place, without long breaks.

Quercus, like Juglans and in contrast to the rest of the sample, did not come to Germany through the Green Card Program. Both Quercus and his wife are holders of the permanent residency permit. They had chosen not to become German citizens, because this would mean losing the Turkish citizenship. He clearly said that if the dual citizenship were issue in German law, they would get German citizenship. Even though both have the right of application for it, they do not consider it, like Juglans. Aside from Juglans and Quercus, ten cases in my study have not lived for eight years in Germany yet. Most of them have asked for a permanent residence permit and there is no barrier to obtain it after five years working in Germany. Nevertheless, nobody declared any demand for German citizenship so far. Mespilus, even though she strongly decided to stay permanently and work in Germany, did not have a plan for naturalization. Fraxinus, who benefited from dual citizen of Turkey and Canada, did not prefer to lose Turkish citizenship. He does not consider German citizenship either, since he has already completed the draft and has working experience in Turkey. Moreover, Quercus said that this was partly emotional, again displaying his nationalism. But he added that there were rational reasons too. In the case of people who had left the Turkish citizenship, the laws and regulations about inheritance and real estate ownership rights were unclear. Furthermore, their retirement time was going to arrive much sooner in Turkey. As such, foreseen inheritance and pension problems seem to restrict the demand of HSL migrant for German citizenship.

---

[3] However it seems that the difference in the spouses' mind in this context is mostly linking with their migration order, not essentially depending on their gender, in comparison with other cases.

After having worked for the same company in different countries, Quercus switched to a big telecom company. While still working there, around two years ago Quercus had a slipped disc at his back. He explained that this is a potential injury for ICT people, due to their prolonged inactivity in front of computer screens. He had spent a year at rehabilitation centers before he was fit again to work. But since then he was not able to find a job. He argued that the reasons were the job crisis and his age. But he added that he was not trying hard anymore. Actually, he and his wife now were involved full-time in Turkish folklore dance studies. He defined himself and his wife as folk dance researchers, and mentioned that they received an award from a EU related institution for their work on Thracian (Trakya) dances. They were now considering publishing it. Accordingly there was no reduction in his workload. Actually he drew parallels between the properties of his previous job and his folklore dance studies. He was used to working in research as an ICT specialist. They are adapted to work since a lot of new projects always kept coming at them. The design of such projects was a difficult and innovative task. He mentioned that due to his age, he was not considered for such positions anymore and he described Germany as conservative when it comes to age. But now he was approaching the folklore dance studies with the same researcher attitude. In order to underline his professional attitude, he compared he and his wife's work to the studies conducted at the Turkish folklore studies department of the universities in Turkey. He argued, compared to their scientific approach, those departments were not even at a high school level. Furthermore during his working years, with his very frequent visits to Turkey, he was aware of the limited developments in the folklore dance studies. With the unemployment following a back injury had prepared the transition from ICT specialist to folklore expert.

When asked about their investments and assets, Quercus suggested that their current ease despite unemployment was a result of their savings. He argued that since he had taken the risk of working as a contractor. Even though he had less job security compared to regular employees, he was able to earn more money. Similar to the most of the interviewees so far, he used to work on a project basis. Obviously, this work scheme had a clear financial advantage for the time he used to work. Actually, he had chosen this scheme due to its temporariness, since after around one year he was going to do his military service. But after that, making good money had replaced that motivation. He stated that in Germany he had made in five years so much money as he would have in Turkey. He compared himself after that to his classmates in Turkey, and argued that most of them were now professors, suggesting he could have taken that path too. The migration had created this difference between he and his friends. He added that he was even considering getting a PhD just for the sake of it. Moreover, the job he had done at companies was not so much different from research at universities; as such he was satisfied in that respect too. All their projects were about untested things, as such, it was very difficult, but with experience, one was learning to become fast at work. Furthermore they had already secured their retirement in Turkey, increasing their confidence. At the moment they were considering and planning to buy one house in Turkey and another one in Germany. Overall, given the monetary advantages of the project-based work in the 1990s Germany, Quercus was not regretting his migration choice, despite the difficulties associated with that work scheme.

Like the rest of the sample except one example, Quercus was not a labor union member. He argued that this was not possible for contractual employees. But he added that unions do not mean much to him, since nobody cares about what they are saying. Remarkably this question reminded him of the labor unions from before, which were very active in the leftist movement in Turkey. He displayed his dislike for them by saying that they were just political toys exploited by other power holders, that is, not serving their function of protecting the rights of the employees. It is interesting to note that Quercus does not criticize the German labor unions as much as the ones in Turkey, even though he views them equally useless.

Acer (29) and Fraxinus (39) did not come to Germany directly from Turkey, like Quercus (47). Unlike the other interviewees in my case, these three men first left Turkey for other countries of destination, in order of the UK, Canada, and Denmark. They are more flexible in crossing the boundaries as labor power than other cases. They last started to work in Germany as the fourth country of working, i.e. third country of destination. Their common features are having working experience in Turkey and being well-trained for the whole HSLM market, not specifically for German labor market. They are more likely to hold graduate degrees or international certificates. It is noticable that they easily decide to move and they have a clear upward mobility through migration career in their biographies, both educational and occupational careers. Furthermore, they work for international companies under more apparently flexible working conditions, and all prefer to speak English as the business language.

According to Quercus and his wife, their German skills were correlated with the structure of their social environment. They had both attended at German language courses. As mentioned before, his wife had even passed the German proficiency exam at the university. She argued that with some practice her grammar would be again perfect. But when it comes to speaking they had no practice. They had no Germans in their social environment. Quercus needed only English in his work environment. Apart from that, they knew a lot of migrants from Turkey due to their folklore connections. But Quercus added that the lack of interaction with colleagues was not exclusive to Germany. He argued that his brother in Turkey, also an ICT specialist, and his wife were spending their time between work and home; they were even visiting the parents only a couple of times a year. Moreover, he added that since German is not their native language, they were not able to express their emotions and thoughts as well as Germans, which is limiting factor in communication. He said that interactions with other migrant couples in Germany were easier. He said: "They are alone, we are alone". He gave the example of his Turkish friends abroad, who were spending time with people from Greece. He, had himself, been spending his time in Belgium with people from Germany who were HSL migrants there too. Once again, it is clear the migrants in a given country mostly interact with each other, with a limited appearance of local people among their social environment. Quercus frequently underlined the richness of the social relations they had established via their folklore dances interest. They both belong to the Founders of the Stuttgart Turkish Folklore Association and have managerial and educational roles at such associations in other cities. They were making tours in Germany, meeting the people interested in folklore dances, including diplomats and other officials. He had also friends from Turkey who used to work at the same companies as him. Due to the international work context containing similar migrants and the professional interest in Turkish folklore dances, Quercus and his wife had a social circle with an absence of German people.

When asked about his relations with guest workers or asylum seekers from Turkey, he approached the issue from his experiences at their folklore association. Interestingly, he referred to guest workers as economic asylum seekers. He said that most people who did come to them are such people. According to him, even though they had damaged Turkey's name, it was understandable that they wanted secure themselves financially. But they had principles regarding political attitudes. Politics should not enter the domain of their activities, and they would never let this happen. Probably, Quercus means here the leftists from Turkey that escaped the 12th of September 1980 military coup and the Kurdish people. He would also not let the Armenian issue be discussed under his roof. His criteria can be considered as a protection for Turkey's dignity and prestige, which once again displays his nationalist point of view.

13. Laburnum, 31, single, female

Laburnum was born in Balıkesir, and she stayed there until the end of high school, identical to Euonymus. Her father had died when she was around five years old. He used to be lawyer, who later took up a government job at the national telecom company (PTT). He met Laburnum's mother, a civil servant (high school graduate), at the telecom company. Her mother's family had moved to Balıkesir from Crete (Girit), underlining the importance of Balıkesir as a migrant receiving city, which was discussed in the analysis of

Euonymus. His mother currently lives in the Erdek, a touristic, coastal district of Balıkesir. Laburnum has an older sister who is a university graduate as well. Her sister and other close relatives live in Istanbul, where she owns a flat too, like Mespilus. Both financially and culturally, Laburnum's family displays middle class characteristics.

Laburnum went to the same high school as Euonymus, namely Balıkesir Anatolian High School. Their first foreign language was English; the second one was German. But after the high school, Laburnum's interest in the German language continued, she took private lessons and attended the Goethe Institute language courses while studying at METU in Ankara. Her major at the university was Industrial Engineering and she was a member of a club consisting mainly of her department-mates. The club has relations with ESTIEM "European Students of Industrial Engineering and Management", an international network aiming at increasing the relations and cross-visits between people studying industrial engineering in different countries. Her first visit to Germany, in 1996, was also related to this network. Already during that first visit, she was impressed by the approach towards work in Germany. Via AIESEC she applied for internship positions abroad, and she completed two such internships in Germany, the first prior to her graduation, and the second following a one-year long work experience after the university. Having two internships in Germany is another coincidental commonality between Laburnum and Euonymus. The current case is yet another example of the function of internships abroad, which can be read as the initial prudential step for becoming migrant labor power.

Laburnum received a job offer from the company where she completed her second internship. Even though she wanted to accept it, she found out that for work permit purposes, she first had to go back to Turkey and wait a month before she could apply. She was critical of this procedure, and did not want to go through the hassle. She returned to Turkey and worked there for five years at several international companies. She argued that the economic downturn in Turkey in 2001 affected the ICT sector. She knew about the Green

Card program of Germany and decided to look for a job there. Since she had taken many ICT related courses during her university years, and had working experience in the field; she could prove her eligibility for a Green Card. It seems, programs such as Green Card function for the receiving country as a call for their reserve labor, which consists of people, who have study or work related experience in Germany.

Laburnum came to Germany in 2003 by means of an ICT company and was granted Green Card. After working two years in Cologne, she moved to Munich in order to join another company. She did have an interesting difficulty during the switch. Even though she had a Green Card valid until 2008, she did not know that her residence permit would be rendered invalid with the quitting of her job. This is partly because in North Rhine-Westphalia the name of her company was not written on Green Card, making her think she could use it anywhere, automatically. After she started working in Munich, she tried to reach the officials at the federal employment office in order to inform that she is now working in Munich. This took a while, and she sent her documents via the labor council of the company. But since she had started working without getting her Green Card approved at the local office, she was actually working illegally, and had no idea about that. She received a call from the employment office, but she argued that the problem was solved in a couple days since she had adopted a dominant stance during the interaction. At the time, Laburnum was still in the probation period of her second job in Germany.

The reasons behind her migration decision are mostly the same as in the previous cases. She said that she could not stand the work atmosphere anymore. Furthermore, working in an international atmosphere such as her work environment in Germany was very important for her. She was accustomed to international and multicultural settings from the university, and now she was actively seeking the same in her working life. Additionally, the technologies they had access to were more advanced than the tools they had been using in Turkey, which increased her satisfaction with her job. Unlike most of the previous interviewees, she argued that she was earning more than the double what she would be earning in Turkey. But still, with her own words: "…the biggest advantage of working in Germany is its contribution to my occupational career."

Laburnum argued that she has a settled life in Germany. With that she meant her job, her flat, and her social environment. But she added that people such as her always have a second plan. She did have savings and her private retirement insurance, and she could withdraw the money in case of need. She stated that she does not have strict plans regarding future, now she had her settled life, but if she were to receive a remarkably better job offer, she would not mind leaving her current life behind. Perhaps not surprisingly, she explained that she used to feel at home in Cologne, especially after coming back from trips. In the end she did have her flat, friends, and her job. Now she was getting used to Munich, and it could be felt that she was going to adapt to her new life without problems. But she also accepted that she was also feeling at home while in Turkey, albeit differently. She defined Turkey as "our country". That is, the common "homeland there, home here" pattern emerges also in the case of Laburnum. After all this, Laburnum interestingly said that she would have to take the decision to stay or return under two particular conditions. If she marries a German, she will stay in Germany. On the other hand, if she marries someone from Turkey, she will go back at the latest after the birth of their child. The birth of the child from a Turkish spouse is seen as a milestone for the return decision, as Ailanthus also stated. Also, we can remember Euonymus' hesitation about this issue. To sum up, Laburnum has a professional attitude toward her life, feeling comfortable where she is, and being ready to change if necessary, with the sole factor that might force her for a definite choice being the birth of a child.

Like Euonymus and Mespilus, Laburnum appears to be a very self-organized person in terms of leisure time. She does a lot of sports, reads every day for an hour, and goes out often with friends. She is the member of an association for young business people in Germany. But regarding associations with members that are migrants from Turkey, she is rather negative. She argues that most of those people join those organizations in order to satisfy their own ego.

She is critical of the fact that such organizations were never useful for their members; that is, they have no contribution to individual careers. The German-Turkish Industry and Trade Chamber was the sole exception for her, and this she explains by the fact that most of their members are "Germans". As such, Laburnum appears to prefer associations with German members. Her self-oriented recreational activities and expectations from organizations suggest a wish to transform her leisure partly into career.

Laburnum's occupational field covers business intelligence systems and reporting solutions. At her first company in Germany, she worked as a manager. Her task was to buy ICT solutions for Turkish companies in Germany. This allowed her to establish many contacts with other migrants from Turkey. But the project she was working on ended she preferred to stay in Germany over returning back to Turkey. Accordingly she found another job in Germany, and was at the time working in Munich for a mid-scale company based in Germany. The main reason behind her decision to stay in Germany is, as mentioned previously, the job satisfaction, which can be discussed under the term "work culture". In this context, she is similar to Sorbus and Quercus, who also cited the "work culture" as different in Germany. For Laburnum, the differences in work culture are not only due to the technological advantages of Germany over Turkey. She argues that the way the people view and deal with their work is different in the two countries and she had observed this already during her internships. With her own words: "Turks work like playing backgammon (*tavla*). Germans work like playing chess. As a result, I wanted to work internationally". People in Germany work more regularly and leave nothing to chance, just like in the game of chess. In Turkey, on the other hand, not all aspects of the work are controlled well, and accordingly there is room for surprises, good or bad. Even though she appreciates the way the "Germans" work, she observes a big change in the last few years. She said that unlike in the 1990s, "Germans" were not working very productively anymore. At the work, they now had "Turkish kind of comfort" and she described them as lazy. Nevertheless, when compared to Turkey the work culture was still favorable.

Once again she used the term ego in this context. She is convinced that the managers in Germany are more work-oriented, understanding, and friendly. The managers in Turkey, on the other hand, are trying to satisfy their own ego, that is, they try to apply their power to their employees by, for instance, making them work longer, even if there is no real need for it. Laburnum's account of ego satisfaction problems and obstinacy of managers in Turkey is reminiscent of Mespilus' complaint about prissiness of managers in Turkey.

Laburnum approached the question on the importance of a regular job from two different angles. She said that if regular job means to go to the same office in order to work on the same tasks everyday, she did not have a regular job. She was working as a consultant on a project basis, and this corresponded to both frequent business trips and changes in the tasks she was responsible for. On the other hand, if a regular job meant to have a secure job, she did not have it either. She explained such security existed only for jobs with low salaries. In her case, if the company would not need her anymore, she could lose her job easily. She mentioned that the ICT sector is the first to feel the effects of an economic downturn. But in the same context, she was not informed about labor unions and councils, and did not know whether there was such a council at the current company. It seems Laburnum internalizes and accepts the non-monotonous working practice together with the relative insecurity of her job.

As a highly educated female migrant from Turkey, Laburnum did have the experience of a "black swan" in a multifaceted way. She did have a very crucial observation. When she speaks with somebody from Germany, who is surprised that she is a highly educated Turkish woman, the person thinks, "She is not like a Turk"; instead of "There are also such Turks then". That is, they do not change their categorization scheme, but just register Laburnum as an exception, as an odd-one out. A common question she is hearing is, whether she came alone to Germany. This suggests the expectation that she must have come since she either married another migrant, or a German person. She confirmed my argument "the image of the Turkish man seemed more negative, but the image of the Turkish woman in Germany was perhaps defined as 'unjustly treated (wronged, mistreated)' (*mağdur*)". Then, she talked about another question the locals ask whether she has a brother. She also mentioned some unpleasant experiences of her Turkish male friends such as nonadmission into the pubs. She repeated they put her into another category after a while following the initial acquaintince. That is, similar to Mespilus' experience, being a female migrant modifies the biases and changes the perceived "difference" to other "Turks".

Four out of five social meetings of Laburnum are with people from Turkey, the rest are with "Germans". She explained that there are only few foreigners at her current company, so she is speaking German most of the time. Overall she defines herself as a person who makes friends easily, and she was already getting along well with her "German" colleagues at work after only six weeks. Moreover, Laburnum comprehends her colleagues' preference for the German language in their leisure time, just as she speaks Turkish with her friends from Turkey.

Since the first company Laburnum worked at did have close relation with Turkey and Turkish companies, most of her friends consisted of "Turks in Germany". She meant by that the descendants of the migrants who came from Turkey in the 1960s and the 1970s. She said that she has more female friends, explaining that with the "ego" problem of "Turkish men", who, even if they are highly educated still resort to aggression easily. With her very close relationship with the younger generations of old migrants from Turkey, Laburnum is one of the outliers in the sample.

14. Sambucus, 29, married, male

Sambucus was born to teacher parents in Ankara. From his third year in school they moved multiple times while his parents were commissioned to different parts of Turkey. His parents are moreover graduates of the Higher Education by Distant Learning program, which is equivalent to a university degree. The educational backgrounds of the parents show a positive stance towards education in general.

At the start of high school, Sambucus and his parents were in Kırıkkale, a small city located at east of Ankara, and he attended the Anatolian High School there for a year. Afterwards they moved back to Ankara, and accordingly he was a graduate of the Yıldırım Beyazıt Anatolian High School in Ankara. At high school he had English as the first foreign language and German as the second. But he argues that at the time he had moved to Germany, his German was next to nothing. But he took German courses at the *Volkshochschule* (Community College) and was considering attending the courses of the Goethe Institute. That is, like many of the interviewees covered, Sambucus had shown interest in learning German after migration.

After high school, Sambucus studied Computer Engineering at METU and there he received also his Master's degree in the same field. He was a teaching assistant for three years at the Department of Computer Engineering in METU and was involved in teaching and certain projects. With a grant, he spent a month in France. He started doing his PhD at METU, but moved to Germany before finishing. At the time he was a PhD student in Berlin and argued that being in academia was important for him even though he accepted that working for the industry had a financial advantage.

Sambucus met his husband at "*Lezbiyen ve Geylerin Sorunları ve Toplumsal Barış İçin Çözüm Arayışları Sempozyumu*" (Symposium of Solution Seeking to Problems of Lesbians and Gays and for Societal Peace) on May 23-24, 2003 which was organized by KAOS-GL, Kaos Gay and Lesbian Cultural Research and Solidarity Association (*Kaos Gey ve Lezbiyen Kültürel Araştırmalar ve Dayanışma Derneği)*, Ankara. As an active member of KAOS-GL, Sambucus was involved in the organization of the event. His husband, a social scientist, was born to a family from Turkey in Germany and was raised here. Sambucus first came to Germany with a tourism visa for three weeks, returned to Turkey afterwards, and came again in the autumn of 2003 with a visa given for business purposes, since he was going to attend a congress (*1.Bundeskongress türkeistämmiger Homosexueller*). Before the expiration of this visa, he married by means of "*Partnerschaftsan-*

erkennung" (Approval of Partnership) in Berlin and received a three-year residency permit since his husband was a citizen of the Federal Republic of Germany. Sambucus actually did not prefer the family unification process, since he considers it as a long and stressful process for the newlywed. Apparently he evaluated the emotional side of a new marriage, and official procedures for the family unification offend the feelings of new pairs. Hence he opted for holding the residency permit after marriage in Germany where he first entered with a temporary visa, in the place of the family unification.

Sambucus argues that the sole reason for coming to Germany was his husband. Similar to most of the interviewees, he observes that otherwise the USA could be an option. Like Juglans, Sambucus' primary, if not only, migration motivation was to be with his partner. Moreover, after receiving the residency permit, he was unable to find a job. He describes his experience as "leaving everything behind in Turkey and coming to Germany".

Sambucus feels himself at home in his flat here in Berlin. He attributes this partly to his experience of living alone while in Ankara for some years, even though he still states that his family would be the biggest advantage of living in Turkey. He thinks food and weather are positive aspects of Turkey in general, but adds that regarding the former; Berlin is better than other cities in Germany. To sum up, given his partner and current work are in Berlin, he has no hesitation to feel at home at his current locus.

Sambucus identifies the main disadvantage of Turkey as the insecurity at work. He, a labor union member in Turkey, states that politics are very important for him and criticizes the fact that one can be fired in Turkey just because of labor union membership. He generalizes this particular rights violation to others, stating that even expressing oneself freely is difficult in Turkey.

> "Please do not say, I am always speaking about politics. However, that is very important for me! My father was always a labor union member. He was also a union founder. When I became a civil servant, I immediately went to the labor union and became a union member. It is okay, I have not experienced so many problems, but

> there is no guarantee not to come across problems. When I wanted to join a demonstration, I could go and nobody asked me why I went to it. But, I know that if my manager would want, he/she can start a discipline inquiry about me. The absence of expressing yourself and freedom of speaking for yourself in Turkey annoyed me a lot. I mean expressing yourself in every field! Not only in the political manner… Speaking about your preference about sexuality is difficult too. You cannot even be free to say what your favorite color is. That bothers me a lot!"

Regarding whether he had met discrimination in Germany, Sambucus gave a "yes and no" answer. On the one hand, he thinks that he had met discrimination especially at the municipality since his German skills were poor. But he argues that it was different at the university, where he had not observed any prejudice. He states that at the university context people do not "ascribe Turkishness" to him, since he was so different from the other Turks they had known. This is another manifestation of the "black swan phenomen", to which Sambucus has a neutral stance.

> "[…] I am not sure why! Probably, because of I am peaceful and quite, they do not expect Turkishness of me (*yakıştırmıyorlar*). I have experienced this, a lot of times. Not only in Germany but also in France, people always say, 'You look Spanish!' [I asked about his reaction in this position.] These people do not want to believe it and say 'You do not have a Turkish accent' or 'You are so easy and comfortable'… I might not say anything against these comments in this kind of position, because the circumstances resulted from very different reasons, such as because of these people's shallowness (*sığlık*) in this context, because they do not ascribe Turkishness to me, or because they do not expect I am from Turkey, etc. Or, perhaps that is really true. I can be different!"

Sambucus was working at the Berlin University of Technology as a teaching assistant and pursuing a doctoral degree. His research topics include computer vision and image processing. He stresses that he needs exclusively English at the work, since the teaching language and the literature are all English. He adds that he'd like to learn German better in order to be able to give lectures in German too. He argues that his experience as a teaching assistant in Turkey renders his current job easier.

Sambucus argues that the working conditions at this university were comparable to METU, that is, flexible working hours and an easy-going professor. He stresses that both in Turkey and Germany, there are differences in that aspect. Moreover he argues that, unlike Turkey, in Germany they are encouraged to participate in many conferences, which enables them to learn about different aspects of computer science in general. While stressing the importance of such an educational capital, he interestingly said that he could understand his friends, who, upon arrival in Germany from Turkey, observe a devaluation of their cultural capital.

Sambucus describes the differences in the ICT sectors of Germany and Turkey in relation to the role of the armed forces in the field. In Ankara, he argues that most of the computer engineers work for the military, with another large group operating in telecommunications. He adds that the application fields in Germany are wider than that with examples such as medical technologies. It is worth adding that his remarks are especially about working in Ankara. Sambucus' observation shows differences also between working possibilities for computer engineers in Ankara and Istanbul. Whereas in the capital city the military is a major employer, in Istanbul the picture seems to be a different, as suggested by the previous interviewees.

Ragarding job security, Sambucus feels at ease. He argues that during the duration of his contract with the university, he will be able to save some money to use in the future, in case he will find difficulties to find another job. Nevertheless, having a regular and secure job is still important for Sambucus, which is supported by his labor union membership in Turkey. He was not well informed about the worker rights representatives in Germany though. He mistakenly said that in Germany having a job meant membership to a labor union automatically, showing the now familiar ignorance of the highly educated migrants in that respect.

Sambucus argues that his social environment mostly corresponded to his husband's social environment, with most of their friends consisting of homosexuals. He is not sure whether that is an advantage or disadvantage. He added that otherwise he had another social at the work environment, but, similar to many previous interviewees, he prefers to define them as colleagues instead of friends. He is now a member of the Association of Gays & Lesbians from Turkey (*Gays & Lesbians aus der Türkei e.V., Türkiyeli Eşcinseller Derneği*) in Berlin. Arguing he does not have much of leisure time, he says that he mostly spends this limited time with his husband or in the asccoiation mentioned above. Furthermore he is a member of professional societies related to his work. He thinks that there are not so many computer engineers from Turkey in Berlin. He has also contact with his alma-mater friend network in other cities of Germany. He concludes that due to his special migration career, he ends up meeting people who have different backgrounds compared to him.

Due to his husband, a second-generation migrant from Turkey, Sambucus has extensive contact with the older generations of migrants from Turkey and especially their descendants. He argues that the Turkish they speak is different. He says that when he coincidentally hears the Turkish they speak, he is not interested much, but if he hears the Turkish of a person who lived in Turkey for a long time, he gets curious about the person. This shows a preference for people, who have a long history in Turkey, similar to him.

Sambucus and his husband have very little contact with their neighbors in Germany, comparable to all the other previous interviewees. He was establishing contact with friends and relatives in Turkey via the internet, either by writing e-mails or having chats. Since his arrival, he had been to Turkey only once, which is explained by his relatively recent arrival in Germany.

15. Rhamnus, 31, married (in the process of divorce), male

Rhamnus comes from the multiethnic city of Şanlıurfa (in southeast Anatolia), where the majority of the population consists of Kurdish people. He defines himself as an Alevi, who is ethnically half-Turkmen and half-Kurdish. His father, after finishing high school, received diplomas from two different Higher Education by

Distant Learning programs, which are, as mentioned in the example of Sambucus, are equivalent to university degrees. He is a former mayor of one of the districts of Şanlıurfa. At the time he was a representative of CHP (Republican People's Party), arguing that in the local elections the voters prefer "serious leftist parties"; but afterwards since there was no difference between CHP and MHP (Nationalist Movement Party) he departed and at the time he was still looking for a new political party to join. He had the parliament in mind. At this point it is important to remember that the Kurdish Alevis, having a closer stance to CHP, experience the contradictions of this tradition with the official ideology represented by the party. Before his political career Rhamnus' father was a high-level civil servant at the municipality until his retirement. His mother, on the other hand, used to be illiterate, but he had taught her to read and write. She is now able to read books and still goes to further courses. He has two university graduate siblings working in different cities and another one, who is still a university student. In summary, Rhamnus comes from a rural middle class Şanlıurfa family, carrying a multiethnic Alevi identity and surrounded by political involvement due to this father.

Rhamnus is one of the first graduates of the Şanlıurfa Anatolian High School. It is one of the most recently opened schools of the type, showing the scarcity of educational opportunities in the city for a long while.

After high school, Rhamnus studied at the Vocational School of Higher Edcuation in Çankırı, and the school was part of the Ankara University. Unlike other interviewees, Rhamnus has a two-year higher education program degree in Computer Programming. He adds that despite the politically sensitive situation at the time he had finished the program with the highest grade of his class. Even though his school was in Çankırı, he lived in nearby Ankara, was an activist participating in the demonstrations such as university fee protests and 1st May (Labor Day) or New-roz (21st of March) type of general meetings.

After having worked in Ankara for a while he moved to Istanbul. He worked there for different ICT-related companies, the last of which being one of the biggest multinational ICT and consulting corporation with headquarters in the USA. Together with the significant need for ICT specialists at the time, he argues that having English competence and mastering certain ICT-skills is enough for progress in career. Furthermore, at the time he moved to Germany, he was in the last year of a Higher Education by Distant Learning program on management. Rhamnus describes his move from Ankara to Istanbul as a natural consequence of being in the ICT business. He says that, in the ICT sector, if one excels, cities like Ankara or Izmir start to look small. Only two of the interviewees do not have experience in Istanbul before their HSLM career: Prunus, from Antakya, who stood by Izmir and Magnolia, from Kayseri, who stood by Ankara, the third and second biggest cities of Turkey, respectively.

One of the main reasons behind Rhamnus' decision to move to Germany was the political situation in Turkey. He was especially stressed by the demonstrations against the F-type prisons (the closed prisons of Turkey) and the weekly meetings of the *Cumartesi Anneleri* in front of the Galatasaray Lycee in Beyoğlu, Istanbul. These demonstrations, in which Rhamnus participated, are the most significant recent protests and public disobedience practices in Turkey, and accordingly deserve a word here. Some convicts held in the F-prisons had started a hunger strike in the autumn of 2000, which later became a "fast to death". Following the so-called "Return to Life" operation by the military convicts, 32 people lost their lives, 30 of them convicts. *Cumartesi Anneleri*, who are the mothers of a group of disappeared persons, who are commonly believed to be victims of the "forced disappearance" tactics practiced by the state and/or army-related illegal organizations. As mentioned above, Rhamnus reported his participation in these demonstrations but added that he was annoyed about inadequate support of the people and the societal insensitivity to this civil disobedience. These socio-political events influenced him unfavorably and he explicitly made decision of going to another country.

> "The time I was working at the bank was one of the shakiest times of Turkey, those were the times when Ecevit (*Bülent Ecevit*) was unable to walk properly anymore, stumbling upon everything. I did have in mind going all the time. I was thinking like 'These people can't govern me, I don't want to live in a country like this, I want a more dynamic country, a more democratic one, I want a more sensible society'. Around those times things like hunger strikes, and the operations against those were in the spotlight, and that there were demonstrations against F-type prisons (*the name of the closed prisons in Turkey*) and alike, and that I was going to those demos for support. I was, for instance going to the front of Galatasaray Lycee (*Galatasaray Lisesi*) to support Saturday Mothers (*Cumartesi Anneleri*). There were only 70, 80 people. All this was depressing me. It was not even possible to talk to people in the streets, everybody was giving each other hatreful looks. In that environment I was uneasy of that atmosphere and identity. [...]"

Rhamnus had first considered moving to the USA and work there. But one of his good friends who wanted to migrate as well went to the USA and found about the difficulties of the work system there with examples such as having two weeks of annual holidays only. After reading about the Green Card program of Germany, he applied for certain positions via internet. Even though it was not as well paid as some other options in other German cities, he chose to move to Hamburg, because the view of the city that he saw from the plane had left a very positive effect on him. Shortly after the interview he quit his job on a Friday and started working in Hamburg next Monday. As a migrant who arrived in Germany in the September of 2001, he is one of the first Green Card holders. But he had never changed his workplace. He is working in the ICT department of a biotechnology and pharmaceutics company based in Germany, which had sales offices in the USA and the UK. He was holding a position similar to an application manager, with roles both in research and decision-making processes. Furthermore he had also his own company with two partners. Interestingly, it was not related to ICT, but was an international wholesale company. But he made clear that he did not think of himself as bound any of the two companies. He declares that he feels like he could leave any time for any place.

Rhamnus was granted the permanent residence permit in October of 2006, but he was hesitant about the German citizenship. Since he had been working in Turkey relatively long time, he had been automatically invested a large amount of money in his retirement. Due to the impossibility of the double citizenship according to the law in Germany, he would have to leave the Turkish citizenship and lose the right for a retirement in Turkey. But he stresses that otherwise the visa problems are quite unbearable and make the German citizenship attractive.

Like the majority of the interviewees in the sample, the compulsory military service appears as a pushing factor in the migration career of Rhamnus. However, unlike other examples covered here, he thinks he will never do it, not even the military service by payment. He was disturbed by the role played by the military forces of Turkey in many types of human rights violations. As such he neither wanted to "pay money for weapons", nor become a figure in the hands of the nationalist and militarist ideology. That is, Rhamnus, bearing clear similarities to Sambucus, is not critical of the military service only, but also of insensitivity to injustice and the lack of minority rights in Turkey. The histories of Rhamnus and Sambucus qualify as examples of migration as a result of indignation.

Rhamnus accepts that nationalism is on the rise in Turkey, but to him the obstacle to reach universal values such as humanism and democracy is different. This stance toward Islam is inseparable from the Republican values and principles of Atatürk that have been the building blocks of the Westernization project, and reflects the official ideology of Turkey. This stance, despite the above cites critique of the official ideology might reflect the contradictions of the Alevi tradition, discussed at the beginning of this section. But despite being overtly critical of nationalism and even more so of Islam, Rhamnus adds that he has not give up on Turkey.

Like all Green Card migrants of the current sample, Rhamnus rules out money as a factor in his migration. He explains that his wage in

Germany is the same as what he earned in Turkey, accepting that this is a huge amount for the standards of Turkey. Rhamnus adds he was not able to use all of his money even if he wanted to. He explained that he was providing financial support for friends and relatives in need, was happy to be doing that. Overall, he expresses that his is more of a decision to "move out of Turkey" than a decision to "move to a certain country". He argues that he feels at home when in Hamburg. While in Istanbul, depending on what he is doing he feels at ease, but when somewhere else in Turkey he misses Hamburg. He especially stresses the everyday life honesty in Germany, such as not having to count the change, or correctness of the expiry dates of products. He was not planning to return to Turkey before his retirement, that is, he has in mind a 10-15 years of migratory presence outside of Turkey. After that he plans to, similar to Fraxinus, move to a small, close-to-the sea village in Turkey, adding he could also do the same in Portugal or Greece. As such, his self-representation reflects neither a permanent migration, nor a determined return, but a person who can go to anywhere at anytime at his will.

Rhamnus was still married, but like many other HSL migrants covered before, he was soon going to divorce. He is aware that this phenomenon was common among migrants similar to him. At the time of Rhamnus' migration, they had been together for two and a half years, and they did not want to erase those years, and got married, since it was only like this that his partner could join him in Germany. She was a nurse, and after coming to Germany she had received in formation related to her occupation and continued working as a nurse here. Furthermore, she was going to university at the time. They had been having problems after the migration and even though they first thought they could solve those, they are now convinced that it is over. Rhamnus argues that the life in Germany is different than in Turkey and how one deals with it determines the future of the relationship. According to him, in Turkey it is normal to ask the partner about what he/she is doing when they are not together at a given time. He justifies this norm-oriented behavior by the compactness of the social circle of couples in Turkey. He argues that the life in Turkey consists mostly of time at work and time at home. Moreover, the partners become easily part of a "big family" together with their friends from work. This presupposes that working spouses as a family unit spend their limited leisure time together within their social environment. Rhamnus observes that it is possible to have more time for himself in Germany, and was now trying out different recreational activities on his own. That is, after migration, the spouses encounter more leisure time without a common social network. As argued in the analysis of the interview with Syringa, there is most of the time a migration order difference between the two partners. Actually the first-order migrant moves with a definite purpose, whereas the second-order migrant moves in order to join the first-order one. Mespilus, like Rhamnus, stressed the importance of "re-organization of leisure time" as "re-creating private sphere" that is actually required for every migrant including single ones. But due to the migration order difference, the spouses start to differ in how they fill this leisure time, especially since the second-order migrants try to "catch up" by looking for a job or by continuing their education.

Regarding the working environment, Rhamnus sees similarities between Germany and Turkey, and describes both as flexible and comfortable. He explains that this is because he is in the ICT sector, adding that their department is "like a company inside a company", which stresses the distinctiveness of the field. Rhamnus thinks the work mentality in Germany restricts flexibility, although the field of ICT is often identified with flexibility independent of the country.

Rhamnus has no fear of losing his job since he is sure he can always find another job if necessary. He was not a labor union member in Germany, and he explains that he did not have much time to investigate those options due to the migration experience. It can be argued that his self-confidence and the adaptation process in general lead to a break in his work-related activism, which was displayed by his labor union membership in Turkey.

Once again the German skills of the highly educated migrant under consideration reflects the needs of the work environment. Rhamnus had learned German after coming to Germany and he had attended both courses and chose to have access to German media only, avoiding Turkish TV and newspapers. Only around five to ten percent of the employees at the company are foreigners and they mostly speak German and at times a mixture of German and English, which he satirized with the phrase “Das ist ein German company”. But the amount of German spoken at the work is not related to the establishment of friendships at work, and Rhamnus argues, identical to most of the interviewees, that the work culture in Germany is different and concludes that colleagues are colleagues and not friends, unlike in Turkey.

Before coming to Germany, Rhamnus had neither friends nor relatives here. He was visiting Turkey, especially Şanlıurfa, often, but irregularly, that is, there were times when he visited Turkey five times a year, but also times two-year gaps between visits. Those visits were mostly due to family related issues such as marriages. Moreover he had frequent phone calls with his family. These suggest that Rhamnus’ relation with Turkey consisted mostly of his family ties.

Rhamnus explicitly states that his relation with later-migrants, that is, other highly educated people is better than the old generation of migrants. Different from the rest of the interviews, he criticizes the older generation of migrants, not on the basis of low education levels or isolation, but dishonesty in the context of political attitudes. His remarks were about people who defined themselves as leftists, just like him. He observes that most of the leftists from Turkey living in Germany are unemployed. According to his value system, people who do not work can serve neither the leftist ideology nor themselves. Clearly his dignification for work stems from Alevi work ethic “The greatest act of worship is to work”, as mentioned in Prunus. Furthermore he stresses that the leftists in Germany, both migrants and locals, are rather ignorant, even about the most prominent figures of the socialist history. As such, after some “fast leftism” during the early phase of his migration, he does not have relations with those people anymore. He was not a member of any association in Germany, but used to be associated with some in Turkey. As a reminder, it can be observed that both Rhamnus and Syringa showed an initial interest in the first generation of labor migrants or refugees who came from Turkey to Germany between the 1960s and 1980s, but they were then disappointed and differentiated themselves from them.

Rhamnus, half-Kurdish, is sensitive about the Kurdish issue and is involved in active discussions on the topic in the virtual communication platforms for highly educated people from Turkey. He argues that the violence and human rights violations in the southeast of Turkey and the discrimination against ethnic minorities in Turkey must come to an end via democratic means as soon as possible. Moreover, he believes that the economy of Turkey would collapse and lead to a state bankruptcy, if the survival of Turkey would not be in the interests of the EU and the USA. It seems, from many angles Rhamnus envisions a negative picture for both the current situation and the future of Turkey.

Rhamnus did not touch on the subject of "prejudice" mentioned by most of the interviewees. His position is similar to Syringa in that respect. Both looked aware of the scarcity of the relations with "Germans", but they still did not use the term prejudice. This is probably because both of them make the case for a worse environment in Turkey regarding discrimination and nationalism.

CHAPTER 5. CONTEXTUALIZATION FOR TYPOLOGY

The research requires comparison between the phenomena derived from the comparative interpretative analyses and the contexts to make the grounded theory strong. As explained in Methodology, the phenomena will be contextualized under the essential components of HSLM: (i) education; (ii) migration; and (iii) work.

Understanding HSLM first requires a comprehensive evaluation of the education system of the country of origin: the growing output of educated individuals modifies the composition of society and, as a result, the migratory potential of this country. In spite of similarities, education systems differ from country to country. I would like to give background information about the main characteristics and stages of the education system in Turkey from a historical perspective. In doing so, we will become familiar with the formation the new, highly educated labor migrants have as well as their patterns of social and familial background. To some degree, I intended to recognize goals and means of educational socialization processes. These show how social institutions and forces affect educational processes and outcomes. The intention of this analysis is an archaeological study of the education system in Turkey in order to understand how people are produced by it. In doing so, I will explain the relevance of development in the education system on HSLM. In order to comprehend individual educational biographies of the participants in the study, secondary and tertiary education will also be focused on.

The thesis will keep in mind the changing migration conditions in the classical European emigration country, Turkey. In this context, the relevance of Turkey's obligatory military service system as a pushing factor cannot be neglected. In Turkey, young men who have worked abroad for at least three years have the opportunity to complete their military service in three weeks in the form of conscription by payment. In this section, I will argue that supplying this option leads not only to a demand for institutionalized temporary expulsion without detriment to any existing right, but also to the implementation of a constant and steady flow of remittances. It will thus be evaluated as a reflection of graduated sovereignty.

The migratory relations between Turkey and Europe (mainly Germany) are not a recent phenomenon. Their foundations and the privileged position of Turkey will be examined in terms of migration politics. Afterwards, the background of HSLM from Turkey will be investigated according to the main historical influences and the key receiving countries of France, Germany, and the USA. Moreover, the thesis will explore HSLM as a consequence of not only internal changes in the emigrant country itself but also transformations of migration conditions in the immigrant country, Germany, in the manner of integration to internationalization and the "flexibilization" of the labor market. This integration will then be detailed in the section of Germany turning into an open house for HSLM. In 2009, the EU finally decided on the Blue Card program to unite all national programs like Germany's Green Card program in order to attract "high-skills" from outside the EU. At the same time, this contributes to Turkey turning into the reserve labor backyard of the EU. While gradually preferring the permanent HSLM, the Federal Republic of Germany, which rejects dual citizenship, still takes a conservative stance towards migration. Nevertheless, the Turkish Blue Card application, which is a revised version of the Turkish Pink Card application, began to protect some rights of the new German citizens in Turkey – ex-Turkish citizens – and are another reflection of the graduated sovereignty of the Republic of Turkey. All these issues will be addressed.

Under the last component of HSLM, work, I will focus on how the flexible mode of production creates a considerable challenge for classical working conditions and sedentary lifestyles in the context of change in recruitment and labor relations in the global labor market. Then, the structure of labor relations in Germany and its difference due to the presence of the social state will be discussed.

The last two phenomena derived from the interview data are the work ethic debate and the gender gap difference in the labor market between Turkey and Germany. Finally, they will be contextualized.

1. Education

1.1. Education System in Turkey

"Her işin başı eğitim"

Education has been designed as one of the basic tools the new Republic used to transform Turkey from the Ottoman Empire into a modernist laic nation state. In actuality, changes in the education system started about one century before the establishment of the Republic of Turkey. It was initially considered a manifestation of progress just before the Tanzimat period (1839-1876). Since then, promoting education has always been emphasized in the political agenda. Lines of thought manifested in the Tanzimat period have since stimulated and shaped education within their own contexts. These mainstreams have continued to exert their influence on the education system to differing degrees, even today. *The current education system in Turkey can be seen as a summary of these relevant periods, or rather their accumulation.* A short clarification of these periods and of their influence on the system is thus essential to understand the whole picture today. The historical background of the educational system in Turkey matters a great deal and can be considered as the pillars on which the current system is built.

In the pre-Tanzimat Ottoman Empire, there were two main arteries of education: royal education and common education run by the *vakıf* (pious foundations/endowed charities). The Palace was exclusively interested in the education of high-ranking military officers, civil servants, and administrators through a process called *Devşirme* ("Janissaries" and "Inner Boys").[1] The Royal Military

[1] The process of *Devşirme* entailed the systematic abduction of young boys between 8 and 20 years old from the conquered Christian lands in order to create loyal statesmen. They were forcibly taken from their families to grow up enslaved and later become the Ottoman elite.

Academy, the Royal Medical Academy, and the Royal School of Administration (Enderun)[2] were free boarding schools in Istanbul with very high level of education to instruct the Empire's governing elite. Except for royal society education, public education was decentralized and administered by various charitable foundations (*vakıf*). In addition to some training schools run by *tarikats* (mystic religious orders), such as *tekke* (dervish lodge) and *zaviye* (small dervish lodge), scientific and religious education was offered to all Ottoman subjects at *sibyan mektebi* (primary education) and *medrese* (secondary and tertiary education). Meanwhile, *sibyan mektebi* was the sole school where no gender restrictions were present. *Medrese* was the widespread popular school, which persisted for more than 500 years in the Ottoman Empire. Some elite *medreses* served to raise the clergy – "the people of Islamic knowledge" (*Ulema*).[3] *Ulema*, who were intellectuals who had graduated from the *medreses*, had a great influence not only on the people, but also on the royal management. Eventually, both the high governmental body and the educated class of Muslim legal scholars comprised the upper class, or more accurately, the intelligentsia of the Ottoman Empire.

After being established with the nation states of Europe in the nineteenth century, nationalism reached the Ottoman Empire. Starting with the Greek national revolt of 1821, nationalist influences among the nations of the Empire began to increase (Zürcher, 1984:7-8). Meanwhile, the Ottoman intelligentsia, especially bureaucrats, were impressed by the idea of Enlightenment and the French Revolution and sought to get rid of the backwardness of the Empire, popularly known as the "Sick Man of Europe" at the time. Therefore, during the reign of Mahmut II (1808-1839), new lines of thought, especially Westernism and Ottomanism, were widely dif-

---

[2] As the first public administration school of the world, Enderun recruited students mostly from gifted Christian boys who came from the communities settled in Rumelia and the Balkans.

[3] *Medrese* was originally a theological school; however, in the Ottoman Empire, education in the *medrese* was also conducted in four faculties: religion and law, language and literature, philosophy, and basic sciences.

fused in Istanbul.[4] The Empire immediately tried to make structural transformations in several fields, including the military and especially with regards to education. After closing the Janissaries corps in 1826, the first reflections of Westernization and nationalization could be seen most clearly in the education of military staff (*harbiye*), and to some extent in the education of medical and civil service staff (*tıbbiye* and *mülkiye*). Meanwhile, 150 students from the Royal School of Administration and Royal Medical School as well as the new Military School and Engineering School were sent to Europe for education in 1830 by the Sultan. Moreover, the Palace allowed some new Western-style schools to enroll children. Primary schools also become compulsory for boys in Istanbul. This subtle shift in education accelerated during Tanzimat.[5]

At the beginning of his reign, Abdülmecit (1839-1861) announced a new public education system as a necessity to destroy ignorance (Kodaman, 1991:10). For the first time, the Royalty took responsibility for education outside of the Palace. Public education was reorganized and centralized with the establishment of the Chamber of Public Education (*Meclis-i Maarif-i Umumiye*) in 1845 and the Ministry of Public Instruction (*Maarif-i Umûmiye Nezareti*) in 1846. By means of the 1856 Reforms, new schools increased and became available to everyone, regardless of gender, ethnicity, and politics. Moreover, non-Muslim minority schools and private foreign-funded schools also began to operate due to the Capitulations.[6] During the reign of Abdülaziz (1861-1876), the Public Edu-

---

[4] In the late Ottoman Empire, there were two pairs of opposing lines of thought: Westernism (*Batıcılık*) versus Islamizm (*İslamcılık*) and Ottomanizm (*Osmanlıcılık*) versus Turkish nationalizm (*Türkçülük*).

[5] Tanzimat was a period of reformation for the reorganization of the Ottoman Empire. It began with the Beneficial Reforms (*Tanzimat Hayriye*), accepted in 1839, and the Reform Edict (*Tanzimat Fermanı*) in 1856. Tanzimat ended with the First Constitutional Era in 1876. The Constitutional Monarchy (*Meşrutiyet*) was accepted through the First Hamidian in 1876 and the prototype of the First Ottoman Parliament, the *Meclis-i Mebusan* by public affairs, as well as the *Meclis-i Ayan* by the Sultan were hence adapted.

[6] Capitulations of the Ottoman Empire were bilateral contracts between the Empire and European countries, particularly France, which gave their subjects rights and privileges in the realms of movement, trade, education, and law. They came to end with the Treaty of Lausanne in 1923.

cation Regulations (*Maarif-i Umûmiye Nizamnâmesi*) were prepared in order to organize public education by imitating the French education system and were published in 1869. Meanwhile, public education had been classified as primary (*iptidai* and *rüşdiye*), secondary (*idadi* and *sultani*), and tertiary education (*darülfünun*). Primary education became compulsory for all children between the ages of 6-11. New secondary education was extremely limited in comparison with *medreses*, but was implemented by fairly good high schools. Actually, some old royal schools were modernized and the new western-style schools were established under the influence of the French *Lycée* (*Lise*) model, mostly in Istanbul during the Tanzimat period.[7] They remain among the best high schools in Turkey. Furthermore, a large number of students were sent to Europe, mostly to France, to receive tertiary education during the Tanzimat period. Even an Ottoman School (*Mekteb-i Osmani*) was opened in Paris in 1857 to provide preparatory classes for them. Other institutions, including homeschooling by the wealthy, also known as "*konak eğitimi*" (the education system in the mansion), also evolved in Tanzimat. This system used tutoring and was common among wealthy families. In addition to the establishment of some secondary schools for girls and a female teachers' training college in this period,[8] the homeschool system provided another

[7] For instance, Galata Palace Royal School, started in 1481, was modernized and called *Lycée Impérial Ottoman de Galata-Sérai* (*Galatasaray Mekteb-i Sultanisi*) in 1868. French was the main language of instruction and many of the teachers were foreigners from Europe. The students included members of all religious and ethnic communities of the Ottoman Empire. Also, there were a number of foreign-funded high schools – seven French, two American, one Austrian, one Italian, and one German in Istanbul, as well as seven American and one French in other cities in Anatolian. They mostly served Christian minorities and foreigners at that time. In addition, high schools training Ottoman Turkish were established, mostly in Istanbul: *Vefa Lisesi* and *Pertevniyal Lisesi* in 1872, *Darüşşafaka Lisesi* in 1873, *Edirne Lisesi* in 1883, and *Istanbul Lisesi* in 1884.

[8] Most of them began education in 1910s, for instance Cağaloğlu High School for Girls (Cağaloğlu Kız Lisesi), Kandilli High School for Girls (Kandilli Kız Lisesi), Erenköy High School for Girls (Erenköy Kız Lisesi), and Çamlıca High School for Girls (Çamlıca Kız Lisesi).

additional educational possibility especially for the daughters of upper-class families, covering the families of *ulema*.[9]

The new western-style schools (*mektep*) created a challenge to *medreses*. Seen as bearers of the oriental education system, *medrese*s were reduced to providing only religious education during this period, whereas *mektep*s were seen as the real place for scientific education. By means of Tanzimat, the constitutive change in the public education regime began to take off. A new form of education, independent from charitable Islamic foundations, was regulated to a certain extent. Furthermore, it coincided with a relatively more favorable environment for the non-Muslim society in the Empire because of the Capitulations.

It is clear that throughout Tanzimat, far-reaching reforms on education were carried out in the name of progress and the new form of education was promoted in connection with its newly attributed role of "creating citizens."[10] However, the pervasive implementation of education was hard for the Orient Empire of Europe to achieve in its downfall. Indeed, education still remained very elitist (Yalçınkaya, 1999; Kaya, 1974:76). It was clearly Istanbul-centered, with Paris as its important periphery. However, it created new elites instead of new citizens. They became influential leaders and thinkers not only of the Republic of Turkey but also of many other former Ottoman states in the Balkans, the Middle East, and

---

[9] Altınöz, Vuslat Devrim. *The Ottoman Women's Movement: Women's Press, Journals, Magazines and Newspapers from 1875 to 1923*. Unpublished MA Thesis. Miami University. Oxford, Ohio, 2003.

[10] The important point in Tanzimat is that education was firstly considered as a required means for the transformation from the ruled (*reaya*) to the Ottoman citizens (*teb'a*) by the Beneficial Reforms. In the Constitutional Monarchy (*Meşrutiyet*), the intention to make education popular was also continued in the state discourse. Said Paşa as the Minister of the Interior and then the Grand Vizier in the reign of Abdülhamit II (1876-1909) explained that education was vital for the effective conduct of public affairs, for a civilized community, and for defense against foreign enemies (Lewis, 1968:180). The mission of education was presented to bring up a new generation of the citizens. As Üstel (2004:32) mentioned, "the child" was perceived as an independent "subject" in Tanzimat and then a potential public subject of the nation ("the child-citizen"). In fact, children as *tabula rasa* were targeted to make them the new "citizen." For the sake of this mission, the new form of education system was promoted in the state discourse in that period.

North Africa. To summarize, Tanzimat brought about the emergence and the rise of the popular scientific ideology and of a new educated ruling elite in the "Sick Man of Europe." As a consequence, Ottoman intelligentsia fell into line in one of three camps: (i) *ulema,* ignorant of Westernization; (ii) super-westernized and ignorant of Islam; and (iii) pro-western and mindful of employing Islam as a modernizing tool instead of a governing role in the society (Hanioğlu, 1995:13-6, 211). The third camp took a stance somewhere between the former two, which were the rather extreme factions dominating intellectual life in the Ottoman Empire. They were first called the "Young Ottomans," and then the "Young Turks."

The Young Ottomans were mostly highly educated Turkish, Kurdish, Armenian, and Greek elites, as well as other ethnicities in Istanbul. They were opposed to the Sultan's regime and engaged in the reinvigoration of the Empire. The prominent figures in the opposition movement, such as Abdullah Cevdet, Ahmet Rıza, İbrahim Temo, and Prens Sabahattin, were influenced chiefly by August Comte, Gustav Le Bon, and Frédéric Le Play. Their *Weltanschauung* can be summarized in two words: science and progress (Hanioğlu, 1995:13).[11] Positivism, which "claimed to be a new religion", was the first ideology for those "who were trying to replace religion with science" (Hanioğlu, 1995:203). Their second ideology was elitism in order to further the creation of a new intelligentsia to remove the Sultan's regime, which they believed to be causing the backwardness of the Empire (Hanioğlu, 1995:206). In addition to their purpose of "replacing the Sultan's regime with a dictatorship of intellectuals", the Young Ottomans also found the "education of the masses" necessary and often underlined the importance of education (Hanioğlu, 1995:207).[12] At this point, they believed the Un-

[11] The "Young Turks" were labeled as "liberals" and "constitutionalists" by many European scholars, whereas their *Weltanschauung* never covered these characteristics (Hanioğlu, 1995:214).

[12] After Tanzimat, education was not only the main field of interest of significant pedagogues such as Rıza Tevfik, Selim Sırrı Tarcan, and İsmail Hakkı Baltacıoğlu but also of many sociologists, philosophers, and politicians such as Prens Sabahattin, Ahmet Rıza, Abdullah Cevdet, and Ziya Gökalp.

ion of the Peoples (*İttihadı Anasır*) could be achieved with Ottomanization of the minorities (Zürcher, 1984:23). The Young Ottomans only embraced positivist scientific education briefly, and their focal point was not only to build a new intellectual ruling elite, but also to provide enough education for the people to adopt their *Weltanschauung*.

FIGURE 1. TANZIMAT PERIOD (1839-1876)

<table>
<tr><th>Line of Thought</th><th>Policy and Application in Education</th><th>Consequences</th></tr>
<tr><td>Ottomanization</td><td>Centralization of public education: Establishment of the Chamber of Public Education in 1845; the Council of Public Instruction in 1846; Public Education Regulations in 1869;
Attempt at popularization: Compulsory primary education</td><td rowspan="2">(i) Emergence of state-controlled Western-type public schools;
(ii) Emergence of new Westernist ruling elite (high-ranking civil servants and military officers) who differentiated from the existing elite – Islamist elite (ulema);
(iii) Divergence between graduates from the orient-education system (medreseli) and graduates from the occident education system (mektepli)</td></tr>
<tr><td>Westernization ("Modernization") including Positivism and Elitism</td><td>Separation of scientific education from religious education due to the establishment of new Western-type schools; Transition to public education imitating French education system in addition to privately-funded schools; Continuation and increase in the numbers of minority and foreign missionary schools set up due to the Capitulations; Opening of secondary schools for girls; European university partnerships - Exchange Student programs; Ottoman School in Paris</td></tr>
</table>

The Young Ottomans founded the Ottoman Committee for Union and Progress (CUP, *İttihat ve Terakki Cemiyeti*) in 1889 in Istanbul. However, since most of the Young Ottomans were sent into exile, the CUP worked as an underground international network of the central branches of Paris, Geneva, and Cairo, besides other branches in the Balkans, North Africa, and Central Asia. The First Congress of Ottoman Opposition took place in Paris in 1902. After the Congress, a shift to nationalism gradually took place until 1906 when the CUP was officially established with a nationalist focus

(Hanioğlu, 1995:211). Afterwards, some non-Turkish members of the Young Ottomans left, preferring their own nationalist movements (Hanioğlu, 1995:211).

While gaining most of the "Young Turks" rather than the "Young Ottomans," the CUP came to power between 1908 and 1918 in the Second Constitutional Era.[13] In this period, the ultra-nationalist high-ranking military officers from Thessalonica,[14] Enver Paşa, Celal Paşa, and Talat Paşa, who were known as the "dictatorial triumvirate" become dominant figures of the CUP by transforming the political opposition struggle into the military coup. Meanwhile, the unionist movement turned into an enforced Turkish nationalist movement in the Empire. For the major figures of the Young Turks at that period, a nation should have a unique language, religion, and culture in order to develop patriotic alliance and national ideals. However, according to Antel (1939:142), this was still too far from the emergence of a national consciousness. To be able to cope, the Young Turks once again, turned to education as the crucial means to promote Turkish nationalism. As the official spokesman of the CUP, Ziya Gökalp (1973:50) initially underlined the importance of a *national* education and training, setting an objective "to bring up national persons," in order "to build a nation."[15] But, the national education "ideal" was not implemented until the Republic of Tur-

[13] Mustafa Kemal was a member of the CUP for a while in the period (Zürcher, 1984:42-68).

[14] The Ottoman Liberty Society was established in 1906 in Thessalonica. Then they joined the CUP.

[15] "Terbiyenin gayesi milli fertler yetiştirmektir. Milli fertler yetiştirmek ise, doğrudan doğruya 'milet yapmak' demektir." Ziya Gökalp was not only a sociologist impressed by Emile Durkheim, Gustave Le Bon, and Auguste Comte, but also an influential ideologue of the CUP. He was influenced by all four lines of thought in the late Ottoman Empire and then he tried to find a balance point between Islamism and Westernism and merged this point with Turkish nationalism instead of Ottomanizm. He suggested taking the "civilization" from the West, referring to technological and scientific progress and "not its non-material aspects": "culture" and "morality" (Berkes, 1959:21). Berkes (1959:22) summarizes his opinions as follows: "As the ultimate reality of contemporary society is the nation, and as national ideals are ultimate forces orienting the behavior of the individuals, so the most urgent task for the Turks consisted of awakening as a nation in order to adapt themselves to the conditions of contemporary civilization".

key came into being, but after the "enforced Turkification" during the war years.[16]

FIGURE 2. COMMITTEE FOR UNION AND PROGRESS (1908-1918)

Line of Thought	Policy and Application in Education	Consequences
Turkish nationalization replaced Ottomanization	Recognition of necessity of unity in education; Development of the idea of National Education; Closing Royal School of Administration (*Enderun*); One-sided removal of Capitulations; **Attention to emancipation of women:** Increased school for girls; University for girls	*[disrupted by the period of wars and "enforced Turkification"]*

The crucial point here is that the Young Turks in power took sides on the national education model in an ongoing debate among intelligentsia.[17] They laid conservative-nationalist ideational foundations in the educational system in Turkey. After the first meeting of the Grand National Assembly (TBMM) against the Sultan's regime in Istanbul, held in Ankara on April 23, 1920, Mustafa Kemal was selected as president of the Assembly. In line with the national education ideal of the CUP, Mustafa Kemal said in the Education Congress (*Maarif Kongresi*) in 1921:

> "I believe that the education and training method that has been followed up until now is one of the major causes of our nation's retrogression. That is why when I am talking about a national education program, I mean a culture that is free of an old era's

[16] These war years were "periods of large population losses and large declines in GDP per capita followed by a rapid recovery in the 1920s. Population of the areas comprising present day Turkey declined by 18 about percent during 1914-1924" (Altuğ et al, 2007:3). Meanwhile, the non-Muslim population was radically reduced from about 20 percent in 1915 to 2.5 percent in 1927, according to that year's census.

[17] As Kadıoğlu (1996) explained, Ziya Gökalp's position denoted a shift from Tanzimat rationalism, inspired by the Enlightenment to the German Romanticism, "by accepting the transcendental reality of society identified with the nation instead of individual reason."

superstitions, and far from influences from the East and the West, but suited for our own national values and history."[18]

Mustafa Kemal emphasized that education should try to arouse and strengthen the necessity to struggle against any antagonistic elements that would weaken a national consciousness and an autonomous spirit (AMAD, 1939:7). "The aim of Turkish education is to train the people who will succeed in this life-and-death struggle; that is, to train the Turkish nation and especially Turkish youth, which are Turkey's greatest asset" (TNCE, 1961:28). In brief, the aim of education was to create "a national code of behavior" (1961:41). İsmet İnönü explained national education in the Congress for Teachers (*Muallimler Kongresi*) in the following manner:

> "We want national education. What does it mean? We can better understand it with its opposite. We can answer the question: what is the opposite of national education. This may be religious education, or it is possible that it is international education. You will give education that is neither religious nor international, but national."[19]

He explicitly defined national education as the inverse of both religious education and international education. Moreover, Baltacıoğlu (1943:177) argued that science is neither carried out for its own sake, nor for society, but for the nation.[20] This chauvinist understanding supporting national "scientific" education has appeared during all periods of the Republic, which was announced on Octo-

[18] The original version is the following: "*Şimdiye kadar takip olunan tahsil ve terbiye usullerini milletimizin tarihi tedenniyatında en mühim bir amil olduğu kanaatindeyim. Onun için bir milli terbiye programından bahsederken, eski devrin hurafatından ve evsaf-ı fıtriyemizle hiç de münasebeti olmayan yabancı fikirlerden şarktan ve garptan gelebilen bilcümle tesirlerden uzak, seciye-i milliye ve tarihimizle mütenasip bir kültür kastediyorum.*" (AMAD, 1939:3-4)

[19] The original version is the following: "*(...) Milli Terbiye istiyoruz. Bu ne demektir? Bunu zıddıyla daha vazıh olarak anlarız. Milli Terbiye'nin zıttı nedir deseler, söyleyebiliriz: Bu belki dini terbiye, yahut beynenmilel terbiyedir. Sizin vereceğiniz terbiye dini değil, milli, beynenmilel değil, millidir*" (Akyüz, 1982:260).

[20] Baltacıoğlu also objects to the *Meşrutiyet* pedogogy, because of its being European-oriented, not being nationally-oriented. Baltacıoğlu (1943:178) suggests that the difference between the two lies in the fact that European-oriented pedagogy is not connected with the life and social practices.

ber 29, 1923 (Gök, 1999:16).[21] The monist understanding in the state discourse has always been spread throughout the education system. The basic structure of the educational system in Turkey is based on national formal education. Since the recognition of the Republic of Turkey with the signing of the Treaty of Lausanne on July 24, 1923, education has been organized and administrated by the Ministry of National Education (*Milli Eğitim Bakanlığı*, MoNE). It was outlined in the Law of the Unity of National Education (*Tevhid-i Tedrisat Kanunu*) on March 3, 1924. The following regulations were introduced through this Law:

> Article 1. All the medreses and schools administered by private foundations or the Ministry of Religious and Foundation Affairs are connected to the Ministry of National Education.
>
> Article 2. The money allocated to schools and medreses from the budget of the Ministry of Religious and Foundation Affairs shall be transferred to the education budget.
>
> Article 3. The Ministry of Education shall open a religious faculty to educate higher religious experts within universities and separate schools to train imams and hatips.

The main target of this law was determined to be the unification of education by proclaiming equal educational opportunities and activating laic education (the exclusion of the teaching of religion and religious symbols from public schools).[22] The law pointed out uncontrolled religion-oriented schools as barriers to laic national education: the Islam-oriented schools, the foreign-funded Christian-oriented, and minority schools. The fact that different cultures of people graduated from these schools was seen as the main obstacle to developing a national culture. With this law, the institutions of the Islam-oriented education system (*medreses*) were completely

[21] The adjective "*milli*" (national) comes from Arabic and was Turkified as "*ulusal*" over the years. As a matter of fact, people following the ideology of "*ulusalcılık*" (nationalism) emerged in Turkey and distinguished themselves from people following the ideology of "*milliyetçilik*" (nationalism). The difference between them may be identified in terms of class stratification. *Ulusalcılar* are mostly from the middle class, *milliyetçiler* from the proletariat.

[22] The aim was to train all children in a national, unique, scientific, laic, widespread formal education.

banned. Like *medreses*, most private, foreign-funded schools which taught in foreign languages, in particular American, French and minority schools, were advised to go with laicism. They were questioned and accused of missionary activities in the name of laicism in the new Republic. Also, the subjects of Turkish language and national history in Turkish became compulsory in their curricula.

The Atatürk[23] period explicitly put forward the characteristics of education in Turkey: laicization and Turkification, which were manifested in a number of events.[24] First, the abolishment of other religious training institutions such as *tekke* and *zaviye* in 1925. Second, the switch from the Arabic alphabet to the Latin alphabet in 1928 and the acknowledgement of Turkish as a common language. And finally, the monopolization of the Turkish language and history by the Society for Research on the Turkish History in 1931 and the Society for Research on the Turkish Language in 1932. These two characteristics can be read as de-/reformed extensions of Tanzimat reforms and the Young Turk's thoughts. Although educational institutions are open to all citizens regardless of their sex, religion, language, and race, these two characteristics of education caused the main problems thereafter.

In the context of Turkey, laicism as one of Atatürk's six main principles is partly different from secularism.[25] The word *laiklik* in Turkish comes from the French word *laïcité,* which is also the core concept of the French constitution.[26] *Laïcité* in France was initially

---

[23] Following the issuance of the surname law in 1934 in Turkey, Mustafa Kemal was legally granted the surname Atatürk. "Atatürk" means the father of Turks. It is done that way "Mustafa Kemal" is used for the military figure before the establishment of the Republic of Turkey and "Atatürk" for the political figure after it.

[24] See Bali, 1999; Aktar, 2000; Yıldız, 2001; and Üstel, 2004.

[25] Secularism asserts the freedom from government imposition of religion upon the people, within a state that is neutral on matters of belief, and gives no state privileges or subsidies to religions.

[26] Article 1 states that "*La France est une République indivisible, laïque, démocratique et sociale*." The term was originally the French equivalent of the term "*laity*", i.e., everyone who is not Catholic clergy. After the French Revolution this meaning changed and it came to mean keeping religion separate from the executive, judicial, and legislative branches of government. The same principle is valid in the constitution of the Republic of Turkey.

established in public education with the 1880s Jules Ferry laws, which established the first free education (1881) and then mandatory and laic education (1882).[27] After about two decades, France accepted the law separating church and state based on three principles: the neutrality of the state, the freedom of religious exercise, and the public powers related to the church. The law states that "The Republic neither recognizes, nor salaries, nor subsidizes any religion."[28] In addition, it continued the ban on wearing conspicuous religious symbols in public education. The laicism principle in the Republic of Turkey is confined to the definition of the separation of religion from state affairs and the freedom of religions as individual faiths. Based on its application, the state has controlled and funded Sunni Islam as the religion of the majority through the Ministry of Religious Affairs (*Diyanet İşleri Bakanlığı*). Including Sunni Islam, all independent religious communities deemed political are nonetheless illegal. It is clear that the laicism in Turkey does not give religions any educational rights and Sunni Islam is under strict government control.

The multi-religious, multi-lingual, and multi-ethnic structure of the Ottoman Empire transformed and unified many peoples under one nation. The Republic of Turkey has recognized the three biggest non-Muslim ethnicities, which are Jews, Greeks, and Armenians, as minorities by the Treaty of Lausanne. However, other religious minorities such as Syrian Orthodox, Roman Catholics, Levantines, Yezidis, and Alevis, as well as other ethnic minorities such as Kurds, Lazs, Tatars, Circassians, Zazas, Arabs, Bulgarians, Albanians, and Roma people were not recognized. There are three problems of recognition in this context. The first problem here is that the Treaty acknowledged *only* non-Muslims as minorities in Turkey. Second, the Republic of Turkey recognized *only some* non-Muslim groups as minorities. The third problem is the application problem of minority rights, as the articles related to education in

[27] Jules Ferry was the Minister of Public Education at that time.

[28] Its application is, however, controversial in the country, especially the exception of the Alsace-Moselle.

the Treaty in 1923 were not violated by the Law of the Unity of National Education in 1924.

> Article 40. Turkish nationals belonging to non-Moslem minorities shall enjoy the same treatment and security in law and in fact as other Turkish nationals. In particular, they shall have an equal right to establish, manage and control at their own expense, any charitable, religious and social institutions, any schools and other establishments for instruction and education, with the right to use their own language and to exercise their own religion freely therein.
>
> Article 41. With regard to public instruction, the Turkish Government will grant in those towns and districts, where a considerable proportion of non-Moslem nationals are resident, adequate facilities for ensuring that in the primary schools the instruction shall be given to the children of such Turkish nationals through the medium of their own language. This provision will not prevent the Turkish Government from making the teaching of the Turkish language obligatory in the said schools.
>
> In towns and districts where there is a considerable proportion of Turkish nationals belonging to non-Moslem minorities, these minorities shall be assured an equitable share in the enjoyment and application of the sums which may be provided out of public funds under the State, municipal or other budgets for educational, religious, or charitable purposes.

The Greeks of Istanbul and the Aegean Islands of Imbros (*Gökçeada*) and Tenedos (*Bozcaada*) were exempted from the 1923 population exchange between Greece and Turkey. Most of the Armenians and Jews have remained in and around Istanbul to the present day. The number of schools of these recognized minorities decreased greatly. In spite of numerous enduring Kindergartens and primary schools, there remained only twelve minority high schools in Istanbul, six Greek, five Armenian, and one Jewish. MoNE administered these schools. Four courses – Turkish language, national history, national geography, and citizenship – were obligatory in all schools and were instructed in Turkish by the teachers of Turkish nationality. In opposition to the treaty, the state did not give any financial support to the minority schools (Yıldız, 2001:280). Furthermore, education in the mother tongue of unrecognized minorities was made impossible by these restrictions. As a matter of fact, the unification of education aimed to make all recognized and unrecognized minorities laic and Turkish in the name of national alliance.[29] The task of education was to create Turkified, secularized youths as determined by Atatürk in the Atatürk period.

Another characteristic of the education system in Turkey is related to progress and being beyond nationality. It can be noticed in Atatürk's speech in 1922:

> "We can't close our eyes and assume that we live in isolation. We can't take our country into a circle and live indifferently to the rest of the world. On the contrary, we will live on the field of civilization as a civilized, advanced nation. Such a life is possible only through science and knowledge. We will take science and knowledge from there where it exists and put it into the head of every single individual in our nation. There are no conditions and restrictions for science and knowledge."[30]

This is reminiscent of the *Weltanschauung* of the Young Ottomans (science and progress) mentioned above. A historical episode that reflects this progress is also very striking. Invited by Atatürk, John Dewey, the founder of pragmatism, visited Turkey in 1924 and in order to prepare a report on education in Turkey. Dewey claimed the importance and necessity of progressive education in his original report; however, the translated version conveyed the issue of a "progressive idea" rather than "progressive education" (Alptekin-Oğuzertem, 2002).[31] This shift of meaning due to the translation

---

[29] The student oath for all formal schools, agreed upon in 1933, indicates a lot about it.

[30] "*Gözlerimizi kapayıp mücerret yaşadığımızı farz edemeyiz. Memleketimizi bir çember içine alıp cihan ile alakasız yaşayamayız....Bilakis müterakki, mütemeddin bir millet olarak medeniyet sahasının üzerinde yaşayacağız. Bu hayat ancak ilim ve fen ile olur. İlim ve fen nerede ise oradan alacağız ve her ferd-i milletin kafasına koyacağız. İlim ve fen için kayıt ve şart yoktur.*" (AMAD, 1939:10)

[31] Progressive education involves two essential components: respect for diversity, indicating that each individual should be recognized for his/her own abilities, interests, ideas, needs, and cultural identity, and the development of critical, socially engaged intelligence, which enables individuals to understand and participate effectively in the affairs of their community in a collaborative effort to achieve a common good. Indeed, Dewey (1915) believed there is an intimate connection between education and social action in a democ-

error prevented the continuity of understanding on progress in the context of education.

Atatürk always pointed out that the future lay in civilization, which for him meant the modern civilization of the West. With every reform in the early republican period in Turkey "was the intention to bring Turkish society completely in line with the Western pattern" (TNCE, 1961:28). Kim (2001:98) mentions that Atatürk "accepted education as an important key to unlock the door to becoming a modernized Western country. Besides, he believed that education itself generated and initiated the necessity of modernization." As a line of thought, Westernism was actively supported in the field of education in the early years of the Turkish Republic.[32] Eventually, there were two main phrases as a binary contradiction in the state discourse of the Republic of Turkey: "to reach the level of the contemporary modern civilizations" or "to catch up with the civilization," pointing towards the West (Westernism) and "to stand on its own feet," referring to antagonism to imperialism (nationalism).[33] The foundation of this discourse was laid in the period from Tanzimat to the fall of the Empire. However, it reached its peak in the 1920s. Therefore, the Republic of Turkey was founded by identifying itself in contrast to the Ottoman Empire, or further, by totally forgetting it. Indeed, the Republic of Turkey has denied its Ottoman past (Robins, 1997:68). It has always had Europeanization on its agenda by way of imitating the Western model. Education in

racy. He believed that school should teach students how to be problem-solvers by helping students learn how to think rather than simply learning routine lessons about large amounts of information (Dewey, 1915; Dewey, 1939). In Dewey's view, schools should focus on judgment rather than knowledge (1915). He also believed that schools should help students learn to live and to work cooperatively with others.

[32] According to Robins (1997:62-4), the Western-type of modernization resembles a kind of assimilation, in fact, westernization in Turkey created "conformism and dependency" rather than "cultural creativity and emancipation."

[33] Although "civilization" is always encouraged in Turkey, the national anthem determines it as "a monster with with only one tooth remaining." It can also be argued that the "chosen trauma" related to being a mandate or a colony since the Treaty of Sèvres in 1920 has been propagated as paranoia of division and it was covered by these phrases. The term "chosen trauma" was first used by Volkan and Itzkowitz (1994:7). Some called it "Sèvres syndrome."

Turkey constantly oscillates between being national and pro-western.

Another main theme of the early years of the Republic concerning education is "state-feminism." Girls had chances to take secondary education in the Tanzimat period with the requirement of being from a family of the upper, "enlightened" class in Istanbul. The Young Ottomans and then the Young Turks developed ideas about emancipation of Ottoman women. During an interview with Ahmed Rıza as the president of the Ottoman Chamber of Deputies, published in the New York Times on November 19, 1911, comparing Ottoman women to their European counterparts, he said:

> "You know, of course, how very backward our unhappy country is in the direction of the education of women. This has been all along the curse of our Fatherland. We have women enough, but we have no life companions, no sisters, no wives, no mothers in the proper sense of the word. I thought what a stupendous benefit would accrue to the whole of our struggling and aspiring empire if an educational centre were created, where sound principles connected with the rational upbringing of Moslem girls, with the sacred duties of properly directed motherhood, could be imparted to our rising female generation."[34]

These sentences summarize the politics on education of girls. In particular, the stress on the gender disadvantage dealt with the ideal of a new pro-western, united society. In this sense, the politics of women's emancipation through education gradually increased and became one of the main topics in the new Republic's political agenda, partly due to social movements of upper-class, educated women.[35] Atatürk greatly encouraged women in Turkey to become educated: "In Turkish society, women have not lagged behind men in science, scholarship, and culture. Perhaps they have even gone

---

[34] "For Emancipation of Moslem Girls: War and Stamboul Fires Delay Lyceum Project of Chamber's New President Admires European System." Constantinpole, November 7, 1911. The New York Times published on November 19, 1911.
[35] See Altınöz, 2003.

further ahead." (Adıvar, 1972:180). In addition, in terms of the unity of education, coeducation was implemented.[36]

Although there were great efforts to popularize education at the turn of twentieth century in the Ottoman Empire, they were extremely limited. In fact, the adult literacy rate before World War I and in the 1920s did not exceed 10 percent (Altuğ et al, 2007:15). Influenced by the popularization politics of the three decades of the early Republic, the literacy rate of those over the age of 15 increased by about 30 percent. Educational popularization politics have consistently furthered such jumps in literacy rates and the rate reached approximately 70 percent by 1980 and 90 percent by 2000. A similar trend can be observed in schooling rates. In fact, the emphasis put on the necessity of education has never changed. This can be seen in two common sayings in Turkey: "Education is a priori" ("*Her işin başı eğitim*") and "Education is a must" ("*Eğitim şart*"). Besides popularization, diversification and intensification (specialization) in secondary and tertiary education have increased, especially since the 1940s.[37] In this respect, new kinds of public high schools have existed with the purpose of training a HSL force. To illustrate, Colleges for Education (*Maarif Koleji*), which were renamed Anatolian High Schools in 1977, began to operate in 1955. For the same intention, Science High Schools began to be established in 1963. Since the 1990s these two types of schools have both private and public examples, and their quantities have gone up significantly. The types of high schools in Turkey will be explained more in the next section.

[36] Single-sex education has continued as well, but mixed education has also been common The author claims that most elite high schools for girls and boys have remained as single-sex schools after the implementation of mixed-education. They have educated children especially from the upper-middle class. These single-sex schools had more influence on the change in gender roles in society in the years since the establishment of the Republic than coeducation. As a matter of fact, these schools have trained people who are relatively more independent from the patriarchy of the state and society.

[37] More specifically, the Law of Gifted Children ("Law of Wonderful Child") in 1948 was also put into action for special musicians and painters.

FIGURE 3. EARLY YEARS OF THE REPUBLIC OF TURKEY (1923-1946)

<table>
<tr><th>Line of Thought</th><th>Policy and Application in Education</th><th>Consequences</th></tr>
<tr><td>Turkish nationalization ("Turkification")</td><td>Centralization: MoNE; Unification: Law of the Unity of National Education; Institutionalization of "Atatürkism" as the official state ideology based on the principles and reforms of Atatürk; Student Oath established in 1933</td><td rowspan="5">(i) Emergence of "Turkified secularized citizens" through common compulsory primary education;
(ii) Reemergence of new Turkish ruling elite as "Republicans" who were highly educated and Westernists;
(iii) Increase in female students and academics</td></tr>
<tr><td>Westernization</td><td>Complete transition to the Westernized school system; Invitation of famous Western experts in education (Dewey in 1924-6; Buyse in 1927; Malche in 1932; Kuhne in 1935); University Reform in 1933; Latin Alphabet replaced Arabic; Foreign language education in curriculum of public schools limited to English, French, and German; Abolishment of Persian and Arabic as choice subjects; Translation of Western masterpieces into Turkish; Employment of refugee academics from Nazi-Germany</td></tr>
<tr><td>Laicization</td><td>Laic education through the abolishment of religious education (including missionary and Islamic schools) in 1924-5; Religious Studies as an optional subject in 1927 and its removal gradually during the 1930s</td></tr>
<tr><td>Popularization</td><td>Continuous emphasis on the importance of education; Increasing numbers of schools; Institutions to improve literacy in adults in 1928 (Millet Mektepleri); public reading rooms in villages 1930-32; Establishment of "people's houses" for public education; The Law of Village Instructors (Köy Eğtimenler Yasası) in 1937</td></tr>
<tr><td>State feminization</td><td>Attention to female education; Implementing coeducation in public education</td></tr>
</table>

Since Atatürk, Atatürkism has become the official state ideology in education and teaching Atatürkism was the first task of national education system. It is very hard to find a teacher who does not follow Atatürkism. Moreover, it is impossible to criticize Atatürk or Atatürkism in schools, indicating that it is clearly the biggest taboo. However, as Turkey became a multi-party system in 1946, it encountered Islamization which was suppressed for many years.[38] In the field of education, its first distinctive influence was to open Islamic Divinity High Schools (*İmam Hatip Lisesi*) which currently educate ten percent of all high school students. In addition to the establishment of these high schools, the subject of religious studies, which was gradually removed in the 1930s, was re-permitted as an optional subject in other high schools. Furthermore, some Faculties of Divinity have been set up since the multi-party regime. It is clear that the Islamization has effected Turkey's education system, although it can be associated with Atatürkism and its laicism principle. In fact, efforts of Islamization in education have remained a debated issue on the political agenda.

MoNE is still responsible for all educational services in the country: drawing up curricula, coordinating the work of official, private and voluntary organizations, designing and building schools, developing educational materials and so on. But since the military coup on September 12, 1980, it has not been responsible for tertiary education. While the University Law of 1946 granted academic autonomy to Turkey's universities, the *coup d'état* and the ensuing military government lead to the creation of the Tertiary Education Council (*Yükseköğretim Kurulu,* YÖK). The Council, in accordance with the Law No. 2547 of 1981, plans, coordinates, and makes policy for tertiary education.

[38] Islamization refers to Sunni-Islamization.

FIGURE 4. INTRODUCTION TO MULTI-PARTY REGIME (1946) UNTIL 1980

<table>
<tr><th>Line of Thought</th><th>Policy and Application in Education</th><th>Consequences</th></tr>
<tr><td>Re-Islamization (in the Sunni branch)</td><td>Opening of Islamic Divinity High Schools and Faculties of Divinity in increasing numbers; Re-permittance of Religious Studies as an optional-choice subject in 1947-8; The Faculty of Divinity</td><td rowspan="3">(i) Return of Islamic elite who joined the existing, Westernist, elite;
(ii) Emergence of middle class through education - “state-oriented militant citizens;”
(iii) Creation of intelligentsia</td></tr>
<tr><td>Atatürkism after the death of Atatürk as (“Nationalist-Westernist”)</td><td>Sustainment of the established education parameters in the early period of the Republic</td></tr>
<tr><td>Further Popularization</td><td>Increasing numbers of schools in Anatolia; Diversification and Intensification - Various Types of Public High Schools: Establishment of Village Institutes for teacher training in 1940 - closed in 1954; Turkish elite “Colleges” (Maarif Kolejleri) in 1955 - named Anatolian High Schools in 1975; Science High Schools in 1963 in order to educate a qualified labor force; Law of Gifted Children (“Law of Wonderful Child”) in 1948</td></tr>
</table>

Since the military coup against the rebellious 1968 generation in Turkey of the 1980s, the articulation of two new ideologies can be observed: the “Turkish-Islamic synthesis” and economic neoliberalism. The Turkish-Islamic synthesis began to be stressed by the Atatürkist military. This ideology, claiming to cooperate with the laicism principle of Atatürk, has three pillars: the family, the mosque, and the barracks. In spite of the fact that that school is not one of the main pillars, the ideology has definitely affected education system. According to Copeaux (1998), the change from the Turkish History Thesis to the Turkish-Islamic synthesis can be noticed in the history books read in schools. Although the subject of religious studies, depending on the present government’s policy, was optional from the beginning of the Republic of Turkey until the 1980 military coup; it has been a compulsory subject in primary and secondary education since 1980. This is stated in the constitution, which was introduced 1982 under heavy influence from the military government. It is actually called "Knowledge about Religious Culture and Morality" (*Din Kültürü ve Ahlak Bilgisi*). The formulation implies, in itself, a comparative study of religions and morality, but in practice, it involves the teaching of Islam, more precisely, Sunni Islam. Furthermore, graduates of Islamic Divinity High Schools have thereafter been eligible to study in all departments of tertiary education.

"Neoclassical liberalism" as a line of thought has emerged in a gradual manner all over the world since the 1970s. In fact, Pinochet's Chile, Thatcher's Britain, and Reagan's America were outcomes of that line of thought. Its early implementation in Turkey started with Turgut Özal who was appointed as the state minister of the economy under the military government (1980-82), the first prime minister after the military coup (1983-88), and then the eighth president of Turkey (1989-93). In Özal's Turkey, the intervention of the state was redesigned to promote greater economic liberty and smaller, individual and social liberty. Actually, the military government, which wrote the Law No. 2547 of 1981 on tertiary education and the 1982 Constitution, has abated academic autonomy, which was granted by the University Law of 1946. By proclaiming that educational institutions, especially universities, have been the center of political ideas and social movements, military leaders, particularly Kenan Evren (the leader of the military government) have perceived them as harmful for Turkey's order and stability. They have attempted to introduce both structural and curricular changes which abolished human rights in education. By means of the Martial Law No. 1402, 3,854 teachers and 120 academics were dismissed from teaching. Meanwhile, a significant number of university students and graduates were sent into exile or fled abroad before and after the coup. Indeed, extreme nepotism in appointing new educational staff was another issue in the 1980s. The 1982 Constitution stipulates that the president appoints university rectors and that the government has the right to set up new universities. YÖK has assigned not only academic titles (lecturers, associate professors, and professors) but also appointed deans of faculties and rectors of universities. Furthermore, the Law No. 2547 of 1981 on tertiary education prohibits all educational staff and matriculated students from belonging to or working for a political party. Clearly, government policies since the coup have institutionalized extensive state interference in educational affairs with the exception of economic manners. Apart from decreasing independence in education by government interference, distinct effects of neoliberalism on education can be summarized as privatization: private universities, increase in the number of private high schools, institutionalization of private establishments preparing students for various exams (*dersane*) and private lessons (tutoring). In the end, the 1980 military coup brought about depoliticization in Turkey while nationalism, militarism, and neoliberalism were growing. Its affect on the education system was to force students to learn by rote memorization. The students affected by this period are called "the 80 Generation", i.e. depoliticized individualistic youth.

Formal public education at all levels primarily receives financial support from the central government, responsible for all educational expenses. In addition, primary education is supported by local authorities, mainly for the construction and maintenance of schools. Some public schools are transformed into private schools. Since the 1980s, they have been increasing. To articulate the allocation of financial support for education in Turkey, some statistical figures are informative. The educational budget makes up about ten percent of the consolidated budget.[39] Nevertheless, educational expenditure as a percentage of GDP per capita for all levels of education combined is 4.34 percent by public sources and 2.63 percent by private and other sources in 2002.[40] In other words, 62.3 percent was financed by public sources (61.4 percent central government revenue and 0.9 percent local government revenue), 37.6 percent was financed by private sources (33.4 percent household funds, 1.9

[39] Source: National Education Statistics, Formal Education 2006-2007.

[40] The World Bank 2005. How Much Does Turkey Spend on Education? Development of National Education Accounts to Measure and Evaluate Education Expenditures.

percent companies, associations, foundations etc., 0.1 percent international resources, and 2.3 percent other sources). Household funds play a crucial role in education.

TABLE 3. HOUSEHOLD INCOMES AND EXPENDITURES ON EDUCATION IN TURKEY (1994)

Household Quintiles by Income	Lowest 20% E	Next 20% D	Next 20% C	Next 20% B	Highest 20% A	**Quasi-Gini Coeffi-cient**
Incidence (%)	**1**	**2**	**3**	**4**	**5**	
Income Shares (%)	4.9	8.6	12.9	19.0	54.9	0.49
Expenditure on Education (%)	2.2	7.1	9.4	18.0	63.3	0.53
Kindergarten - Primary Education	0.8	1.5	22.4	13.1	62.2	0.54
Secondary Education	0.0	0.1	0.5	1.0	98.4	0.79
Higher Education	0.2	16.5	9.9	22.0	51.4	0.43
Other Education	1.2	6.2	8.7	21.8	62.1	0.55
Educational Materials	7.5	13.5	18.4	25.8	34.9	0.27

Source: State Institution of Statistics (1995)

TABLE 3 shows income shares and ratios of total expenditure on education according to household quintiles in Turkey in 1994. It is worth remembering that the lower quintile a household is, the more of children it has (the poorest 20% about 3, the richest 20% about 1). It is explicit that education expenditure is a major factor that demonstrates the separation between rich and poor households. In particular, the significant difference among household quintiles in terms of education expenditure in secondary education is arresting. Parallel to that, "other education" shown in TABLE 3 refers to non-formal (extended) education, covering private tutoring and cram schools, which are known in Turkey by the name of *dershanes*. In the last years, they are the main reason that private out-of-pocket expenditures are not comparable to public ones on education, in addition to private school fees.

In spite of a Turkish-Islamic synthesis with the coup, the Military has not abandoned Atatürkist ideology. On the contrary, it has accelerated the propaganda of Atatürkism and Atatürkist nationalism with the repetition of his symbol.[41] It managed the campaign of delivering "One statue of Atatürk to every district and one bust of Atatürk to every school" ("*Her ilçeye bir Atatürk heykeli, her okula bir Atatürk büstü*"). In the martial period, the subjects of Reform History of the Republic of Turkey and Atatürkism (*T.C. İnkılâp Tarihi ve Atatürkçülük*) became compulsory for the eighth grade and the subject of National Security (*Milli Güvenlik*) for the tenth grade. The course "Turkish Reform History," which every student should take in the third and fourth semesters of tertiary education, was renamed "Atatürk Principles and Reform History" (*Atatürk İlkeleri ve İnkılâp Tarihi*) in 1981. Furthermore, six Institutes of Atatürk Principles and Reform History (*Atatürk İlkeleri ve İnkılâp Tarihi Enstitüleri*) were established in 1982 under the university structures.

It is impossible to enter any school or university and to open any school book in Turkey without seeing an image of Atatürk, who is commemorated as the first main teacher of the Republic of Turkey. All over the country, at least one bust of Atatürk must be situated in every school's courtyard. In each classroom above the blackboard, a portrait of Atatürk is hung. On one side, his speech to the Turkish Youth can be seen and on the other, the National Anthem. Every student in the junior high school must recite Atatürk's speech to the Turkish youth as follows:

> "Turkish youth!
>
> It is your first duty to protect and to defend forever the Turkish independence and the Turkish Republic.
>
> It is the very foundation of your existence and future. This foundation is your most precious treasure. In the

[41] In addition, it is generally believed that Atatürkism was restored in education on "February 28, 1997" by the National Security Council against the Islamist government.

> future, too, there may be enemies both from within or outside who try to deprive you of this treasure. If one day you are forced to defend the Republic and its independence then you must perform your duty without regard for personal cost or the circumstances you are in. These circumstances may be extremely unfavorable. It might be that the enemies who endeavor to end the Republic and your independence have been victorious throughout the world. It may be that, through force and deception, all the fortresses of your beloved fatherland are occupied, all its shipyards captured, all its enemies dispersed and every part of your country invaded. Even worse and more serious however, might be a situation in which those who hold power in your country are careless, who lead in the wrong direction or even betray the country. It is also possible that those in power may profit from the enemies intention. The nation may be exhausted and have collapsed in misery and poverty.
>
> Young people and the future of Turkey! Even under these circumstances it will be your duty to save the Turkish Republic and its independence.
>
> The power you need to do it with is to be found in your noble blood!"

On Monday mornings and Friday afternoons, flag ceremonies are held with all the teachers and students present in the courtyard or playground of each school until tertiary education. In addition to flag ceremonies on Mondays and Fridays, primary school students say the pledge in chorus every day. Article 12 of the guidelines for primary education by MoNE dictates the student pledge. The Article 12 says that students in primary education must pledge as a whole by observance (supervision) of teachers every day, before class. Primary school students are obliged to recite the student oath:

> "I am a Turk, I am honest. I am a hard worker. My rule is to protect those younger and to respect my elders, and to love my country and my nation more than myself. My goal is to enhance and to get higher. May my life be a present to the Turkish people. Oh, honorable, unreachable Atatürk! I give my oath to continue towards reaching the targets you showed, to walk on

the road you have opened, in the country you created.
How happy I am to say I am a Turk."[42]

Except for students with foreign nationality, every student has to pledge this oath. The oath aims at the repetition of Turkishness, honesty, diligence, constitution, societal cohesion, country, nation, goal, and sacrifice for nation.

FIGURE 5. THE MILITARY COUP 1980-DATE

Line of Thought	Policy and Application in Education	Consequences
"Turkish-Islamic synthesis"	Compulsory Religious Studies lessons in primary and high schools; Entrance of graduates of Islamic Divinity High Schools to all departments of tertiary education; YÖK; Nepotism in appointing educational staff who stand close to the "Turkish-Islamic synthesis"; Dismissing many academics and teachers under the premise of marital law	**(i)** Depoliticization while growing relevance of militarism-nationalism-economic liberalism ("the 80 Generation"); **(ii)** Inequality and injustice of education - Educational career mostly affected by social stratification; **(iii)** Increase of students and university graduates
Neoliberalization	Private universities; Increase in the number of private high schools; Private establishments preparing students for various exams *(dersane)*; private lessons; YÖK; Merging of different types of high schools	
Atatürkist nationalization saved by the military and militarization	National Security lessons in high schools; Atatürkism lessons; Atatürk Institutes; Uniformization; Proliferation of nationalist figures, images, and ceremonies; Atatürk bust placed in every school; "Atatürkist education;" Atatürkist indoctrination; Restoration of Atatürkism in education in the duration of "February 28; 1997" against Islamist government by the National Security Council	

---

[42] The original version: "*Türküm, doğruyum, çalışkanım. Yasam küçüklerimi korumak, büyüklerimi saymak, yurdumu, milletimi özümden çok sevmektir. Ülküm yükselmek, ileri gitmektir. Ey büyük Atatürk! açtığın yolda, gösterdiğin hedefe durmadan yürüyeceğime ant içerim. Varlığım Türk varlığına armağan olsun. Ne mutlu Türküm diyene!*"

1.2. Stage of Secondary Education

The attendance of secondary education in Turkey is around fifty percent of the relevant age group. Secondary education in Turkey was divided into two stages until 1997: the junior high school (the middle school, *Ortaokul*), lasting minimum three years, and the senior high school (*Lise*), lasting minimum three years. Meanwhile, there were two different scales for secondary school in Turkey until 1997. The first scale of high school included both stages within its own scope, which were called *Lise* as well. The second scale separated the senior high school (*Lise*) from the junior one (*Ortaokul*).

School types in secondary education are extremely complex due not only to the continuous emergence of new regulations but also effectuated new types or schools and their mergence with older types over time. Using data of existing schools in Turkey from 1997, I re-categorized high schools with relevant levels (see FIGURE 6). The first level of separation is high schools are public or private. The second is whether or not it is a vocational-technical high school. The third level of separation is whether it is Anatolian, Science or none (normal). The secondary education system is thereby separated into five main types of high schools:

(1) Public **General** Normal High School offers the standard common type of public secondary education.[43] They included the State Boarding High School (*Devlet Parasız Yatılı Lisesi*), selected mostly by children from rural areas or poor families and providing free food and lodging during the term, Super High School (*Süper Lise*) for successful graduates from the junior high school, in addition to Public Evening High School (*Akşam Lisesi*) for the non-relevant age groups.

(2) **Vocational and Technical** High School (*Meslek-Teknik Lisesi*) as another common type of public high school which focuses on a certain type of vocation in addition to the standard lessons outlined

[43] Terms of "Public High School" or "Regular State High School" (*Normal Lise, Devlet Lisesi*) are sometimes synonymously used instead of General High School (*Genel Lise*).

for secondary education.[44] Free boarding is possible. There are relatively few private versions and they will be evaluated in the category of Private High Schools.

FIGURE 6. HIGH SCHOOL CATEGORY LEVELS AND HIGH SCHOOLS IN TURKEY (1997)*

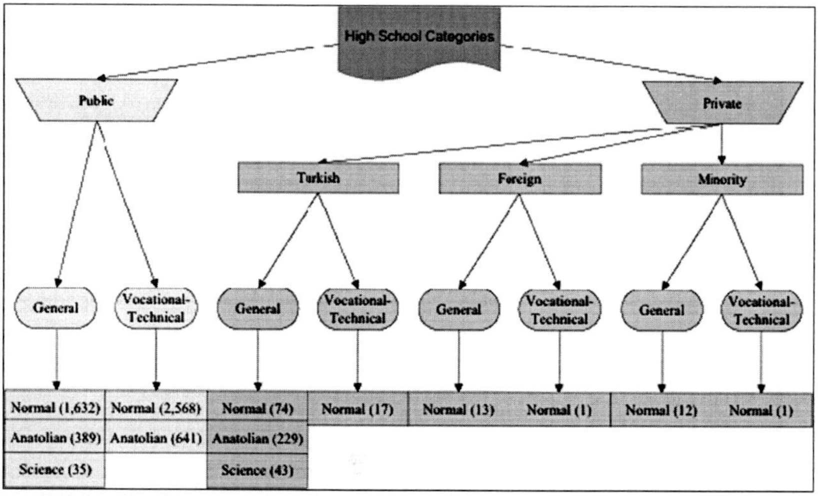

*High school category levels were created by the author. Numbers of high schools are based on MoNE Data 1997.

(3) **Anatolian** High School (*Anadolu Lisesi*) as a type of public high school which provides additional skills in a selected foreign language (English, German or French) by instructing a certain part of science courses in the foreign language.[45] Free boarding is pos-

---

[44] To name a few, Tourism Vocational High School (*Turizm Meslek Lisesi*), Industrial Vocational High School (*Endüstri Meslek Lisesi*), Electrical Vocational High Schools (*Elektrik Meslek Lisesi*), Anatolian Technical High School (*Anadolu Teknik Lisesi*), Islamic Divinity Students High School (*İmam Hatip Lisesi*), Teacher's Training High School (*Öğretmen Lisesi*), and so forth.

[45] In 1955, MoNE designed a new model of high school, called Secondary Education College (*Maarif Koleji*), and established six high schools in six different cities (Istanbul, İzmir, Eskişehir, Konya, Samsun, and Diyarbakır) with a purpose of providing a nationwide secondary education in a foreign language. In 1975, they are recalled by Anatolian

sible. There are relatively few private versions and they will be evaluated in the category of Private High Schools.

(4) **Science** High School (*Fen Lisesi*) as a type of public *senior* high school which focuses on science education including education in foreign languages.[46] Free boarding is possible. There are relatively few private versions and they will be evaluated in the category of Private High Schools.

(5) **Private** High School (*Özel Lise*), established by private enterprises and charging an average fee of about 4,000 US Dollars per year.[47] All Foreign and Minority High Schools are privately-funded.

All graduates from the junior high school have the right to continue General High Schools. But, there are different exams for admission to the so-called State Boarding, Vocational-Technical, Anatolian, and Private High Schools after primary school education; and to Science High School after junior high school education.[48] The exams for admission to these high schools were independent from each other, meaning that you would not be able to get into a Private High School with the points you had scored in the Anatolian High School exam. To do so, you would have to take the Private High School exam. The same held true for Anatolian High Schools. Before the exams, you had to list the schools according to preference and the lowest minimum entrance score required. In order to get into any of the schools you had to score either the same as or above the lowest minimum score required by your preferred schools. If

High School. The numbers of this type of high school are 87 in 1993, 452 in 2003, and 775 in 2005.

[46] Since 1964, Science High Schools have been founded to give education in order to create "superior brain power" in accordance with the First Five Year Development Plan in 1963. (Devlet Planlama Teşkilatı, 1963, p.456.)

[47] All foreign high schools (*Yabancı Okullar*) are privately- funded, such as American, French, Italian, German, Austrian high schools, and so on. They are evaluated as Private High School.

[48] The regulation procedure of these exams occasionally changes in Turkey. Nowadays there is only one centralized exam for high schools called the Entrance Exam for Secondary Education (*Ortaöğretim Kurumları Giriş Sınavı-OKS*) after eight-year obligatory grade school education.

you did achieve that score then you would earn the right to admission (as "*asil*"). If not, then you would get on the waiting list ("*yedek*"). If the pupils who got in as "*asil*" did not exercise their right to register to the school listed, then that would open up the possibility for "*yedek*" pupils to register at that school. It is generally believed that the demand for admission to Private High Schools is high among upper-middle class, to Anatolian High School and Science High School among middle class, for Vocational-Technical High Schools among lower-middle class, and for State Boarding High School among peasantry and poverty-stricken families. However, Anatolian High School and Science High School are the most attractive types of high school. Consequently, it can be argued that admission to Anatolian and Science High Schools is controlled by a very competitive entrance examination in which only about ten percent of students succeed. Students who either do not take or pass the exam either go on to General, Vocational-Technical, or Private High Schools, or drop out of schooling all together. As a matter of fact, differences in secondary school quality are not only the norm but also "a source of pride for some: the elite Anatolian and Science High Schools are highly prized components of the Turkish education system".[49]

> "At present, the examination system tends to exacerbate the inequality of access to quality education beyond the primary level. Families with economic means send their children to private tutoring courses to improve their chances of passing both the high school and university entrance exams. Most families and students, who do not have such financial means, have less of an opportunity to access a high-quality education." [50]

It is very clear that graduates from Science High School, Anatolian High School, and Private High Schools are very successful in the university entrance exams.[51] Specifically, the percentage of graduates of Science High School who are accepted to pursue a Bachelor's of Science degree is approximately 59, 42 among graduates

[49] World Bank, 2005:5.
[50] World Bank, 2005:5.
[51] Source: ÖSYM and National Education Statistics, Formal Education.

from Anatolian High School, 18 among graduates of Private High School, eight among graduates of General High School, and two among graduates of Vocational-Technical High School. Interestingly, unlike other types of high school, the success ratio of graduating students in General High School (approximately three percent) is significantly less than the general ratio. That shows that most of them need and spend extra preparation for the university after graduation from high school. Furthermore, as most graduates from Private High School prefer to go abroad in order pursue tertiary education, some do not take the university entrance exam in Turkey. Taking the numbers into consideration instead of the ratios, the largest quantity remains graduates from General High School. Particularly, it can be evaluated with the numbers of graduates from secondary education between 1986-2004 as seen at TABLE 4; around half graduated from General High School, 41.85 percent graduated from Vocational-Technical High School, 4.71 percent from Anatolian High School, 2.98 from Private High School, and only 0.31 from Science High School.

TABLE 4. GRADUATES FROM SECONDARY EDUCATION IN TURKEY (1986-2004)

Years	Total	General* (%)	Vocational-Technical (%)	Anatolian (%)	Science (%)	Private** (%)
1986	220.941	54,84	41,33	1,28	0,13	2,43
1987	226.453	52,83	43,23	1,39	0,17	2,37
1988	246.358	53,50	42,17	1,61	0,16	2,57
1989	253.143	54,09	41,26	1,78	0,17	2,71
1990	279.056	52,09	43,32	1,69	0,18	2,72
1991	335.544	52,79	42,14	1,98	0,14	2,96
1992	361.868	53,31	41,22	2,10	0,21	3,15
1993	474.982	55,44	39,54	2,27	0,16	2,58
1994	448.762	55,46	38,76	2,44	0,25	3,08

Years	Total	General* (%)	Vocational-Technical (%)	Anatolian (%)	Science (%)	Private** (%)
1995	472.838	48,88	43,52	3,87	0,23	3,49
1996	531.303	52,75	41,82	2,78	0,18	2,46
1997	663.612	59,03	36,37	2,00	0,14	2,45
1998	476.698	48,60	46,99	2,61	0,19	1,61
1999	534.174	42,53	49,26	3,94	0,41	3,86
2000	490.053	43,91	46,24	5,04	0,59	4,22
2001	480.870	42,08	47,79	6,47	0,48	3,18
2002	497.095	41,06	43,40	12,30	0,54	2,70
2003	517.759	46,45	37,31	12,44	0,59	3,21
2004	675.125	50,83	34,62	10,27	0,51	3,76

* Graduates from State Boarding High School, Public Super High School and Public Evening High School are included.
** There are some private Vocational-Technical High Schools, Anatolian High Schools, and Science High Schools. They are also included.
This table was prepared using annual statistical reports from YÖK and MoNE.

According to PISA 2003 (Programme for International Student Assessment),[52] between-school variance in student performance (68.7) is the highest variance among OECD (Organization for Economic Cooperation and Development) countries and about twice the OECD average (33.6). The variance within schools (56.5) is below the OECD average (67.0). The student performance average of Turkey (423) is quite low compared to the OECD average (500). Regional and gender differences in scores are relatively less conspicuous than socio-economic differences and the between-school and within-school components of variation in a comparison with other countries. According to the final report on Turkey, the average performance of students from Science High School is about 700 with a small standard deviation, 630 from Police College with

[52] The OECD's PISA surveys, which take place every three years, have been designed to collect information about 15-year-old students in participating countries.

a small standard deviation, 500 from Anatolian High School and Private High School with large standard deviations, 450 from Anatolian Vocational and Technical High School, 420 from General High School, and 370 from Vocational and Technical High School with large standard deviations.[53] Association of student performance with socio-economic background (more than 22.0) is very significant (OECD average 17.0). That is, the greater the socio-economic advantage, the greater the advantage in student performance. The impact of socio-economic background is extremely high in comparison with other OECD countries. The PISA 2003 Report (2004:186) underlines those countries especially Mexico (57.3) and Turkey (54.1) "with a low average level of socio-economic background and a wide distribution of socio-economic characteristics face particular challenges in meeting the needs of disadvantaged students".[54] Moreover, PISA reveals not only inequitable learning opportunities according to the relationship between socio-economic background and student performance but also inequality in learning opportunities promoted by national education systems according to the relationship between socio-economic background and school performance. As the highest percentage across OECD countries, 56 percentage of the variance in student performance in Turkey can be explained by students' study programs, the international index of economic, social and cultural status, and the between-school component of variation (OECD average 26.4).

Students normally choose one foreign language (English, French, or German) in General and most kinds of Vocational and Technical High Schools. Still, the numbers of teachers and facilities for supplying good quality foreign language instruction are generally not enough in these types of schools. In all Anatolian, Science, Private, and some Vocational and Technical High Schools there are however one or two years or extra preparatory classes at the beginning to teach one foreign language (English, French, or German) and in the following years, all science lessons are taught in that foreign

[53] EARGED, 2005.
[54] OECD, 2004.

language. Most of these three types of high schools give education in English and teach German as a second foreign language. It is clear that learning German as a second foreign language in high school, or even as a first foreign language in some General public high schools, is not enough but provides a basis. However, learning German as a first foreign language in some certain high schools is much appreciated. There are about 40 Private or Anatolian High Schools whose teaching language is mainly German and partly Turkish as well as lectures of English as a second foreign language[55]. Most of them are located in Istanbul. *Istanbul Lisesi*, *Cağaloğlu Anadolu Lisesi*, *Üsküdar Anadolu Lisesi* (Anatolian High Schools), as well as *Alman Lisesi* and *Avusturya Lisesi* (Private High Schools) are the most apparent ones in Istanbul. In Ankara, there is one private high school whose teaching language is German, mostly for children of diplomats. In Izmir, *Bornova Anadolu Lisesi* is also notable in the context of German language teaching. Some graduates of these high schools start directly at universities in Germany by means of the Abitur.

Biographical information about secondary education is a key indicator about *family background* in the context of the education system in Turkey. On the one hand, which type of high school a person attends signalizes her/his family's political-economic position in social stratification because it exposes their political point of views and their capability to afford fees and school expenditure (economic capital). Similarly, the choice of high school for their children indicates the family's social-cultural position, since they are giving weight to the children's education (cultural capital). Furthermore, this information clues us in on *social formation*. Biographical information about high school indicates which kind of curricula they have (cultural capital) and what kind of social networks they are in (social capital).

[55] Webpage: Schulen: Partner der Zukunft http://www.pasch-net.de [06.09.2009]

1.3. Stage of Tertiary Education

In addition to universities, tertiary education in Turkey includes two-year vocational schools (*Yüksek Okul*), offering Associate's degrees, and the Open University (*Açık Öğretim*), offering two-year and four-year distance learning programs. Universities are composed of faculties offering Bachelor's of Science/Art degrees and graduate schools offering advanced professional programs (*Master's of Science/Art degrees* and *Doctorate of Philosophy*). As there have been more applications than quotas since at least 1975, there is a strict admission system of *numerus clauses* in tertiary education in Turkey.[56] As a matter of fact, the number of students applying for admission to tertiary education has increasingly exceeded the number of available spaces. For entrance to all institutions of tertiary education, it has been obligatory to take the tertiary education entrance qualification test in Turkey since 1974, which is designed, administered, and evaluated by the Center for Selection and Placement of Students (*Öğrenci Seçme ve Yerleştirme Merkezi, ÖSYM*).[57] In fact, all high school graduates have the right to participate in the centralized examination. It then determines candidates for the enrollment of each university and faculty after evaluating the grades of related subjects, their high school results, and their preferences according to the admissions capacity of each faculty.

Applicants are increasing, as a continuously growing portion of the population in Turkey take the entrance exam each year (See TABLE 5). It is not uncommon for more than a million applicants to take the exam. In other words, approximately one person out of every four in the theoretical age group 18-21 applies for this exam (See Table 2). However, no more than one-third of the candidates to tertiary education can be admitted, as seen at TABLE 5, which leads to increased competition. In order to qualify for admission, students start studying for the entrance exams as much as two years

[56] The *numerus clausus* is currently used in countries and universities where the number of applicants greatly exceeds the number of available places for students.
[57] The Center was established in 1974 and affiliated with YÖK in 1981.

in advance. Even if an applicant qualifies for admission, the individual's actual score determines whether s/he may study a chosen discipline, or must take up a less preferred one. Thus, many young people spend at least one year studying at a private institution (*dershane*) and/or taking private courses during and following high school in order to pass the exam successfully. Total expenditures by families in Turkey on the university entrance exam preparation for their children are approximately 3 billion US Dollars every year.[58]

TABLE 5. APPLICANTS AND PLACEMENT FOR TERTIARY EDUCATION (1994-2004)

Year	Theoretical Age Group (18-21)	Applicants	Bachelor's of Science Degree 4 years +	Bachelor's of Science Degree (%)	Tertiary education (%)
1994	5.093.000	1.249.965	130.460	10,44	29,67
1995	5.228.000	1.265.103	139.744	11,05	30,35
1996	5.184.000	1.399.061	137.540	9,83	29,47
1997	5.142.000	1.398.595	147.850	10,57	31,99
1998	5.102.000	1.355.707	153.348	11,31	31,06
1999	5.063.000	1.478.365	153.223	10,36	30,34
2000	5.025.000	1.414.223	160.247	11,33	31,11
2001	5.371.000	1.471.197	166.963	11,35	32,04
2002	5.355.000	1.534.902	169.835	11,06	40,01
2003	5.288.000	1.502.605	187.192	12,46	36,91
2004	5.192.000	1.786.883	192.632	10,78	32,17

* This table was prepared using annual statistical reports from YÖK and MoNE.

Prior to 1984, public universities charged no tuition. Tertiary education Law No.2547 introduced tuition to Turkey starting with the 1984-85 academic year. The tuition fee is 250-450 US Dollars an-

[58] Source: Ankara Chamber of Commerce, *Ankara Ticaret Odası.*

nually for public universities and 5,000-15,000 US Dollars for private universities. A number of university students receive loans from the Tertiary Education Credit and Hostels Institution (*Yurt-Kur*) for education and tuition fees. Some successful students also receive additional scholarships from public and private institutions. As seen at TABLE 5, barely more than 32 percent of applicants each year were admitted to an institute of tertiary education, including vocational schools of tertiary education and the Open University. Among all applicants, around ten percent are admitted for a Bachelor's of Science degree. In other words, only one out of every ten applicants annually has a chance to be a university student. Nonetheless, there is a significant difference in terms of the level of competitiveness among the universities. In order to facilitate the exploration of this difference, it is necessary to picture the history of universities in Turkey.

The historical outline of universities in Turkey can be separated into four main periods (TABLE 6). The first period lasts from 1923 until 1971. In this period, nine universities were established. Their geographical distribution is overarching enough, and reflects the historical roots of tertiary education in Istanbul after the last period of the Ottoman Empire. Three universities were established in Ankara both because of its status as the capital city and its central location of the country. Erzurum, Izmir, and Trabzon, as the largest cities of the East, West, and North respectively, each had one university. These universities developed and contributed to the university culture in Turkey. Most of the universities established in the first period are still the best ones, their success due to their deep roots.

The second period (1972-1981) is characterized by the establishment of new universities on a larger scale: the period of deployment in Anatolia. In this period, new universities were founded in ten different cities in Anatolia: Diyarbakır, Adana, Eskişehir, Sivas, Malatya, Elazığ, Samsun, Konya, Bursa, and Kayseri. They also give a geographically homogenous picture. The level of these public universities is intermediate.

TABLE 6. NUMBER OF UNIVERSITIES, BY TIME PERIODS, CITIES, AND PUBLIC/PRIVATE

	-1971	1972-1981	1982-1991	1992-2001
Turkey	**9**	**19**	**29**	**76**
Public	9	19	28	52
Private			1	24
Istanbul	**3**	**3**	**6**	**22**
Public	3	3	6	6
Private				16
Ankara	**3**	**3**	**5**	**9**
Public	3	3	4	4
Private			1	5
Izmir	**1**	**1**	**2**	**5**
Public	1	1	2	3
Private				2
Other Cities	**2**	**12**	**16**	**40**
Public	2	12	16	39
Private				1

The third period (1982-1991) signals the re-centralization period in the history of tertiary education. In this period, six universities in the biggest three cities and four universities in four other cities (Antalya, Edirne, Van, and Gaziantep) were established. The university in Ankara was founded as the first private university (Bilkent University) in Turkey, and it has entered the realm of the most successful universities in Turkey. The other five new universities in Istanbul, Ankara, and Izmir can be evaluated as the secondary successful universities.

Finally, the fourth period (1992-2001) of the university history in Turkey is marked by an increasing number of new foundations at the public as well as private level. This last period shows two characteristics. The first is related with the proliferation of small public universities in 23 different cities. Interestingly, twenty of them were established in the West. The second characteristic of the last period is the proliferation of new private universities in Istanbul (15), Ankara (4), and Izmir (2). In the last period, there was a rise in the number of not only private but also public universities.

It can be clearly argued that entrance to *Orta Doğu Teknik Üniversitesi* (*ODTÜ*, Middle East Technical University-METU), *Boğaziçi Üniversitesi* (Bosporus University), and *Bilkent Üniversitesi* (Bilkent University, the first private university), *Istanbul Teknik Üniversitesi* (Istanbul Technical University, ITU), and *Marmara Üniversitesi* (Marmara University) is the most highly competitive. Of the top scorers out of people who took the university entrance exam, almost all prefer these universities.[59] But there are some departmental exceptions and institutional variations, especially amongst less competitive universities, in particular new private universities. According to overall ranking of universities in the context of engineering departments, the most competitive ones are still the aforementioned universities: Middle East Technical University, Bosporus University, Bilkent University, Istanbul Technical University, and Marmara University. The first three are all English language universities. Additionally, the option teaching language in all departments of the Engineering Faculty in ITU is English, whereas the compulsory language at the department of Economic Informatics and Management in Marmara University is German. When we take departments of engineering, e.g., computer engineering and electronic-electrical engineering, into account, the top public universities are Bosporus University (Istanbul), Middle East Technical University (Ankara), Istanbul Technical University (Istanbul), Hacettepe University (Ankara), and Ege University

[59] For example, universities preferred by the top 100, 1000, and 2000 out of the 1.5 million in 1999. Available at http://www.milliyet.com.tr/1999/07/15/haber/hab02.html

(İzmir) and the top private university is Bilkent University (Ankara).

1.4. Summary

> "Das Erziehungssystem hat eigene Formen des Umgangs mit Paradoxen entwickelt. Es nennt sich zu diesem Zwecke ‚Bildungssystem'. Dabei geht es vor allem darum, die Paradoxien zu entstören und sie so weit zu invisibilisieren, daß sie unbemerkt bleiben können. Oder anders gesagt: die unergiebige Kurzzeitoszillation im Paradox muß ersetzt werden durch Problemstellungen, die mit Hoffnung auf Lösung der Probleme ausgestattet sind" (Luhmann, 2004:241).

Accordingly changing policy, and its application in education, the education system is chronologically separated into five periods: the Tanzimat Period (1839-1876), the Period of Committee for Union and Progress (1908-1918), the Early Years of the Republic of Turkey (1923-1946), the Introduction to Multi-Party Regime (1946-1980), and The Military Coup 1980-date. After evaluating these periods as well as the secondary and tertiary education systems, it can be said that the Turkish education system has *nationalist*, *modernist*, and *non-egalitarian* features.

Its nationalism began with Ottomanization and continued with Turkish nationalism, enforced Turkification, and Atatürkism. Education is a means of social control to improve the self.[60] Hence, it is goal-oriented communication and introduces social formation, which is the result of becoming a member of society. As a forward-looking process, education has the property of "anticipatory socialization" (Musgrave, 1979:24).

Its modernist feature is closely related to the unique republicanism of this territory and history. The uniqueness lays in the combination of principles such as positivism, westernization, laicization,

---

[60] Social control, in Mead's words, is the expression of the 'me' over the expression of the 'I' (Mead, 1934: 210). According to Mead (1934), the self arises in the "internalization" of the "generalized other" within the dialectic between the "me" and the "I". Mead also thinks that the self has references not only to others but also "toward the various phases or aspects of the common social activity or set of social undertakings in which, as members of an organized society or social group, they are all engaged" (Mead, 1934:154-155).

and islamism. This extraordinary blend has given rise to religious enlightenment – "the rationalization or Turkicization of Islam" in Berkes' words – and accordingly, Turkish Islam has a certain "Protestant" character, according to Tapper and Tapper (1991).[61]

Finally, the non-egalitarian character of the Turkish education system stems from inequalities of opportunity and educational quality. Durkheim (1956:70-1) argues:

> "[I]t is society as a whole and each particular social *milieu* that determine the ideal that education realizes. Society can survive only if there exists among its members a sufficient degree of homogeneity; education perpetuates and reinforces this homogeneity by fixing in the child, from the beginning, the essential similarities that collective life demands. But on the other hand, without a certain diversity all co-operation would be impossible; education assures the persistence of this necessary diversity by being itself diversified and specialized."

Although popularizing education with the principles of "access and equity" has been aimed at in every period since the establishment of the Republic of Turkey, educational participation still remains discriminatory with regard to gender and geographical locations, and it is remarkably elitist; in other words, it depends mostly on the socio-economic status of family. In order to give and overall picture of education in Turkey in 1997, some key data is required: the literacy rate was 80.46 percent, the schooling rate (the portion of school attendees within a given age group) for primary education was 97.10 percent, the schooling rate for secondary education was 46.52 percent, and the percentage of university graduates was 4.72.[62]

2. Migration

2.1. Relevance of the Military Service System in Turkey

Like many nation states, the Republic of Turkey has a compulsory military service system. Article 72 of the 1982 Constitution states that "National service is the right and duty of every Turk. The

[61] Berkes, 1964:483; Tapper and Tapper, 1991:79.
[62] Source: T.R. Prime Ministry State Planning Organization (Devlet Planlama Teşkilatı).

manner in which this service shall be performed or considered as performed, either in the Armed Forces or in the Public Service, shall be regulated by law." The further legal basis of conscription is the Law on Military Service (1111/1982) and the Law for Reserve Officers and Reserve Military Servants (1076). According to the Turkish legal system, every male, Turkish citizen who reaches the age of 20 is obliged to join the army to perform military service. Compulsory conscription in Turkey applies to all male citizens between 20 and 41 years of age.[63] The length of mandatory military service is fifteen months. University graduates may perform twelve months as reserve officers, or six months as short-term privates for those who have not been enlisted as reserve officers. Certain professional groups (doctors, teachers, civil servants, and also computer engineers) may be permitted to perform special services in the army. One may be legally exempt from service (draft exemption) under the following conditions: (1) he is *prove*n to be handicapped, homosexual, mentally ill, or not healthy;[64] (2) any Turkish citizen who possesses dual citizenship and who lived abroad before the age of 18 and performed military service in another country. Exemption on this ground is only possible if the length of military service that has been performed in another country is considered to be comparable to the length of service in Turkey. As a matter of fact, dual citizens completing the military service in Germany, Austria, Denmark, Finland, France (people born in 1979 and older), Israel, Sweden, Switzerland, Italy (people born in 1985 and older), Norway, Greece, Tunis, or Syria, have been exempt since July 5, 1993.[65] Moreover, men who are enrolled in universities or vocational training programs are allowed to evade their draft until they

[63] According to Article 1 of the Military Act (1111/1927), every male Turkish citizen is obliged to carry out military service. Women are not conscripted in Turkey, but are allowed to become officers in military schools.

[64] This person is called *Çürük* (disabled) as well. Being draft-exempt in this way is not easy, since homosexuality or a disability should be diagnosed with a medical certificate by an army hospital. The disability criteria are having an incurable illness or losing sixty percent of service capacity.

[65] Source: The official website of the Ministry of National Defense. The Department of Recruitment (Milli Savunma Bakanlığı, Askeralma Dairesi Başkanlığı: ASAL) [visited July 15, 2008]

have completed these programs. However, the completion of another, similar degree, e.g., another Bachelor's, Master's of Science, or PhD. Students may postpone their military service up to the age of 29, or up to the age of 36 in the case of postgraduate students. Men who have not fulfilled their military service by the age of 41 and who have not been draft-exempt may still be called up after the age of 41.

Neither conscientious objection and nor civil service are recognized in Turkish law. Since the 1990s in Turkey there have been a small number of conscientious objectors who have publicly stated their refusal to carry out conscription. But, they are usually then subject to criminal prosecution. Although the European Court of Human Rights ruled in favor of the first conscientious objectors of Turkey, the government of Turkey has never considered introducing legislation on conscientious objection.[66] In fact, a brochure published by the armed forces in 1999 stated:

> "In our laws there are no provisions on exemption from military service for reasons of conscience. This is because of the pressing need for security, caused by the strategic geographic position of our country and the circumstances we find ourselves in. As long as the factors threatening the internal and external security of Turkey do not change, it is considered to be impossible to introduce the concept of 'conscientious objection' into our legislation".[67]

The Government of Turkey has continuously reduced the length of military service and it plans to increase the number of professional soldiers in the future, but it has no plans to abolish conscription.[68] The Government justifies military service as an important aspect of

[66] See the chamber judgment Osman Murat Ülke vs. Turkey (The European Court of Human Rights) http://www.echr.coe.int/Eng/Press/2006/Jan/Chamberjudgment%C3%9ClkevTurkey240106.htm [July 15, 2008 visited]

[67] Additionally, to the United Nations (1999), "[t]he Government of Turkey takes the view that conscientious objection to military service is not recognized in the Universal Declaration of Human Rights nor the International Covenant on Civil and Political Rights. The Government of Turkey has reservations on General Observation No. 22 (48) of the Human Rights Committee, as well as all resolutions adopted by the Commission on Human Rights concerning conscientious objection."

[68] UK Home Office Immigration and Nationality Directorate: Country Report, October 2004.

the principle of equality before the law.[69] It believes that "allowing any person or group to be excluded from performing compulsory military service would compromise the application of the law."[70] Nevertheless, obligation of conscription to men (gender difference) and the application of the three-week-draft by payment (class difference) remain in conflict with the principle of equality in the Constitution.

For Turkish citizens who have worked abroad for at least three years (1,095 workdays), a basic military training of 21 days is offered instead of the full-term military service if they pay a certain fee in foreign currency.[71] It is called *military service by payment* or *military service by payment with foreign currency* (*bedelli askerlik, dövizle askerlik*). The annual average number of drafts by payment due to working abroad has been about 10,000 since 1980.[72] Military service by payment is restricted to Turkish citizens who have worked abroad for at least three years. In the history of the Republic of Turkey, a provisional clause has existed ten times. The last three were in 1987, 1992, and 1999. Unlike the routine military service by payment, their yields were deposited into a different account by the Ministry of Finance, instead of the Defense Industry Support Fund.[73] The biggest annual amount of military service by payment was after the earthquake on August 17, 1999.[74] Based on

---

[69] United Nations, Economic and Social Council, E/CN.4/2000/55, December 17, 1999.

[70] United Nations, Economic and Social Council, E/CN.4/2000/55, December 17, 1999.

[71] The amount of payment was 10,000 old German Marks, is now 5,112 Euros (cash or on at most four credits) before 38 years of age and 7,668 Euros (cash) after 38 years of age. Source: Ministry of National Defense.

[72] Approximately 349,000 men joined the army to perform military service by payment between 1980-2002, according to the response of the Minister of National Defense Sabahattin Çakmakoğlu to the parliamentary question by a the member of the parliament, Dengir Mir Mehmet Fırat, in May 2002. Approximately 222,000 of them did it due to working abroad for three years.

[73] http://www.tbmm.gov.tr/sirasayi/donem21/yil01/ss188m.htm [visited July 6, 2008]

[74] This exceptional draft opportunity to help the economy for the reconstruction and rehabilitation of suffered cities drew considerable interest. Only men born before January 1, 1973 are able to apply for this exceptional draft and applications needed to be made before May 4, 2000. If the person was older than 27 years of age, the amount was 15,000 German Marks; if older than 40 years of age, 20,000 German Marks. Source: Ministry of National Defense.

the general staff press release in April 2004, a total of 125,834 men (18,433 men in 1987-89, 35,111 men in 1992-93, and 72,290 men in 1999-2000) did exceptional military service by payment. Not surprisingly, draft by payment attracts considerable attention.

As in many countries, the military is often presented in the media as "the most trusted institution" in Turkey. However, this perception is the result of field research, which is worthless due to their controversial conceptualization and contextual difference of the abstract variables in comparison. As in many countries, the military is often presented in the media as "the most trusted institution" in Turkey on the basis of some field researches in spite of their controversial conceptualization and contextual difference of the abstract variables in comparison. The dominance of the military is, however, not a speculation but rather a mainstay in the context of Turkey. Certainly, the army has had significant power since the establishment of the Republic of Turkey. It became visible through routine discrete military coups and interventions in the last half century. Moreover, it has been consolidated in the face of continuous stress. Furthermore, the military has become a political power, while not only preserving the status quo against leftists, but also reducing the Kurdish question into the war against the PKK and secularism into the struggle with the Islamists. Explicitly, the military has damaged social democracy and the principles of equality and liberty of conscience. It has always claimed a dominant role in society, while legitimizing its own existence with the purpose of "protecting the country and its official ideology from enemies inside and outside". Its authoritarian power has actually caused a widespread societal anxiety as well as cowed silent resistance strategies. Military in Turkey is like a typical father figure in a traditional family, who expects all his sns to perform military service. The sons address their father, the military, with deference to his authority, thereby reproducing this authority again and again. Some sons do not show deference and resist the reproduction of their father's authority. In Turkey, a large surveillance system works in the name of military service. For instance, a person liable for military service needs to present documentation annually in order to be able to postpone it. Also, additional documentation required from all academic institutions in Turkey must be forwarded to the government to prove whether male students are attending lectures and writing exams. Unlike female students abroad, male ones must present their official transcripts and verifications of enrolment from their academic institution to the Turkish embassy in the country of residence. The military service status is always open to be questioned, e.g., when a man stays at a hotel, when he applies for a driver's license, or when he crosses boarder of Turkey. Furthermore, it is explicit that completing one's conscription brings with it status and prestige. In other words, being a conscience objector (*vicdani retçi*), a draft evader (*asker kaçağı*) – an evader of enlistment (*bakaya*) or an examination evader (*yoklama kaçağı*) – being exempt from the draft (*askerden muaf*), or being deferred (*tecilli*) indicates social deprivation in different levels. When a man applies for a job or an academic position or even decides to marry, he will commonly be questioned whether he has served in the armed forces. Moreover, having performed long-term or short-term military service, or deferred military service by payment can be read as an indicator of socio-economic status.

Although not having completed the draft appears to be a social stigma, most people tend to try to find ways to avoid it. In other words, legally deferring military service, as well as evasion from enlistment and draft is very common in Turkey. It is generally known that a considerable portion of men who enroll in a tertiary education institution or who procure a forged medical certificate are believed to be exempting themselves or deferring from military service. Most of them wait for an opportunity for conscription by payment or try to go abroad to work for that purpose. Statistics surrounding this theme are naturally difficult to find, but the average of the people who meet their military obligation compared to the population of military age is 58 percent, according to a report of the Turkish Grand National Assembly.[75] That is, 42 percent do not ful-

[75] To the draft of law about including a provisional clause into the Law on Military and reports of National Defense, plan and budget committee on October 4, 1999. http://www.tbmm.gov.tr/sirasayi/donem21/yil01/ss188m.htm [visited July 6, 2008]

fill the obligation, either by legally deferring service due to their health, or through education like postgraduate studies, higher education entrance exams, or illegal evasion. According to the General Staff, the number of draft evaders in Turkey is about 200,000 and the number of men living abroad and having still not carried out their draft was about 226,000 in December 1998.[76] Based on the military age range of 20-41 (total liable men 14,306,525), there are currently circa 1 million men (7 percent) who do not carry out military service due to their status as deferred, a draft evader, or an evader of enlistment.[77]

One entry about draft by payment in a very popular online dictionary in Turkey, *Ekşi Sözlük*, conveys important points of view.

> "In Turkey, where there are people selling some of their organs like their kidney or their spleen in order to be disabled to avoid the service, the existence of a draft by payment is a must. People who try to find a way to avoid military service by payment are not the children of ministries saying, 'I am proud of my Range Rover' and performing their military service in the front of a waterside residence in Yeniköy. In order to evade the draft, they pursue academic careers or go abroad and work there to struggle for the same rights as a *Dönerci* in Germany. Their argument is that 'We do not want to lose our work in Turkey where there high unemployment in the name of conscription. We are from the educated strata. If need be, we can take out a loan and work to pay back the debt in order to get rid of this difficulty. Moreover, there are enough soldiers in this country and it is not war time, so we can and we want to do more beneficial works rather than expending twelve months in vain. We ask for the right that {the wealth} have. They have the right to military service by payment, since they are born in another country, they are double citizens, they are not of help to the country, and they cannot even speak Turkish. After all, they have the right. After carrying out military service by payment, they only visit Turkey for a cheap holiday. We demand this right for ourselves as well.'"

---

[76] Hürriyet Newspaper on December 21, 1998.
http://webarsiv.hurriyet.com.tr/1998/12/21/85584.asp [visited July 7, 2008]

[77] According to the response of the Minister of National Defense, Vecdi Gönül, in June, 2008 to the parliamentary question about "conscientious objection" by the member of parliament Akin Birdal.

Seeing the military service as a pushing factor from Turkey appears to be a relevant characteristic for understanding HSLM. The problem of compulsory military service crosses contexts of educational, working, and migratory careers. In this thesis, it is henceforth relevant to examine the military service problem under the migration story dimension. With regard to the struggle against conscription, the motivation towards educational preferences, especially Master's of Science degrees, and working in an emigrant country resemble a silent societal resistance. That is, highly skilled men develop strategies to protect themselves from the official pressure to do military service by using their social environments. In addition to this silent resistance, there is a relatively small social movement (political resistance) in support of conscientious objection. The absence of the right to conscientious objection or even an elective civil service option in the Turkish legal system seems to be a crucial push factor among highly qualified men, although migration creates some restrictive alternatives and becomes a limited solution. From an economic perspective, people spend more on education to become highly skilled than to become low-skilled. This implies costs not only for the state and families, but is, at the same time, an investment for their future and that of the labor market. The state appears anxious about losing highly skilled people, yet at the same time it points out emigration paths for them. Moreover, the family institution expects the child will reimburse its expenditures on education with symbolic capital, and support this path. If they prefer long-term military service, they participate in drawing of lots and their place of duty is determined by lot or according to the occupational necessity of army. At the end, they are inducted as reserve officer. If they prefer short-term service, they will become an ordinary soldier. They are then recruits for the first three months. The military (-state) expects a longer period of service from university graduate men to meet its professional requirements and grants them a sum of money, similar to a salary, which is a lot lower than the going wage on the market. Although they mostly handle different kinds of duties, excluding active combat, during the military service period, they generally find their time in service to be dispensable. As a consequence, draft evasion is an institutionalized phenomenon in Turkey for highly educated people. Furthermore, going and working abroad in order to solve this problem is seen as an institutionalized phenomenon without prejudice: institutionalized expulsion. The term "brain flight" might be coined to describe this phenomenon, drawing from popular terminology with the word "brain". Certainly, the presence of compulsory military service constitutes a serious causal condition of HSLM.

As a result, a lot of male university graduates try to keep student status in Turkey in order to delay military service. As previously mentioned, continuing tertiary education allows one to delay conscription. Still, it is not an ultimate solution for escaping from service, but serves to lengthen the period of anxiousness. The second possibility for postponing military service obligation is to work abroad. Working abroad for three years extends the delay and makes military service for three weeks by payment possible. Furthermore, completely being rid of Turkish military service rather than postponing it and then having a right to the military service by payment is only possible by becoming a citizen of another country. Yet, with a new citizenship comes another military service duty.

2.2. Migratory Relations of Turkey with Germany in Europe and its "Privilege"

I would first like to touch on the Ankara Agreement and its importance in dealing with migrant workers from Turkey. As a first step in the establishment of the European Community (and the EU), the European Economic Community was founded by means of signing the Treaty of Rome by France, West Germany, Italy, Belgium, the Netherlands and Luxembourg, which are known informally as the Common Market (the Six), on March 25, 1957.[78] The Republic of Turkey first applied for associate membership in the Community in July of 1959. The Community responded by suggesting the establishment of an interim association before full accession. This led to

[78] The "Economic" was removed from its name by the Maastricht treaty in 1992, which at the same time effectively made the European Community the first of three pillars of the EU, called the Community (or Communities) Pillar.

negotiations which resulted in the "Ankara Agreement" (The Agreement Creating an Association between the Republic of Turkey and the European Economic Community) on September 12, 1963. The Agreement entered into force on December 1, 1964 aiming toward the full membership of the Republic of Turkey into the Community through the three-phase establishment of a customs union (preparatory stage, transitional stage, and final stage) which would serve as an instrument to bring about integration between the Community and the Republic of Turkey.

The Ankara Agreement discussed the progressive establishment of a Customs Union, which would bring the Parties closer together in economic and trade matters.[79] However, the Ankara Agreement excluded the Republic of Turkey from the European Economic Community decision-making mechanisms and precluded the Republic of Turkey from recourse to the European Court of Justice for dispute settlement. It envisaged the free circulation not only of goods, but also of workers, establishment, services (including transport) and capital between the parties. In the context of this study, I want to give more information about the issue of "free movement of workers" in the Ankara Agreement in 1963.[80] Article

[79] In the preparatory stage, the European Economic Community was to offer financial aid to Turkey. Under the First Financial Protocol, which covered the period 1963-1970, the Community provided the Republic of Turkey with loans worth 175 million European Currency Units. The trade concessions which the Community granted to the Republic of Turkey under the form of tariff quotas proved less effective than expected. Nonetheless, the Six's share in Turkish imports rose from 28.8 percent in 1964 to 44 percent in 1973. The Community enlarged to include Denmark, Ireland and the United Kingdom in 1973, the Nine's share in Turkish imports was 55 percent in 1973. As well, the Six's share in Turkish exports slightly increased from 33.5 percent in 1964 to 37.4 percent (the Nine's share was 46.4 percent) in 1973. These percentages are calculated from the data in the General Agreement on Tariffs and Trade L/4126 on December 20, 1974. See the full text http://192.91.247.23/gatt_docs/English/SULPDF/ 90910043. pdf On November 13, 1970, the so-called "Additional Protocol" established a timetable for the abolition of tariffs and quotas on goods traded between Turkey and the Community. Therefore, the period between 1970 and 1995 was seen as the transitional stage of the Agreement. On December 31, 1995 the customs union between Turkey and the EU came into effect. "The final stage", as defined in Article 5 of the Agreement "shall be based on the customs union and shall entail closer coordination of the economic policies of the Contracting Parties."

[80] The free circulation of establishments may also be relevant in the context. Yet, it is now ignored since it is out of the research interest.

12 of the Agreement states that "[t]he Contracting Parties agree to be guided by Articles 48, 49 and 50 of the Treaty establishing the Community for the purpose of progressively securing freedom of movement for workers between them."[81] In other words, all Articles related to the free movement of workers admitted in the Treaty of Rome for the six founding members were valid for the Republic of Turkey, except for Article 51 [42 EC], which dealt with the social security of workers.[82] Furthermore, Article 36 of the Additional Protocol on November 13, 1970 envisaged the free circulation of people between the parties in the following 12 to 22 years. In addition, Article 37 of the same Protocol (working conditions and wages) and Article 39 (the social security) protected rights of workers from Turkey working in the countries of the Community.[83] Simultaneously in the background, the large scale of labor migration from Turkey to Europe (particularly to Germany) was underpinned by liberal immigration regimes at the time of economic boom and labor shortage. The 1963 Ankara Agreement and the 1970 Additional Protocol are not known well enough by migrant workers and public servants to use the migrant worker rights derived from them. Some juridical courts have clarified the relevant issues. During that legal process, the Agreement and the Protocol provided privilege rights for employees and employers from Turkey different from those of other non-EU countries.

In the 1960s, Turkey signed intergovernmental contracts with some European countries, including Germany, the UK, the Netherlands, Austria, Belgium, France and Sweden. For instance, large-scale labor migration from Turkey to Germany started with an agreement signed by the Turkish and West German governments in 1961. The contract attempted to provide an expansion of the German industry with temporary unskilled labor. It was expected that these workers,

---

[81] The relevant Articles of the Treaty of Rome referred now respectively to 39, 40 and 41 in the European Community Treaty, or the Treaty on EU, which is signed in Maastricht on February 7, 1992, and entered into force on November 1, 1993.

[82] For the relevant Articles in the Treaty of Rome: http://www.hri.org/docs/Rome57/Part3Title03.html#Art48

[83] For the full text of the Protocol: http://www.tuerkischebotschaft.de/tr/index.htm

known as "guest workers", would return to Turkey after a German economic boom. It was also expected that "they would return to Turkey with new skills and help reorient the Turkish economy from rural agriculture to industry" on the side of the Turkish government (Kirişçi, 2003).

Turkey is generally considered to be the country from which most classical labor migrants came in the 1960s and 1970s and from which numerous asylum-seekers entered since the late 1970s. It is also perceived to be the starting point for the current marriage migration. This also forms a substantial context for the discussions in the EU over the question whether and in which period the country can become a member of the EU.[84] Along with unskilled labor migrants, skilled labor power has gradually migrated from Turkey to Europe since the 1960s. However, hardly any attention has been paid to this connection so far. It can be argued that HSLM on a

---

[84] With the EU due to decide whether to start accession negotiations with Turkey by December 2004, both the question of migrants from Turkey in European countries and prospects of further migration from Turkey to Europe have become major issues. On the one hand, some believe that there are a large number of migrants from Turkey who suffered integration problems in their host communities. This belief brings about anti-immigrant feelings in a number of EU member countries and concerns about further immigration. On the other hand, some maintain that the previous migrants have actually integrated well by contributing to job creation, running their own business, and joining policy at the local, national and even European level. In addition, it is already known that the EU usually sets long transition period for new candidates after starting negotiation about their membership. Turkey's possible membership in medium term is to achieve alignment with the *acquis* as regards recognition of professional qualification under the title of free movement of persons (APT, 2003). Therefore, most think that the right to free movement for Turkish nationals within the EU would not be realized during this period. In fact, the full mobility of workers from Turkey might not come for another 17 years. "By that time the labor markets will be strongly affected by the ageing of the population (not only among the EU-15, but also the new members). There might thus be actually labor shortages, instead of the wide-spread unemployment that is the rule today" (Derviş et al., 2004:67). It is possible that if Turkey joins the EU, emigration may no longer be as attractive to Turkish workers (Derviş et al., 2004:67). It is also possible that many Turkish nationals may return to Turkey as seen in the cases of Greece, Spain and Portugal, if Turkey were admitted as an EU member (Kirişçi, 2003). Also, some analysts suggest that as the Turkish economy expands with EU membership, the pressure to emigrate will diminish (Erzan et al., 2004). According to their model, they estimate only 1-2.1 million people would migrate from Turkey to the other EU members with the right to free movement between 2015 until 2030, if Turkey joined the EU. Otherwise, this number would become 2.7 million (Erzan et al., 2004).

global level is accelerating increasingly, while other kinds of migration are declining due to being controlled. It can be generally assumed that HSLM from Turkey will become larger whether or not Turkey will be admitted as an EU member. Additionally, we should remember the provision of "Turkish preference" under which, if the necessary labor cannot be found in the member states or EU employment market, it shall be sought on the Turkish employment market or from unemployed workers from Turkey already present on the territory of the Member State in question, rather than from another third country. Article 8 of "The Decision No 1/80 of the Association Council of 19 September 1980 on the development of the Association" states as follows:

> **1.** Should it not be possible in the Community to meet an offer of employment by calling on the labor available on the employment market of the Member States and should the Member States, within the framework of their provisions laid down by law, regulation or administrative action, decide to authorize a call on workers who are not nationals of a Member State of the Community in order to meet the offer of employment, they shall endeavor in so doing to accord priority to Turkish workers.
>
> **2.** The employment services of the Member State shall endeavor to fill vacant positions which they have registered and which the duly registered Community labor force has not been able to fill with Turkish workers who are registered as unemployed and legally resident in the territory of that Member State.

Although the Ankara Agreement and the relevant protocols have never been properly put into practice, this legal base is known through the judgments of the European Court of Justice. In particular, Süssmuth et al. (2004) also touched upon the significance of HSLM from Turkey in the Germany context and put into perspective in the economized migratory relations between these two countries.

> „Gleiches gilt für die groβe türkische Gemeinschaft in Deutschland. Ihre Mitglieder kennen die Kultur und Sprache potanzieller Kunden und Geschäftspartner, was eine wichtige Voraussetzung für unternehmerisches Handeln mit der Türkei ist, die zu den am schnellsten wachsenden Märkten in Europa gehört. Allein der deutsch-türkische Handel ist in den vergangenen Jahren zweistellig gewachsen. Aber nicht nur die Bundesrepublik würde davon profitieren, wenn die Potanziale der Zuwanderer besser genutzt

> werden. Auch die Einheimischen, vor allem die gering Qualifizierten, haben zur Zeit erhebliche Schwierigkeiten, einen Arbeitsplatz zu finden. Zusammen mit der Tatsache, dass es künftig beispielsweise über den (humanitär begründeten) Familiennachzug eine stetige Zuwanderung von gering Qualifizierten geben wird, verdeutlicht dies, dass neue Wege gefunden werden müssen, um diese Menschen besser in den Arbeitsmarkt zu integrieren. Zu diesen neuen Wegen zählt auch die verstärkte Zuwanderung von hoch Qualifizierten und Qualifizierten." (Süssmuth et al., 2004:178).

Clearly, the necessary HSL of the EU, specifically Germany, will be primarily sought from the potential HSL power in Turkey under the right set of circumstances.

2.3. Historical Background of HSLM from Turkey

HSLM from Turkey cannot be easily isolated from its historical background and shifting patterns of interdependence in the world system. It is in this context that the various phases and particular issues of the related HSLM will be examined. Like any other sending country study, there are a number of specific topics, stemming from certain particular historical and social factors, which need further interpretation.

Brain migration from Turkey dates back to the decline of the Ottoman Empire, "the Sick Man of Europe", under the influences of the central powers of Europe. This history draws an analogy of modernization, or the so-called westernization. Since the early 19th century, the Empire attached importance to raising a Westernist Ottoman intelligentsia and ruling class to get rid of its backwardness. The French Empire was seen as their guide, since French impact on the Ottoman domestic policy and French language dominance in the renewed education system was intense.[85] In fact, the school system was designed according to the French counterpart.[86] In 1830,

[85] Due to the Capitulations, some European empires, but notably the French Empire, provided various extraterritorial rights in exchange for trade opportunities. During the 19th century, "the trade on the Levant" was developed; the French post offices were opened in various cities of the Ottoman Empire to facilitate communication for business interests; and the community of the Levantines was expanded under protection of their religious and educational institutions.

[86] See the Section of Education.

150 students from the Royal Schools of Administration, Medicine, Military, and Engineering were first sent to Europe, specifically to France, by Sultan Mahmut II (1808-1839). A significant number of French teachers and academics immigrated to the Ottoman Empire to teach students of the upper-middle class families in Istanbul. Simultaneously, the number of governmental-sponsored students in the French Empire increased, and then an Ottoman School was opened in Paris in 1857. In summary, the 19th century can be read as the inception of brain migration as a form of brain circulation with student-teacher exchange, and can be seen as the experimental phase of the HSLM system. This phase's influences can still be seen not only in the education system but also in continuing elitism of modern-day Turkey, standing as the extension of the Young Turks and inherited from previous generations.

Apart from the French impact on the Ottoman Empire in the 19th century, the two decades around the turn of the century were marked with growing German influence. Although the relations between Istanbul and Berlin grew closer in the Bismarck Age, this close partnership began at the time of the Prussian Empire (1871-1918), particularly in the context of military. The German mission was to modernize the Ottoman Army, requiring defense policy to handle the so-called "*Orientalische Frage*". In this context, the German contribution targeted military and engineering schools. Along with this partnership, the Prussian Empire administered the Ottoman railway system construction with the financial backing of the Deutsche Bank. This intensified political and economic interactions. Therefore, the French-dominated high school system in the Ottoman Empire started to witness the start of German influence. The German High School (*Alman Lisesi-Deutsche Schule*), which was established in 1868 for the children of German traders, artists, engineers, and diplomats living in Istanbul, developed in this period and the number of students grew to 600 in 1893. The other German-speaking school in Istanbul was the Austrian High School (*Avusturya Lisesi-Sankt Georgs Kolleg*), founded in 1882. But more importantly, Istanbul High School (*Istanbul Lisesi-Deutsche Auslandsschule*) was established in 1884 for Ottoman children. Its teaching language was determined to be German. Its student populace exceeded 600 in 1891, and grew to 1,600 in 1913 with the addition of 22 teachers sent by the German Ministry.

Historians speculate that the influence of both the French and Prussian Empires were related by their colonial efforts in the Ottoman Empire before World War I (Stürmer, 2000:91). It can be claimed that the railway, as a symbol of Germany's intention to gain a foothold in Istanbul and Anatolia, prevailed over the post offices, which were a symbol of French power in the Ottoman Empire. In fact, the Young Turks, who held significant power in the last period of the Ottoman Empire, had close relations with the Prussian Empire, and this became a direct alliance at the start of World War I. Many alumni of Istanbul High School became the key figures of the war years and of the establishment of the Republic of Turkey. Following Atatürk's instructions, the school moved to the building of the former Council of Ottoman Revenues and Debts Administration *(Düyun-u Umumiye)* in 1933. This movement, like the school itself, carries crucial symbolic meaning, marking the intimacy with the Weimar Republic (1919-1933). French architects designed the building in 1882. It was eventually used to take over the surveillance and control of the public finances by the British-French consortium in order to regulate the Capitulations, which destroyed the political stability and economic unity of the Ottoman Empire. However, Turkish-German relations were ruptured in the period of the Nazi Germany (*Dritte Reich*, 1933-1945), and during World War II. The German education in Istanbul High School was accordingly suspended in 1942.

The breakdown of Turkish-German relations did not lead to a migration gap; on the contrary, it brought about the acceptance of Jewish refugees. Atatürk and his Minister of Education, Hasan Ali Yücel, a former prominent teacher of Istanbul High School, initiated a new era of brain immigration to Turkey in the 1930s. They actually took advantage of Hitler's dismissal of Jewish educators and scientists and admitted hundreds of exiles from Nazi-Germany to Turkey.[87] The contribution of these refugees to the development of tertiary education life, particularly at Ankara University and Istanbul University was remarkable (Shaw, 1991 and Shaw, 1992). The brightest faculties of these universities (medical faculty and faculty of administrative sciences) can trace their success back to these scholars. In the first half of the 20th century, Turkey insisted on remaining outside World War II to cover the remaining costs from World War I and it tried to increase the amount of educated people in spite of its financial bottleneck. The recessive German-Turkish political relations became stronger after the declaration of the Federal Republic of Germany (1949-1990).

Unlike French high schools' dominance in Istanbul in the end of the 19th century, a similar number of American high schools was spread in the other big cities in Anatolia, as well as Istanbul. In the second half of the 20th century, the American influence on Turkey began to increase, although German and French influence remained. After World War II, the USA provided economic aid, machines, and goods to the sixteen countries in Europe, including Turkey, under the Marshall Plan.[88] Based on the recommendations of the Plan, Turkey began agricultural mechanization and development of highways in the 1950s. Simultaneously Turkey's political and economic loyalty to the USA and their American lead military relations dramatically increased.[89] From 1956 to 1963, the METU in Ankara was opened with American initiative and financial support to train people in English in order to create a HSL force in the fields of basic sciences and engineering, like the two best universities: Bosporus University (formerly Robert College)

---

[87] The Ottoman Empire also experienced two great waves of Jewish immigration in the 16th and the 19th centuries.

[88] The Marshall Aid Plan consists of the UK, France, Belgium, Portugal, Ireland, Greece, Turkey, Holland, Luxembourg, Switzerland, Iceland, Austria, Norway, Denmark, and Sweden.

[89] Turkey was seen as a politically important periphery country in the time of the Cold War by NATO countries, notably the USA, since its geographical proximity to the Union of Soviet Socialist Republics (USSR) and Middle East. The cost of Turkey's membership to NATO in 1952 was not allowing the establishment of American military bases in Turkey, but also sending a Turkish brigade to the Korean War.

and Istanbul Technical University.[90] HSLM from Turkey to the USA has been composed mostly of students and graduates from these three universities.

According to a 1968 UN Report (1968:60-5), the number of HSLM engineers, medical doctors, natural and social scientists from Turkey between 1962 and 1966 is 535 to the USA, 161 to Canada, and 134 to France. However, this report does not give information about HSLM to the other countries. Using the UN data and the admission figures to the USA in 1967, Franck (1970:301) estimated the global annual outflow rate of HSLM from Turkey in the early 1960s as 375 in his study. This is somewhat conservative since it underestimates the number of HSLM to Germany. It is generally known that the USA attracted the highest numbers of engineers and scientists from Turkey in the 1960s, but at the same time the majority of migrants with occupational backgrounds in medicine and education moved to Germany.[91] For instance, the number of medical doctors and practitioners from Turkey in West Germany in the year of 1964 was 832, followed by the USA with 607.

HSLM from Turkey to Germany began to be institutionalized in the 1950s. The Institute of World Economy in the University of Kiel informed the Turkish Ministry of Foreign Affairs about their intention to accept interns from Turkey. As a response to this demand, in 1956, 25 highly skilled people from Turkey departed for Germany. Furthermore, another agreement was signed in 1957. A program, sponsored by the Chamber of Artisans of Hamburg, was announced with the motto: "Citizens helping citizens" (*Bürger hilft Bürger*) (Abadan-Unat, 1976:13). In 1957 when the president Theodor Heuss visited Turkey, the Bilateral Collaboration Agreement on Culture and Education between the Federal Republic of Germany and the Republic of Turkey was signed. As a result, the curriculum of Istanbul High School was changed back to German

[90] Until 1971, there were nine universities in Turkey (See the section on Tertiary Education for details).
[91] At this I would like to remind again the reader that the best universities in engineering and science are BU, METU, and ITU, and their teaching language is English. All these brought about rise in the Anglo-American share of HSLM from Turkey.

in 1958. In the same year, about 150 skilled Turkish workers with high school degrees came to Cologne to work for Ford Factory. They were warmly received and have since been referred to as "Heuss-Turks" ("*Heuss-Türken*"). All of these factors gradually initiated recruitment of HSL from Turkey in West Germany. Nevertheless, the phenomenon of crowding rendered the perception thereof less probable because a very big number of un- or semi-skilled workers from Turkey came to Germany after the recruitment agreement in 1961 ("*Anwerbeabkommen*"). In fact, the number of workers abroad from Turkey in 1973 is estimated to have been approximately 800,000, of whom 100,000 were skilled workers. 80 percent of these workers abroad were in West Germany and the rest worked in other European counties. Statistics also reveals the presence of about 3,000 highly skilled workers from Turkey in West Germany. Crowding occurs when the proportion of highly skilled migrants to the net migrants is difficult to be expressed as a percentage. However, the significance of this movement becomes visible if it is expressed as a proportion of the whole HSL potential of Turkey at that time. More than 3.3 percent of Turkey's 90,000 highly educated laborers was employed in West Germany. The year 1973, when the energy crisis boomed due to the rise of oil prices, can be marked in the context of labor migration as "*Anwerbestopp*" (Ban on recruitment). This shows that labor migration not only depends on national policies, but also to a high degree on economic interdependence between national economies (Abadan-Unat, 1976:4-5).

The period between 1956 and 1972 marked the initial phase of HSLM from Turkey. Unlike other Mediterranean countries, Turkey exported about a quarter of its highly educated labor in the late 1960s and about half in the early 1970s (Abadan-Unat, 1976:11). Clearly, the liberal emigration politics Turkey had introduced (Oğuzkan, 1976:103) in order to decrease the imbalanced distribution of labor power backfired since it had the exact opposite influence on the imbalance (Aydınoğlu, 1976:110). HSLM in this period increased this gap considerably. Considering influential works of Oğuzkan (1976), Abadan-Unat (1976), and Aydınoğlu (1976), I roughly estimate the number of HSLM (excluding skilled workers from Turkey between 1956 and 1972) as around 10,000. Of these, 3,200 were in Germany, 2,000 in the USA, 800 in the UK, 600 in Canada, 600 in France, and the rest scattered around the world.

In the academic year 1962-63, the total number of students in Turkish tertiary education was around 70,000. This number grew to more than 175,000 in the academic year 1972-73 when the quantity of secondary education graduates preferring to continue their education (140,000) exceeded the annual student capacity of tertiary education (37,000). This indicated both the potential of student population for growth and insufficiency of capacity in universities. Between 1972 and 1981, ten new universities were opened in Turkey.[92] Also, two-year tertiary programs and televised teaching began. Despite these rapid advances and innovations, Turkey did not recover from the student overflow. However, the distinction of the period 1972-1981 is not only the increase in government-sponsored students abroad but also the rise in the number of students abroad outside this program (Oğuzkan, 1976:92).[93] The number of Turkish students abroad was 8,336 in 1971 (1,424 out of them were government-sponsored) and grew to 13,668 in 1972.[94] In addition to the inadequate capacities of universities, the political instability in the period between 1972 and 1981 is a significant "push" factor. Around the awful military coup in 1980 a large number of university students, graduates, teachers and academics went abroad, especially to Europe, seeking asylum or as an exile. The conjectural

---

[92] See the Section of the Stage of Tertiary Education.

[93] The government-sponsored study-abroad program was regulated on the basis of the law numbered 1416 (Law Regarding Students to be Sent to Foreign Countries, *Ecnebi Memleketlere Gönderilecek Talebe Hakkında Kanun*), enacted in April 1929. It was administered by MoNE. Until 1972, the non-return rate of participants of the Turkish state-scholarship program was more than 8 percent (Uysal:1973:71). Regarding this result, Oğuzkan (1976:95) describes the state scholarship program as "a major source of brain drain".

[94] Approximately 45 percent of them were in Germany, 19 percent in the USA, 11 percent in the UK, and 8 percent in France. Milli Eğitim Bakanlığı. *Yurt Dışı Devlet Öğrencileri Bilgi ve İstatistiği, 1971* (Information and Statistical Data on Study-Abroad Program, 1971). Ankara: Bakanlık, 1971, p.69.

amount of the highly educated exiles in that period is 30,000.[95] These exiles constituted a large amount of undocumented HSLM. This kind of HSLM can be called "brain exodus" or "brain hemorrhage".

In the period between 1982-1991, ten new universities were established and privatization in education began. Since 1992, there has been a boom in the number of universities. Forty-five new universities were opened until 2001, more than half of which are private.

Going abroad to study and to work has been a more globally accepted phenomenon since the 1990s. Despite an increase of the politics of fear ("security politics") regarding migration, the mobility of students and graduates has been encouraged more politically (and hence accelerated) in the last two decades. Many advanced economies have not only modified their skilled migration programs to make them more attractive, but also shifted their policies on student mobility from a purely educational basis to one linked to longer-term interests in the future recruitment of HSL. They facilitate legal regulations, such as student visas and work permits as well as the portability of grants and loans. In the period between 1994-2005, 1,755 students were sent abroad with state funding. However, YÖK declared the scholarship program unsuccessful since many of those students chose not to return to Turkey.[96] Still, the number of government-sponsored students abroad in the academic year 2005-2006 increased to 392.[97] Güngör and Tansel (2006) argue that the compulsory service requirement attached to this scholarship increased the probability of student return.

In the middle of the 2000s, Turkey had approximately 2,000,000 total enrollments in tertiary education.[98] As shown in FIGURE 7,

---

[95] Some other realistic estimates of Güven (2007): about 30,000 (9,400 public servants, 3,854 teachers, 120 academicians) were fired, 388,000 could not get passports, and 14,000 were denaturalized.

[96] http://www.yok.gov.tr/duyuru/2006/turkey_higher.pdf

[97] Türkiye Eğitim İstatistikleri 2005-2006.

[98] Turkey began to appear as a receiving country of student migration with about 13,000 in 2004 and 16,500 in 2006, 20 percent of whom come from the EU and its candidate

the number of students abroad from Turkey is more than 50,000 around the same time, making Turkey the seventh highest ranking country in terms of gross outflow of students.

FIGURE 7. TOP DESTINATIONS FOR OUTBOUND MOBILE STUDENTS FROM TURKEY IN TERTIARY EDUCATION (2005)

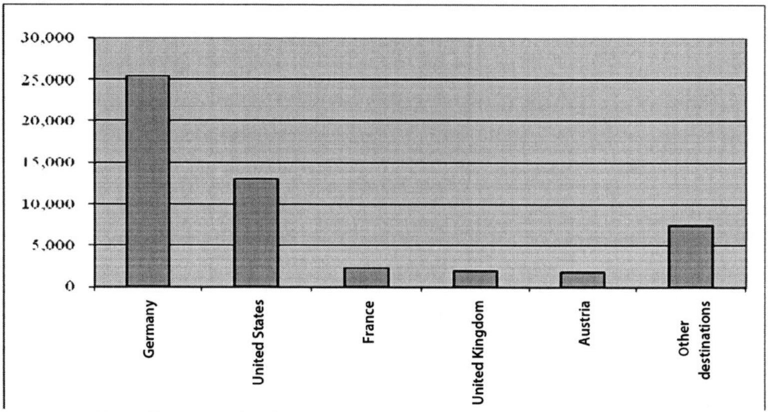

Data Source: OECD and UNESCO Institute for Statistics
Total Number: 52.027

According to these OECD and UNESCO (United Nations Educational, Scientific and Cultural Organization) statistics, Germany is the largest receiver of Turkish students.[99] However Germany owes this high ranking to the so-called "*Bildungsinländer*" who comprise two thirds of the overall total.[100] In the case of "*Bildung-*

countries but notably from Asian Republics. Sources: UNESCO, 2006: Yüksek Öğretim İstatistikleri 2006-2007.

[99] According to UNESCO statistics, 52,048 students from Turkey studied abroad in 2004, mainly in Germany (27,582), the United States (11,398), France (2,273), the UK (1,960), and Austria (1,820). Source: UNESCO, 2006. In 2005, the OECD statistics state that the total number is 52,027: 25.421 in Germany, 13.029 in the USA, 2.283 in France, 1.913 in the UK, 1.857 in Austria, and 7.524 in other countries.

[100] In the context of Germany, the category of "foreign students" consists of "*(auslandische) Bildungsausländer*" and "*(auslandische) Bildungsinländer*". The former group covers students who move to Germany after obtaining the qualification to enter the higher education system in a different country. The latter group, on the other hand, includes

sausländer", we see Turkey at only the fifth position among the sending countries in 2007, whereas they were first until 2000.[101] The outflow statistics, produced by YÖK, correct the distorted image of Germany in the HSLM picture, despite the fact that it does not cover the students abroad with scholarships. The total number of private students from Turkey studying abroad as of October 2, 2006 was 19,658.[102] As the host country for 17 percent of the students from Turkey living abroad, Germany comes second after the USA which has a share of 18 percent.[103] The amount of women among tertiary students in Turkey is more than 40 percent, but the amount of female students abroad is less than 10 percent.[104] The OECD Database on all students abroad (both *Bildungsinländer* and *Bildungsausländer*) shows that female students from Turkey account for about 27 percent of foreign enrolment in tertiary education. The gender imbalance in favor of male students in tertiary education abroad is clear. It is obvious that the chances to go abroad are less for women than men.

Hunger (2003:18) introduces some official statistics about highly-qualified migrants in the USA based on their educational level in 1990. According to these statistics, 19,285 highly qualified mi-

---

those people without German passports who go through normal phases of the education system in Germany to gain the same right. *Bildungsinländer*" with Turkish passports are a consequence of migration history between Turkey and Germany, including labor migration, refugees, and family unifications. They are, however, products of German education system.

[101] Today China is the biggest sending country to Germany, followed by Bulgaria, Poland, and Russia (http://www.wissenschaft-weltoffen.de/daten ; Quelle: Studentenstatistik Statistisches Bundesamt; HIS-Berechnungen). In comparison with these countries, the number of "*Bildungsausländer*" in Germany from Turkey, France, Austria, South-Korea, Spain, and Italy have not radically changed in the last ten years.

[102] National Education Statistics, Formal Education 2006/07. YÖK.

[103] The following four countries are Azerbaijan with 16 percent, France with 12 percent, the UK with 7 percent, and Kyrgyzstan with 7 percent. About 50 percent have been educated in EU member or candidate countries. The data is impressive: the USA received 56 percent of students from Turkey for graduate study (28 MA, 28 PhD), the UK 53 percent (46 MA, 7 PhD), Germany 44 percent (40 MA, 4 PhD), France 18 percent (12 MA, 6 PhD), and the Central Asian Republics only 2 percent.

[104] It may be a result of a bias in the registration system, since male students must be registered as students abroad in order to postpone their military services, but females have no any obligation to register themselves as students. Still, they display this general tendency.

grants out of 41,605 from Turkey (approximately half of them) live in the USA. The amount of university graduates who migrated from Turkey to the USA consisted of approximately 1.5 percent of the net HSLM to that country (Carrington and Detragiache, 1998:13-8). The proportion of university degree holders among Turkish migrants in the USA is circa 40 percent in the 1990s. This is more than twice as much the tertiary school enrollment ratio in Turkey (Özden, 2005: 235). Based on the USA population census in the year 2000, the share of those holding a Bachelor's of Science degree or above among the migrants from Turkey in the USA was 43 percent, and the share of those holding a Master of Science degree or above is 23 percent. In 2003, there were 20,000 people from Turkey in the USA, and more than half were university graduates.

I argue that upper middle class families prefer to send their children to the USA or EU countries (mostly Germany, the UK, and France) in order to complete a Bachelor's of Science degree after completing elite high schools. Moreover, if their children do not perform well in the university entrance examination in Turkey, middle class families prefer universities in the Central Asian Republics (mostly Azerbaijan and Kyrgyzstan) as a second choice. In order to undertake graduate study abroad, a student must have certain achievements, such as a good cumulative grade point average (CGPA) or language skills. Furthermore, students from Turkey mostly go to the USA or EU countries in order to receive MA degree and overwhelmingly go to the USA for PhD degrees.

The ERASMUS (European Region Action Scheme for the Mobility of University Students) program has supported the academic mobility of students and teachers within the EU since 1987. Having been an associate member of the EU since 1963, Turkey joined the ERASMUS program in 2004. Turkey's primary student exchange partner in Europe is Germany, ahead of the Netherlands, France, and Italy. About one quarter of ERASMUS students from Turkey prefer to go to Germany. Likewise, one quarter of the ERASMUS students who come to Turkey are from Germany.[105] In the academic year 2004-2005, the outflow from Turkey equals 1,142 students, whereas the figure for inflow from the ERASMUS program is 299.[106] In the next academic year, the numbers are 2,852 and 894 respectively.[107] It is predictable that as the numbers of ERASMUS increase, student mobility will continue.

HSLM from Turkey started to be institutionalized around 1960 in the above-mentioned circumstances. While analyzing the historical background of HSLM from Turkey, I saw three main receiving countries (France, Germany, and the USA). Their influential existence in the HSLM is partly constructed by their impacts on the Turkish education system. These impacts shape key patterns of HSLM and its potentiality. I would like to symbolize them with the post office, the railway, and the highway, respectively, each of which are connected to their historical meaning in Turkey. The first HSLM pattern is brain circulation. The migrants are like return receipt requested mail. The second HSLM pattern is brain export that is deliberate and gradually growing. The last HSLM pattern is brain drain that quickly sweeps the migrants away.

2.4. Germany Turning into Open House for HSLM

In February 2000, German Chancellor, Gerhard Schröder, announced the introduction of a so-called "Green Card" program for foreign ICT specialists as the defining moment.[108] Then, the Fed-

---

[105] http://www.daad.de/presse/de/2007/8.1.1_1107_engl_ERASMUS.pdf Deutscher Akademischer Austauschdienst e.V.

[106] Erasmus Statistics, 2004-2005.

[107] Erasmus Statistics, 2005-2006.

[108] The name was borrowed from the US Green Card. Nevertheless, the US Green Card means that an immigrant has the right to live and work in the USA *permanently*. After five years the immigrant can apply for American citizenship. This regulation therefore differs clearly from the German Green Card, which is in the form of a *temporary* work permit. The German Green Card is to the H1-B visa in the USA, which is a temporary visa for highly skilled workers. The original name of the Green Card program in Germany is „*Verordnung über Aufenthaltserlaubnisse für hoch qualifizierte ausländische Fachkräfte der Informations- und Kommunikationstechnologie* (IT-ArGV)". Officially, it is also called the Emergency Program to Cover Need for Skilled IT Labor („*Sofortprogramm zur Deckung des IT-Fachkräftebedarfs*").

eral Republic of Germany began a temporary relief program on August 1, 2000, which is particularly designed to enable ICT specialists from non-EU countries to meet labor demands of its market. The German labor market had the opportunity to hire up to 20,000 non-EU member ICT specialists for a maximum of five years until 2005.[109] In the "Green Card" program, ICT professions include the fields of software development, multimedia development and programming, the development of circuits and ICT systems, and ICT consultancy, as well as systems, internet and network specialists. As a matter of fact, ICT specialists with university degrees – Bachelor's or Master's degrees – in any ICT-related subject were eligible to apply for a "Green Card". In addition, ICT specialists without a university degree could only work in Germany if the employer agrees in writing to pay an annual salary of at least 100,000 DM (German Marks; 51,000 Euro) before taxes and deductions. In order to hire a non-EU-citizen ICT specialist, the company had to apply for a work permit at the employment office. The employment office then verified within a week whether (i) a skilled German or an EU-citizen could meet the requirements of the firm; (ii) the person the firm wanted to hire was qualified for the position; and (iii) the employer was offering the foreign specialist the same working conditions and wage as a comparably qualified German ICT specialist would receive. The Green Card also applied to foreigners graduating from German universities, who had to leave the country after their graduation before the Green Card came into force. During the five-year period of validity of the Green Card, it was possible to change to another ICT job with a different firm. In that case, no further checks were made as to whether a German or EU-citizen ICT specialist would be available for the job and would therefore have priority in filling the vacancy. Self-employment was only possible under certain circumstances. A

---

[109] In fact, the deadline to apply for a working permission under the Green Card program was originally July 31, 2003. However, this deadline had been extended by the German government to the end of 2004, when a new immigration law started to regulate work and residency permits for highly skilled, non-EU workers seeking employment in the country.

spouse could only take up employment after a one-year waiting period.

The Green Card program aimed at temporary HSL immigration from outside of the EU. The new Immigration Act replaced it in 2004. Since the new migration law in Germany came into effect in 2005, HSL migrants are eligible to instantly receive a permanent residency permit (*Niederlassungserlaubnis*) if their total yearly income is a minimum 86,400 Euro. At the end of 2008, it was reevaluated and the required yearly income was decreased to 63,600 beginning in 2009. This shows that the Federal Republic of Germany is gradually improving permanent HSLM instead of temporary one.

There have been some special programs in the last few decades by most receiving countries of HSLM in order to attract highly skilled people to their country. Most of them, like the Green Card program in Germany, appear encouraging for temporary migration. But it is fairly easy to be turned into a permanent migrant, due to the chance at a *Niederlassungserlaubnis* after completing the duration of the Green Card. Moreover, the new migration act has facilitated more permanent HSLM. At the same time, the EU tried to give up the competition, and put consensus in this context with a new program called the "Blue Card" to attract foreign workers with highly valued skills into the European labor sector.

2.5. Appreciation of Dual Citizenship and Difference of Turkish-German Context

In the frame of a nation state, nationality is defined as a legal bond between a person and a state which grants the state jurisdiction over the person, and grants the person the protection of the state. Under international law and *lex causae* ("cause for the law") principles, it is traditionally the right of each state to determine who its nationals are. In fact, every state has a nationality law generally included in the public law to define the ways in which that country's nationality and citizenship are transmitted, acquired or lost. Nationality laws in continental Europe are based upon the Napoleonic Code.[110] The term "citizenship", used by most countries of central and Eastern Europe, is used synonymously with the term "nationality", which is common throughout Western Europe. Although citizenship mostly purports the legal sense of nationality, to be a national but not a citizen (i.e., be legally subject to a state and entitled to its protection without having rights of political participation in it) and to have political rights without being a national of a state are possible in some countries outside continental Europe. But, in most countries, a non-citizen is a non-national and called either a "foreigner" or an "alien". In this study, I prefer to use the word "citizenship" rather than nationality, since nationality often evokes a sentiment of inalterable essence and may be understood as a synonym of ethnicity. Citizenship can be perceived as an entity which can be lost, changed, and gained, and hereby defined by relations with a state. However, some specific terminology such as "nationality law" will not be changed in this thesis.

Within the complex variety of citizenship, it is clear that there is not always a one-to-one relation between people and states. As distinct from national citizenship, people may have subnational citizenships (e.g. citizenship of a commune and citizenship of canton in Switzerland) and supranational citizenships (e.g. EU citizenship and Commonwealth citizenship). Furthermore, statuses of statelessness[111] (mostly refugees[112]) and multiple citizenships (mostly dual citizenship) exist. These two statuses are still contentious at the national and international levels. On the one hand, various international conventions[113] work to reduce statelessness, paying re-

[110] See the full text from the web site:
http://www.napoleonseries.org/research/government/c_code.html

[111] There are two types of statelessness: *de jure* and *de facto*. *De jure* statelessness is where there exists no recognized state in respect of which the subject has a legally meritorious basis to claim nationality. *De facto* statelessness is where the subject may have a legally meritorious claim but is precluded from asserting it because of practical considerations such as cost, circumstances of civil disorder, or the fear of persecution.

[112] Statelessness most commonly affects refugees although not all refugees are stateless, and not all stateless persons may be able to qualify as refugees.

[113] See 1954 Convention Relating to the Status of Stateless Persons (The Office of the United Nations, High Commissioner for Human Rights)

gard to Article 15 of the Universal Declaration of Human Rights (UDHR) adopted by the United Nations General Assembly (A/RES/217, on December 10, 1948 at Palais de Chaillot, Paris). It states: (1) Everyone has the right to a nationality. (2) No one shall be arbitrarily deprived of his nationality nor denied the right to change his nationality. On the other hand, a lot of conventions have aimed at reducing multiple citizenships.[114] Nevertheless, it can be argued that multiple citizenship status is currently becoming a more accepted phenomenon in the context of globalization. As a multilateral treaty, the European Convention on Nationality (E.T.S. No. 166, signed on November 6, 1997, in Strasbourg) is strong proof of this acceptance. Being the most comprehensive convention dealing with nationality law, it covers issues not only of nationality but also of statelessness and multiple nationalities.[115] Unlike previous conventions, it explicitly preambles:

> "noting the varied approach of States to the question of multiple nationality and recognizing that each State is free to decide which consequences it attaches in its internal law to the fact that a national acquires or possesses another nationality... [and] agreeing on the desirability of finding appropriate solutions to consequences

---

(http://www.ohchr.org/english/law/ stateless.htm), 1961 Convention on the Reduction of Statelessness (http://www.ohchr.org/english/law/ statelessness.htm), etc.

[114] See Convention on Certain Questions Relating To The Conflict Of Nationality Laws signed on April 12, 1930, in the Hague (http://www.coe.int/t/e/legal_affairs/legal_co-operation/foreigners_and_citizens/nationality/documents/ legal_instruments/Conv%20conflict%20nationality%20The%20Hague%2004_1930.pdf); Convention on the Exchange of Information relating to Acquisition of Nationality signed on September 10, 1964, in Paris (http://ec.europa.eu/justice_home/judicialatlascivil/html/pdf/conv08_ciec_en.pdf); and Convention on the Reduction of Cases of Multiple Nationality and on Military Obligations in Cases of Multiple Nationality (ETS No. 043, signed on May 6, 1963, in Strasbourg, http://conventions.coe.int/ Treaty/en/Treaties/Html/043.htm).

[115] See its full text on the web site: http://conventions.coe.int/Treaty/en/Treaties/Html/166.htm It was signed by Member States of the Council of Europe: Albania, Andorra, Austria, Belgium, Bulgaria, Croatia, Cyprus, Czech Republic, Denmark, Estonia, Finland, France, Germany, Greece, Hungary, Iceland, Ireland, Italy, Latvia, Liechtenstein, Lithuania, Luxembourg, Malta, Moldova, Netherlands, Norway, Poland, Portugal, Romania, Russian Federation, San Marino, Slovak Republic, Slovenia, Spain, Sweden, Switzerland, "the former Yugoslav Republic of Macedonia", Turkey, Ukraine and United Kingdom.

> of multiple nationality and in particular as regards the rights and duties of multiple nationals."

The convention evidently seems to embody the debate about the desirability of multiple citizenships. In fact, multiple citizenship status may be seen as a challenge to the extant *Master Nationality Rule* that is a result of Article 4 of the Hague Convention on Certain Questions Relating to the Conflict of Nationality Laws of 1930. Article 4 affirms: "A State may not afford diplomatic protection to one of its nationals against a State whose nationality such person also possesses." Notwithstanding the direct opposition to multiple citizenship, The Hague convention protects the right of states which forbid it, or permit but do not recognize it, under their nationality laws. As a consequence, the phenomenon left to the related nationality laws of countries to decide is still controversial in the global level. There are different implementations in countries concerning multiple citizenship status to their nationality laws. Before browsing these implementations on a country level, acquisition of citizenship will be generally elaborated.

The acquirement of citizenship varies with different but not necessarily mutually exclusive criteria according to countries. This is based on three main phases of life: (i) birth; (ii) marriage;[116] and (iii) migration (adoption and naturalization). Citizenship is automatically bestowed at birth to people on the basis of two discrete principles or a combination of them: *Jus sanguinis* ("right of blood") and *Jus soli* ("right of soil"). *Jus sanguinis* is a right by which citizenship can be recognized to any individual born to a parent who is a citizen of the related state, whereas *Jus soli* applies to any individual born in the territory of that state. The classical example of *Jus sanguinis* is Germany prior to January 1, 2000. The traditional example of *Jus soli* is France prior to the 1992 reforms. These two principles are more well known in the context of the German-French debate on nationality derived from Johann Gottlieb Fichte's conception of "objective nationality" vs. Ernest

[116] Marriage to a citizen of a state may lead to gaining its citizenship. Not married foreign men, but foreign women are eligible for citizenship of her husband in some countries (e.g. Iran).

Renan's conception of "subjective nationality" (although France and Germany have still not implemented the pure forms of these principles). Like most other countries, they use today both principles at different scale for ascribing citizenship in order to be able to cope with blurred lines between them. Especially for cases of birth in the territory to stateless parents, unknown parents, or parents who cannot transmit their nationality, *Jus soli* is privileged instead of *Jus sanguinis* by dint of international treaties. The New World (e.g., the USA, Canada, Argentina, Brazil, etc.) actually prefers *Jus soli* to develop and increase their own citizenry. But, it can be observed that *Jus sanguinis* is still the more preferred means to acquisition of citizenship in the Old World (including most European countries with benefits of maintaining national identity as well as ethnic homogeneity). Peculiar legal regulations based on *Jus sanguinis* in nationality laws, such as facilitating naturalization of diaspora populations in the context of "ethnic/blood origin" and preventing people from traveling to a country with the intent of gaining citizenship for a child (e.g., Ireland since June 24, 2004,[117] India since July 1, 1987, Malta since August 1, 1989, and New Zealand since January 1, 2006) are becoming common.

Citizenship may also be acquired through naturalization as a consequence of migration. Naturalization refers to the act whereby a person obtains citizenship not at birth but later, and it usually takes place upon meeting specific state-defined requirements. Basic requirements generally include legal status as a permanent resident held by the applicant for a determined period and promises to obey the state's laws, to which an oath or pledge is sometimes necessary. In addition, some countries ask for renunciation of the person's previous citizenship. Unless resolved by denaturalization or renunciation, naturalization can bring about multiple citizenship.

Almost all countries in the English-speaking world are more liberal towards the multiple citizenship status. Canada has clearly accepted multiple citizenship since February 15, 1977 by its substantially

---

[117] 27th Amendment of the Constitution Act 2004 http://www.irishstatutebook.ie/2004/en/act/cam/0027/index.html

revised nationality law.[118] Also, Australia has not had any restrictions on multiple citizenship since April 4, 2002. Prior to 2002, multiple citizenship was also possible but in restricted circumstances. The USA (there is no definition in the Immigration and Nationality Act but the case Kawakita vs. the USA, 343 U.S. 717 (1952) of the United States Supreme Court determined dual citizenship as a "status long recognized in the law") and the UK (since the British Nationality Act of 1948) recognize and maintain multiple citizenship by their citizens. If their citizenship is acquired via naturalization, there is no need for renouncement of former citizenship. An oath of citizenship must be taken in order to become the USA citizen.[119] Also, people over the age of 18 who wish to become a UK citizen must take the oath of allegiance,[120] the affirmation of allegiance,[121] and the pledge in a citizenship ceremony.[122] New Zealand has also allowed multiple citizenship status since the creation of New Zealand citizenship on January 1, 1949., East Asia is more conservative towards the status of multiple citizenship. Countries like Japan, China, Singapore, South Korea, North Korea, and the Philippines do not permit multiple citizenship. Moreover,

[118] The oath of Canadian citizenship is as follows: "I swear (or affirm) that I will be faithful and bear true allegiance to Her Majesty Queen Elizabeth II, Queen of Canada, Her Heirs and Successors, and that I will faithfully observe the laws of Canada and fulfill my duties as a Canadian citizen."

[119] "I hereby declare, on oath, that I absolutely and entirely renounce and abjure all allegiance and fidelity to any foreign prince, potentate, state, or sovereignty of whom or which I have heretofore been a subject or citizen; that I will support and defend the Constitution and laws of the United States of America against all enemies, foreign and domestic; that I will bear true faith and allegiance to the same; that I will bear arms on behalf of the United States when required by law; that I will perform noncombatant service in the Armed Forces of the United States when required by the law; that I will perform work of national importance under civilian direction when required by the law; and that I take this obligation freely without any mental reservation or purpose of evasion."

[120] "I (name) swear by Almighty God that on becoming a British citizen, I will be faithful and bear true allegiance to Her Majesty Queen Elizabeth the Second, her Heirs and Successors, according to law."

[121] "I (name) do solemnly, sincerely and truly declare and affirm that on becoming a British citizen, I will be faithful and bear true allegiance to Her Majesty Queen Elizabeth the Second, her Heirs and Successors, according to law."

[122] "I will give my loyalty to the United Kingdom and respect its rights and freedoms. I will uphold its democratic values. I will observe its laws faithfully and fulfill my duties and obligations as a British citizen."

some Arabian countries do not either, and even implement criminal penalties. French nationality law has allowed multiple citizenship since 1973, but the other citizenship must be a partner state and signatory to European Convention on Nationality. South Africa did not recognize the status until 2004, but has recently permitted multiple citizenship to a certain extent. The Netherlands began recognizing multiple citizenship to some extent on April 1, 2003. In Morocco, a person having a dual nationality does not lose Moroccan nationality.

German citizenship may be obtained by naturalization by those with permanent residence who have lived in Germany for eight years. Additional requirements include an adequate command of the German language and an ability to be self-supporting without recourse to the social state. Furthermore, a central naturalization exam (*Einbürgerungstest*) has been in place in Germany since September 2008. Under a new law in 2000 of the Federal Republic of Germany, obtaining citizenship by means of the principle of *jus soli* and the naturalization process were made easier, although dual citizenship is more restricted. Applicants for naturalization are normally expected to prove they have renounced their existing citizenship, or will lose this automatically upon naturalization.[123] It is explicit that if migrants from Turkey to Germany prefer to obtain German citizenship, then they must renounce their Turkish citizenship, although Turkey permits double citizenship. Therefore, Turkish citizenship is also of concern.

Turkish citizenship is defined in Article 66 of the Constitution of the Republic of Turkey - 1982 Constitution.

> *s1* Everyone bound to the Turkish state through the bond of citizenship is a Turk.
>
> *s2* The child of a Turkish father or a Turkish mother is a Turk (*This sentence was abolished on October 3, 2001-Act 4709 Article 23*).

[123] An exception applies to those unable to give up their nationality easily (such as refugees). A further exception applies to citizens of EU member states.

> *s3* Citizenship can be acquired under the conditions stipulated by law, and shall be forfeited only in cases determined by law.
>
> *s4* No Turk shall be deprived of citizenship, unless he commits an act incompatible with loyalty to the motherland.
>
> *s5* Recourse to the courts in appeal against the decisions and proceedings related to the deprivation of citizenship, shall not be denied.

Turkish nationality law, which was last revised on February 11, 1964 (Act Number 403), is based primarily on the principle of *jus sanguinis*, like German nationality law. Article 1 states that "Children who are born to a Turkish citizen mother or a Turkish citizen father in or outside of Turkey shall be Turkish citizens effective from the moment of its birth". Still, the principle of *jus soli* exists in the Law. Article 4 reads that "Children, who were born in Turkey, but cannot acquire Turkish nationality by birth by virtue of their mother and father, shall be Turkish citizens effective from the moment of their birth". Like German citizenship, Turkish citizenship may be acquired by birth, descent, marriage or naturalization. In 1981, the Republic of Turkey amended its Nationality Law by Act No. 2383 to permit dual citizenship, taking into consideration the existence of the Turkish population abroad caused by labor migration and citizenship policy in most European countries. If Turkish citizens acquire an additional citizenship, the Republic of Turkey may grant a permit which protects their Turkish citizenship. It is clear that this amendment is mostly targeted towards Turkish citizens who live in a country whose state accepts dual citizenship. But, Turkish citizens residing in Germany, Austria, Denmark, and Sweden still face a dilemma as to which citizenship to choose. On June 7th, 1995, the Republic of Turkey amended Article 29, thereby regulating consequences of renouncement of Turkish citizenship in the Nationality Law by Act No. 4112. This amendment presupposes worries of some Turkish citizens abroad, who cannot obtain dual citizenship because of the nationality law restrictions in their resident country about being subjected to proceedings for foreigners in Turkey. Moreover, this amendment aims to solve the question of their refusal to renounce Turkish citizenship.[124] Article 29 is modified as follows: "The persons losing Turkish citizenship in accordance with this Act shall be treated as foreigners as of the date of loss of nationality. However, the persons who acquired the Turkish citizenship by birth and who acquired a foreign citizenship after an authorization of renunciation issued by the Council of Ministers, and their legal heirs, shall continue to benefit from the same rights on matters such as *residence, travel, working, inheritance, acquisition and transfer of movable and immovable goods*, the same rights as Turkish citizens, unless provided otherwise for the protection of the national security and the public order in Turkey. Provisions of Articles 33 and 35 remain reserved. [italics mine]" Pre-Turkish citizens, "foreigners having special status", continue to enjoy the same rights vested in Turkish citizens by means of a "pink card" on the matters in Article 29 after they acquire another citizenship as a result of obtaining *permission for renunciation.* Still, these "foreigners" having special status experienced some difficulties in the so-called pink card application due to ambiguities and contradictions with the foreigners law and the law of title deed. Afterwards, Article 29 was again modified by Act No. 5203 Amendment to the Turkish Nationality Law on June 29, 2004 as follows:

> "Persons who lost Turkish citizenship are treated as foreign persons starting from the date of loss. However, the ones who were born as Turkish citizens and have taken permission documents of quitting (renouncing) citizenship from the Ministry of Internal Affairs and their legal heirs registered in their quitting documenn re-

[124] It is stated in debates about this amendment that "Our citizens abroad wish to acquire the nationality of the state where they reside and work; but the respective states require the renunciation of Turkish nationality; whereas our citizens who had to obtain permission to renounce Turkish nationality in order to be able to acquire the nationality of the state of residence are made subject to the status of a foreigner in Turkey in accordance with Article 29 of the Turkish Nationality Act; this practice however has given rise to our citizens in question giving up their desire to acquire foreign nationality and thus the Act No. 4112 has been precisely drafted for the purpose of removing this difficulty." (See "Türk Vatandaşlığı Kanununun Bir Maddesinde Değişiklik Yapılmasına İlişkin Kanun Tasarısı ve İçişleri Komisyonu Raporu (1/846)" (Draft Statute Concerning the Amendment of an Article of the Turkish Nationality Act and the Report of the Ministry of Interior Commission (1/846)), TBMM Tutanak Degisi, C. LXXXVIII, S. Sayısı 842, p. 1.)

main protected by their acquired rights regarding social security, *except for citizen's rights of drafting, voting, joining public duties and importing house furniture and vehicles* on condition of the sentences concerning the national defense and public order of the Republic of Turkey. They continue to benefit from the rights acknowledged for Turkish citizens in exactly the same way by virtue of the related laws regulating their usage. Provisions of Articles 33 and 35 remain reserved. [trans. and italics mine]"[125]

The related people are given "the document about the usage of rights acknowledged with the Act No. 5203". The document, currently called "blue card" instead of "pink card", is obligatory to show during procedures with an identity card showing citizenship.

Between 1995 and 2000, there was an increase in the number of naturalizations of Turkish citizens in Germany, which I contend is because of Act No. 4112 Amendment to the Turkish Nationality Law and due to the effect of refugees from Turkey. There has been a decrease in the number since 2000, which I argue is because of difficulties in the implementation and use of the "pink card" and the new barrier against dual citizenship by amendments to the German Nationality Law in 2000. I estimate that there has been a rise in the amount of transformation from Turkish citizenship to German citizenship in Germany since 2005 by means of Act No. 5203 Amendment.

The Republic of Turkey began to draw more attention to people having Turkish origin in Germany with the AKP government. For the last years the prime ministers of the origin and destination countries (Erdoğan and Merkel) have more frequently come together in the front of the public of "people with Turkish migration

[125] "Bu Kanun gereğince Türk Vatandaşlığını kaybeden kişiler, kayıp tarihinden başlayarak yabancı muamelesine tâbi tutulur. Ancak doğumla Türk Vatandaşı olup da, İçişleri Bakanlığından vatandaşlıktan çıkma izni alanlar ve bunların vatandaşlıktan çıkma belgesinde kayıtlı reşit olmayan çocukları; Türkiye Cumhuriyetinin milli güvenliğine ve kamu düzenine ilişkin hükümler saklı kalmak kaydıyla, askerlik hizmetini yapma yükümlülüğü ve seçme-seçilme, kamu görevlerine girme, muafen araç veya ev eşyası ithal etme hakları dışında, sosyal güvenliğe ilişkin kazanılmış hakları saklı kalmak ve bu hakların kullanımında ilgili kanunlardaki hükümlere tâbi olmak şartıyla Türk vatandaşlarına tanınan haklardan aynen yararlanmaya devam ederler. Kanunun 33 ve 35 inci madde hükümleri saklıdır."

background in Germany". More importantly, Erdoğan also visits to the town of Ludwigshafen in August 2008, scene of a recent tragic fire that killed five children and four adults all of whom are Turkish descent, and to the city of Hannover in April 2009 to attend the 65th birthday party of former Chancellor Gerhard Schröder gives more insights. During his both visits, he gave speech to the Turkish-origin community in Germany. Especially in the second visit he met with representatives of Turkish non-governmental organizations and left three main words: Turkish descents in Germany should learn German and think little of naturalization to be German citizen, all German citizens of Turkish descent should cast their votes in the elections, and Turkey is ready to build a strong bridge with Turkish descents in Germany.[126] I claim that these messages are traces of the emerging graduated sovereignty of the Republic of Turkey as the sending country.

3. Work

3.1. Relevance of Change in Recruitment and Labor Relations

It is necessary to explore the so-called "contractor firm" encountered in the interviews. However, this and similar kinds of companies should be examined in the broader context of private employment and recruitment agencies. They are a relatively new phenomenon on the labor market in the last two decades. These firms are referred to under a variety of names: recruitment company, third party recruiter, placement firm, employment agency, staffing company, labor provider, leasing firm, employee leasing, staff leasing, co-employment, employment exchange, hiring out of labor, contract work agency, temporary work agency, overseas recruitment agency, and so on. Additionally, the related terminology such as outsourcing, off shoring, on shoring, near shoring, on boarding, internet recruiting, headhunting, executive search, executive recruitment, talent staffing, professional employer organization, and body shopping became part of the labor market lexicon during the

[126] He added, "There are nearly 70 thousand Turkish employers in Germany. Their investments reached to 7.5 billion euro and their annual sales climbed to 33 billion euro. They employ 33 thousand people in their companies. We are proud of them."

1980s. Whereas there are only slight differences among them at best, all of them indicate a new age of recruitment processes and labor relations in the market. Consequently, the change in recruitment and employment with private agencies should be evaluated in detail.

Recruitment (employment, placement, staffing, and hiring) refers to the process of finding a person who can fulfill the requirements of a solicited position or required function. Recruitment is basically the process of matching a person to a job. Therefore, the employment relationship is established between a person called an "employee" (frequently referred to as "a worker") and an "employer", for whom the employee performs work under certain conditions in return for remuneration. The employment relationship as a legal notion is traditionally established through a labor agreement between these two parties (employee and employer), and hence their reciprocal rights, benefits, and obligations are defined in the context of labor law and social security.

Taking improving labor productivity and efficiency into consideration, Taylor first put forward recruitment as one of the tasks of administration to select the right person for the right job. Taylor (1911:59) suggested:

> "Now one of the very first requirements for a man who is fit to handle pig iron as a regular occupation is that he shall be so stupid and so phlegmatic that he more nearly resembles in his mental make-up the ox than any other type. The man who is mentally alert and intelligent is for this very reason entirely unsuited to what would, for him, be the grinding monotony of work of this character. Therefore the workman who is best suited to handling pig iron is unable to understand the real science of doing this class of work."

Consequently, selecting employees with appropriate abilities for each job is determined to be an administrative task, thus leading to the emergence of a division of labor between employees and administrators who are different from owners and organizers. This conception has lead to the creation of internal recruiters, now known as "human resources" (HR). Some have argued that the modern concept of HR (Human Resources) was an organizational development stemming from the human relations movement rather than the efficiency movement of Taylorism. Aside from Taylorism, which is known as scientific management, the development of HR is perceived to have been heavily influenced by Fordism and the reorganization of the productive process. The HR department, which in the past was known as the personnel office or just personnel, entered into business life in the 1960s and has become a staple within organizations. Its function covers not only recruiting but also interviewing, orienting, firing, exit interviewing, employee disputes, contracts, benefits, calculating salaries, organizing personal or occupational development programs for the personnel, etc. Here, however, the internal recruiter role of HR departments is the issue. HR staff mostly work inside organizations, and deal with matching a person to a job in the name of the organization. More importantly, the employment relationship intermediated or actually facilitated by the HR department is still a legal labor agreement of a definite nature between employee and employer, i.e., a bilateral agreement. Aside from the HR department as the internal recruiter, there are also external recruiters: public employment service and private employment agencies. Public employment service tries to intermediate and facilitate employment relationships between job seekers and enterprises looking for employees. After matching employer to employee, this public service is finished, and not a party in the employment relationship like the internal recruiter. Moreover, private employment agencies provide similar recruitment operation as service enterprises. However, they carry out operations on behalf of individuals or enterprises under private law, under contract, and in exchange for financial compensation.

As a relatively new phenomenon in the labor market, private employment agencies have emerged in the last few decades. The first private employment agency in the world, Engineering Agency, was opened in 1893 in the USA. Thereafter, some agencies were established only for artists, models, and writers. However, the initial boom of these agencies took place in the 1960s in the USA, and their growth and importance have rapidly increased since the 1990s in many countries around the world.[127] Most continental European countries resisted agreeing to private employment agencies for a long period because of a ban on such agencies in their national laws and the 1949 International Labor Organization (ILO) Convention No. 96 (the Free-Charging Employment Agencies Convention). On the one hand, International Confederation of Private Employment Agencies (CIETT) urged the European Commission to file a complaint about national regulations on the liberalization of private employment agency work, especially against Italy, Spain, and Germany in 1992. Besides these three countries, Greece, Finland, Sweden, and the Netherlands then started to take further steps within the regulations of national laws in order to recognize these agencies. On the other hand, CIETT seemed to be canalizing the ILO official position regarding the private employment agency sector, transitioning from the strict prohibition to formal recognition. The 1949 ILO Convention No. 96 was revised by the 1997 ILO Convention No. 181 on private employment agencies.[128] The 1997 ILO Convention No. 181, whilst having preambles such as "being aware of the importance of flexibility in the functioning of labour markets", "recognizing the role which private employment agencies may play in a well-functioning labour market" or "recalling the need to protect workers against abuses", states the necessity of the legal activation of these agencies. The Convention is also accompanied by Recommendation No. 188.[129] Twenty countries including some countries in Europe have already ratified the 1997

[127] Their chronological development can be seen through the establishments of their associations: American Staffing Association (founded in 1966), Independent Staffing Alliance (founded in 1962), Association of Executive Search Consultants (founded in 1959), Association of Canadian Search, Employment and Staffing Services-ACSESS (The Association of Professional Placement Agencies and Consultants (founded in 1962) and The Employment and Staffing Services Association of Canada (founded in 1968) were merged in 1998), International Confederation of Private Employment Agencies – CIETT (1967), European Confederation of Private Employment Agencies – Eurociett (1992), International Association of Labour Migration – IALM (founded in 2004), and Association of Labour Providers – ALP (founded in 2004).

[128] http://www.ciett.org/fileadmin/templates/ciett/docs/Text_ILO_Convention_181.pdf

[129] For text of the Convention: http://www.ciett.org/fileadmin/templates/ciett/docs/Text_ILO_Recommendation_N__188_on_Private_Employment_Agencie.pdf

ILO Convention No. 181 and its accompanying recommendation: Albania, Ethiopia, Finland, Japan, Morocco, the Netherlands, Panama, and Spain in 1999; the Czech Republic and Italy in 2000; the Republic of Moldova in 2001; Georgia and Portugal in 2002; Hungary in 2003; Belgium, Lithuania, and Uruguay in 2004; Bulgaria in 2005; Algeria and Suriname in 2006. Furthermore, CIETT has tried to convince states to change national legislation and regulations for the private employment agencies according to the 1997 ILO Convention No. 181, while suggesting that the national legislation take into account specific circumstances and capacities. Furthermore, national associations and international confederations of private employment agencies have already determined various standards of the terms and conditions of employment contracts as well as a code of practice (professional ethics, business ethics). For instance, charging employment seekers a fee, which is prohibited in all of the EU-15 countries, is forbidden by the CIETT's code of practice. It can be concluded that the continental countries have been endeavoring to integrate the new recruitment phenomenon and its agencies in the last decade. Yet it is important to recognize the non-ratification of the International Convention on the Protection of the Rights of All Migrant Workers and Members of their Families (adopted in December 18, 1990 by the United Nations Office of the High Commissioner for Human Rights (UNHCHR)) by any major migrant-labor-receiving countries, or any member of the EU.[130] Article 1 of the 1997 ILO Convention No. 181 establishes the definition of the private employment agency:

> 1. For the purpose of this Convention the term *private employment agency* means any natural or legal person, independent of the public authorities, which provides one or more of the following labour market services:
>
> (a) services for matching offers of and applications for employment, without the private employment agency becoming a party to the employment relationships which may arise therefrom;

[130] For text of the Convention: http://www.ohchr.org/english/law/pdf/cmw.pdf For an elaborative investigation of the reasons behind the non-ratification status related to this Convention in France, Germany, Italy, Poland, Spain, the United Kingdom, and Norway, see MacDonald and Cholewinski (2007).

(b) services consisting of employing workers with a view to making them available to a third party, who may be a natural or legal person (referred to below as a "user enterprise") which assigns their tasks and supervises the execution of these tasks;

(c) other services relating to jobseeking, determined by the competent authority after consulting the most representative employers and workers organizations, such as the provision of information, that do not set out to match specific offers of and applications for employment.

2. For the purpose of this Convention, the term "workers" includes jobseekers.

3. For the purpose of this Convention, the term *processing of personal data of workers* means the collection, storage, combination, communication or any other use of information related to an identified or identifiable worker.

It is hard to determine types of private employment agencies since their differences are intermingled and blurred. The new broad terminology used to describe them demonstrates this difficulty. It can still roughly be said that there are two different types of agencies according to their function and mode of operation. The first type of agency's service is to mediate a contract between the job seeker and its client company looking to hire an employee to fulfill a fixed-term job vacancy ("temporary employment") in order to charge a fee from the company. In its function, the first type of agency is not different than internal recruiters and public employment services. The first type of private employment agency coincides with item *a* in Article 1 of the 1997 ILO Convention No. 181. The second type of agency recruits and hires the employee on its own, and then lends or hires the person as a temporary employee to its clients ("employee leasing"). This type fits item *b* in the Article 1 of the Convention. The second type of agency is their employer and is responsible for remuneration of the employee's labor. The agency's employee is often ineligible to apply for internal openings in the client firm. Almost all interviewees use the term "project" frequently, as can be seen in the interviews. Its usage sometimes points to this form of leasing.

It may be useful to define similarities between agencies. A basic similarity amongst private external recruiters is that their main task is to provide coherent contacts between their client companies and the candidates they recruit for a position. They occasionally offer a permanent work position to the job seekers, but almost all offered positions at their client companies are for a certain period of time (temporary, contractual, seasonal) ranging from one week up to two years.[131] The job position can be full-time, part-time, or on an hourly basis. They may also offer consultancy or other administrative services such as HR consultancy, sales or business development for their client companies. All their offerings can be seen as management services often called outsourcing. Outsourcing refers to the act of delegating a number of non-core operations to an external actor. Private employment agencies, which generally work for more than one company, respond, deploy, and provide specified requirements of their clients including HR. Many specialize in a particular profession such as ICT, accounting, health care, domestic, technical, or secretarial labor.[132]

Two characteristics of private employment agencies of great importance to the current thesis are their affect on labor migration and their focus on skilled labor. Their services are often offered internationally. In this context, they operate in international labor migration. There is also a common argument that employee leasing is an easier way to overcome some legal barriers of recruiting migrant labor.[133] The new recruitment processes are especially widespread in executive and professional job positions. Executive and professional searches, or informal headhunting, are common worldwide. In fact, most agency workers are university graduates.[134] In particu-

[131] Although under qualified employees work with contact in a relatively short period (2-3 weeks), high-qualified personnel work a fixed-term which ranges from two months up to six months or more (Nyström, 2005:203).

[132] For details on temporary employments in Germany including employment for highly skilled labor, see Bolder et al., 2005. Moreover, for the related literature, see http://www.igzeitarbeit.de/ seiteinfoliteratur.htm [June 15, 2008 visited]

[133] Nyström (2005:199) touched on this issue in her article on Sweden.

[134] For Sweden, Nyström (2005:200) actually states "[a]lmost half of all agency workers are university graduates and women dominate the group". However, she expresses that

lar, the ICT sector seems to be the field in which the private agencies have become most integrated. Almost all other sectors have required ICT to adapt their operations to the information society. However, the size of the required labor force for the ICT is hard to predict. For instance, some contingencies, like Y2K (the year 2000 problem, or the millennium bug), created a shortage of skilled labor. As well, some contingencies, like the dot-com boom (dot-com bubble), initially resulted in rapidly increasing new Internet-based companies, and then a big recession. In other words, large segments of the ICT labor force have become redundant at times. Consequently, fixed-term work, hiring out of temporary labor, or project-based contracts began to dominate the ICT sector. The typical contract period for ICT specialists is six months, which is known as a probationary period. However, the contracts are repeated as long as needed by the company and the agency unless any conflicts arise among the parties.

A new phenomenon in the labor market is not only fee-charging from the recruitment process, but also a change of the typical employment relationship. The existence of private employment agencies alone has not caused this change, but has encouraged the labor market to become more flexible. These agencies cultivate all types of labor market flexibility: (i) external numerical flexibility (temporary or fixed-term employment contracts), (ii) internal numerical flexibility (overtime, part-time work and irregular working times; working time flexibility), (ii) functional flexibility (task and job rotation, outsourcing), (iv) wage flexibility, and (v) flexibility of place.[135] In fact, private employment agencies support new forms of employment relationships within a flexible labor market. Depending on the type of private employment agency, the noticeability varies. For example, commercial law and standard contract law

---

women mostly engage in typical women's jobs such as nursing, education, secretarial, and domestic labor.

[135] The first four well-known types of labor market flexibility are designated by Atikson (Atikson, 1984; Atkinson and Meager, 1986). Additionally, Reilly (2001) and Wallace (2003) make mention of locational flexibility. For an elaborated study on working time flexibility, see also Chung et al.. (2007).

rather than employment law and labor law start to dominate the recruitment process in the labor market. Moreover, employment relations have not only been open-ended and bilateral, but also closed-ended and triangular. The agencies exist as a new party in employment relations, besides the employer, and the employee.

The change in labor relations can be described as two mutual dependencies. On the one hand, the rise in unemployment rates and spontaneously increasing demand for highly qualified labor reveal flexible labor relations. On the other hand, these relations bring about the popularization of part- and short-time (un)employment and accordingly rise in turnover rates. As a consequence, life-long work guarantees become nearly nonexistent. It is hard to have seniority in the same firm. The trend is towards a continuously growing list of former employers on curriculum vitae.

3.2. Structure of Labor Relations in Germany: an Amalgam of Social State and Flexibility

Etymologically, *Sozialstaat* in German ("social state"), whose rough equivalent in English is "welfare state" (*Wohlfahrtsstaat*) has been coined as a contrast to the "warfare state" of Nazi Germany. Although the terms "social state" and "welfare state" are used interchangeably in some literature, there are some distinctive differences in their objectives. On the one hand, the "social state" identifies a state that ensures "social protection" under the idea of societal solidarity and equality.[136] Germany is generally considered to have had the first social state, followed by the Scandinavian countries. In fact, this model was seen as a middle way between communism and capitalism during the Great Depression.[137] On the other hand, the "welfare state" is interpreted as a model in which the state assumes primary responsibility for the well-being of its citizens. Therefore, any state with the capacity to provide welfare is a "welfare state" but not necessarily "social state". An early version of the welfare state appeared through socioeconomic reforms called

[136] The term "social security" is mostly used synonymously with "social protection".

[137] For the term "welfare state" see O'Hara (1999:1245).

“*xin fa*” (new policies) in China in the 11th century. Wáng Ānshí, the prime minister at that time, believed that the state was responsible for providing its citizens with indispensable goods for a modest standard of life. But, modern welfare states, including Saudi Arabia, Kuwait, and the United Arabia Emirates, all distribute their wealth to their citizens. In many present-day welfare states, especially in continental Europe, welfare services are in fact not only provided by the state, but also by civil society, i.e., non-governmental organizations, or through a combination of these agencies. It is believed that current welfare services lead to the regulation of the informal economy, and influence how their citizens consume and spend their time.[138] The welfare state is generally identified as a distinctive combination of democracy and capitalism. Although the two terms “social state” and “welfare state” are very controversial, it can be argued that their meanings are intermingled.

The term “social security”, derived from “social state”, mainly refers to “social welfare services”. It is concerned with received benefits and services, which covers retirement pensions, disability insurance, survivor benefits, and unemployment insurance. The term may also mean income maintenance in the case of interruption of employment, including retirement, disability, and unemployment. In addition, it may mean social services such as medical care, aspects of social work, and even recruitment by public agencies. Occasionally, the term is used to refer to basic security, i.e., access to basic necessities, such as food, clothing, shelter, education, and medical care. Still, all these examples indicate a system of regulation and redistribution of national wealth to protect the living standards of citizens. In other words, it is a set of benefits to reduce socially recognized deprivations, including poverty, old age, disability, unemployment and so forth.

In the Federal Republic of Germany, the framework of legal commercial employee leasing has been determined from 1972 onward by the Employee Leasing Law (*Arbeitnehmerüberlassungsgesetz,*

[138] See Esping-Andersen (1999) and Rice et al. (2006).

AÜG).[139] In fact, private employment agencies are officially permitted in Germany with some restrictions in the frame of licensing prerequisites, special regulations for employment relationships, and social security laws. It can be said that the relevant legal framework is somewhat elaborate, although it has been renovated two times in the last years. Moreover, it includes definite exceptions for some leasing situations; in particular, there is no limitation for inter-corporate leasing. In fact, the legal framework causes "a rather dangerous environment with many hidden risks for those transgressing" according to Shüren (2005:67,76-77).[140] The leaser firm must establish an employment relationship with the leased person for an unlimited time period (§ 9, No. 2, AÜG). In other words, the leaser is responsible for paying the leased person during the entire leasing period, not simply during his/her working time. As a result, hiring a worker in line with demand "just once without the intent of doing it repeatedly" signifies a fake leasing contract (Shüren, 2005:69). The maximum duration of a legal employee leasing was two years until January 2002, whereas it became possible without time limit in January 2004. Moreover, the leased employee must be paid exactly the same wage and given the same fringe benefits (social security benefits) as other employees of the lessee's company after one year (§ 10, ¶ 5, AÜG). Furthermore, the leased employee, like all employees, has a right to an annual minimum four weeks vacation, as well a right to paid sick leave for a maximum six weeks in case of sickness and a parental leave regulated by the Maternity Protection Act. The leased employee also has the right to vote for the works council (*Betriebsrat*) of the lessee's firm after three-months employment (§ 7, sent. 2, BetrVG).[141] As a result, the leaser bears the economic risk if there is no opportunity to hire out of the employee, whereas there is an inclination to shift this risk to the employee by the "synchronization" of the hiring periods with the employment contract (Shüren, 2005). Such synchronization is

[139] For the text of AÜG (*Gesetz zur Regelung der gewerbsmäßigen Arbeitnehmerüberlassung*): http://bundesrecht.juris.de/a_g/BJNR113930972.html [June 15, 2008 visited]
[140] See also Schüren. *Kommentar Zum AÜG*. 2003.
[141] *Betriebsverfassungsgesetz, BetrVG* (Work Council Constitution Act).

prohibited (§ 3, ¶ 1, No. 3, AÜG and 5; § 9, No. 2, AÜG), but the related prohibition does not cover the possible synchronization strategies of the firms, it is difficult to identify them. The AÜG includes regulation dealing with not only employment relations of native leasers but also transnational employee leasing taking place in Germany (§ 3, ¶ 2-5, AÜG).

> § 3, ¶ 2 Die Erlaubnis oder ihre Verlängerung ist ferner zu versagen, wenn für die Ausübung der Tätigkeit nach § 1 Betriebe, Betriebsteile oder Nebenbetriebe vorgesehen sind, die nicht in einem Mitgliedstaat der Europäischen Wirtschaftsgemeinschaft oder einem anderen Vertragsstaat des Abkommens über den Europäischen Wirtschaftsraum liegen.
>
> § 3, ¶ 3 Die Erlaubnis kann versagt werden, wenn der Antragsteller nicht Deutscher im Sinne des Artikels 116 des Grundgesetzes ist oder wenn eine Gesellschaft oder juristische Person den Antrag stellt, die entweder nicht nach deutschem Recht gegründet ist oder die weder ihren satzungsmäßigen Sitz noch ihre Hauptverwaltung noch ihre Hauptniederlassung im Geltungsbereich dieses Gesetzes hat.
>
> § 3, ¶ 4 Staatsangehörige der Mitgliedstaaten der Europäischen Wirtschaftsgemeinschaft oder eines anderen Vertragsstaates des Abkommens über den Europäischen Wirtschaftsraum erhalten die Erlaubnis unter den gleichen Voraussetzungen wie deutsche Staatsangehörige. Den Staatsangehörigen dieser Staaten stehen gleich Gesellschaften und juristische Personen, die nach den Rechtsvorschriften dieser Staaten gegründet sind und ihren satzungsgemäßen Sitz, ihre Hauptverwaltung oder ihre Hauptniederlassung innerhalb dieser Staaten haben. Soweit diese Gesellschaften oder juristische Personen zwar ihren satzungsmäßigen Sitz, jedoch weder ihre Hauptverwaltung noch ihre Hauptniederlassung innerhalb dieser Staaten haben, gilt Satz 2 nur, wenn ihre Tätigkeit in tatsächlicher und dauerhafter Verbindung mit der Wirtschaft eines Mitgliedstaates oder eines Vertragsstaates des Abkommens über den Europäischen Wirtschaftsraum steht.
>
> § 3, ¶ 5 Staatsangehörige anderer als der in Absatz 4 genannten Staaten, die sich aufgrund eines internationalen Abkommens im Geltungsbereich dieses Gesetzes niederlassen und hierbei sowie bei ihrer Geschäftstätigkeit nicht weniger günstig behandelt werden dürfen als deutsche Staatsangehörige, erhalten die Erlaubnis unter den gleichen Voraussetzungen wie deutsche Staatsangehörige. Den Staatsangehörigen nach Satz 1 stehen gleich Ge-

sellschaften, die nach den Rechtsvorschriften des anderen Staates gegründet sind.

3.3. Work Ethic and Culture

The interviewees almost always open with a subject regarding work ethic and culture. Thus, flexible labor relations bring about a change in work culture. To explore this alteration, emergence of work ethic in human life and its evolution in the current labor relations should be explained. Work culture refers to attributing a social value to labor affiliation and the share of work in life. Work ethic is a set of values based on the moral virtues of hard work and diligence.[142]

In the Ancient World and the Middle Ages, that is, in pre-modern societies, there were different bases of labor relations and human beings were not subject to work ethic, but simply they did have work culture. Human beings were, and still are, need of a kind of discipline in order to deal with the anarchy of nature. This dealing in the self-imposed discipline brought about the emergence of culture. In this old work culture, only physical work was postulated as work, but philosophizing as leisure. This approach to the matter gradually changed until the emergence of modern societies.

Attempting to solve the anarchy of nature, human beings acknowledged the absence of any ultimate victory over nature, and this gave rise to the inner chaos of human beings. They have had "the permanent need to combat inner anarchy without expectation of victory" (Sennett, 1999:101). Therefore, the self-discipline of the farmers as deteriorating psychic beings transformed into "practical stoicism". While the time schedule of monotheistic religions such as the ringing of church bells and the five calls a day of muezzins from mosques regulate worship for the inner order, it supports time organization of work for the external order. In the Middle Ages there was a belief that work before the great beyond should be interpreted as plight and punishment, as Augustine of Hippo men-

[142] It should not be confused with the term "business ethics" which is a form of applied ethics that examines principles and moral problems that arise in a business environment.

tioned. Self-disciplined use of one's time and delay of gratification began to be perceived as human virtue. Work is still appreciated as burden rather than desire. In other words, people determine their values through work, in the form of "worldly asceticism", as Weber called it in his famous article on work ethic, *The Protestant Ethic and the Spirit of Capitalism.* Human beings, who worked before as a requirement of nature, start to work as a requirement of culture. This new socially coded work culture, by introducing work ethic, is based on individualism and defines who the virtuous human is through their approach towards work.

The shift of working to eat to eating for work requires discrete motivation. This is the desire for self-realization of human beings. That is, it paves the way for *homo faber,* who individually creates her/his own history. Throughout the Enlightenment, the existing approach towards daring to know and rationalizing social acts, including stoic praxis, actually changed perception of work. It is no longer seen as a burden but as a desire. From this perspective, Sennett (1999:102) criticizes Weber's study in neglecting the contradiction of self-discipline and self-fashioning and only focusing on their combination. Weber started his query with why "modern culture" was a current reality in western countries and then focused on understanding „*spezifisch gearteten Rationalismus der okzidentalen Kultur*" (specific-natured rationalism of occidental culture). By evaluating the relation of the substance of Christian faith to work ethic, he tried to explain "occidental rationalism" in work. He explores that the Protestant work ethic sees work as duty and responsibility, which people must not question. Work is then socially constructed as the focus of life, and leisure or free time revolve around it. Weber (1904/1905) described the view of the Protestant work ethic intermingling with capitalism in the sixteenth century:

> „Jener eigentümliche, uns heute so geläufige und in Wahrheit doch so wenig selbstverständliche Gedanke der Berufspflicht, einer Verpflichtung, die der einzelne empfinden soll und empfindet gegenüber dem Inhalt seiner ‚beruflichen' Tätigkeit, gleichviel worin sie besteht, gleichviel insbesondere ob sie dem unbefangenen Empfinden als reine Verwertung seiner Arbeitskraft oder gar nur seines Sachgüterbesitzes (als ‚Kapital') erscheinen muss –

> dieser Gedanke ist es, welcher der ‚Sozialethik' der kapitalistischen Kultur charakteristisch ist [...] Die Fähigkeit der Konzentration der Gedanken sowohl als die absolut zentrale Fähigkeit, sich der Arbeit gegenüber verpflichtet zu fühlen, finden sich hier besonders oft vereinigt mit strenger Wirtschaftlichkeit, die mit dem Verdienst und seiner Höhe überhaupt rechnet und mit einer nüchternen Selbstbeherrschung und Mäßigkeit, welche die Leistungsfähigkeit ungemein steigert. Der Boden für jene Auffassung der Arbeit als Selbstzweck, als ‚Beruf', wie sie der Kapitalismus fordert, ist hier am günstigsten".

Weber concludes that the individual's will to work easily attaches to the spirit of capitalism by rationalized asceticism. Both Weber and Sennett are in the same camp while indicating "the driven human being". However, Sennett's question here to is how human beings will to work and why they organize their life according to work. His answer is that human beings, by becoming the corporate conformists, expose their predictable and reliable character in the name of self-justification. *Homo faber* dares to take the place of the holy Creator by appreciating her/his reason, knowledge, and experience in order to make his/her life. Due to the Renaissance, human beings have recognized that they have to and have made history. Therefore, this recognition turned into a re-defined motivation to hard work and be diligent for their future. The deep-rooted practice of stoicism has been of assistance to this motivation.

Capitalist labor relations continuously maintain the existing work culture. According to the capitalist work ethic, workers are driven to exhibit good work performance (working hard and playing by the rules). If they do, they are selected for promotion. If workers fail to exhibit good work performance, they are regarded as failing to provide fair value for the wage. Marx's theory of alienation, which initially provided an economic-political dimension in the framework of the labor relations of capitalist production, exposes the problems of the workers. That is the state of feeling separated from one's milieu, process of production, products of work, and self. Consequently, labor estranges not only nature from human beings but also human beings from themselves. Furthermore, it is believed that slacker and hippie cultures have challenged these values since the nineteenth century. They noted how "alienation" of the workers was destructive to work ethic because the workers of these subcultures saw no point in doing any more than the minimum. Later, the Taylorism revised the notion of work ethic to include giving up control over the work process to "scientific management" so that the workflow process is rationalized. The notion of work ethic has thereafter been included within the acknowledgment of management control. Taylorism presents a task-oriented optimization of work by analyzing workflow processes in order to improve labor productivity. This understanding is often mentioned along with Fordism.

Fordism, which is specific to automobile manufacturing, has four key elements. First, it is characterized by a distinctive division of labor – the separation of different work tasks between different groups of workers. Second, parts and components are highly standardized. Third, it is organized not around groups of similar machinery, but machines arranged in the correct sequence required to manufacture a product. Finally, the various parts of the production process are linked together by a moving conveyor belt – the assembly line – to facilitate the quick and efficient fulfillment of tasks. Consequently, a system like Frankenstein governs its producer, *homo faber*. Disciplined work is considered to be a moral duty, a social obligation, and the route to individual success. Foucault defines discipline as an act of self-punishment, by seeing modernity as disciplinary society. As a matter of fact, work ethic is constructed under social control as a belief in the moral benefit of work and its ability to enhance character. It includes being reliable, having initiative, and maintaining social skills. By Gorz's account (1989), the ideology of work assumes (i) the positive relation between the amount of individual work and the quality of life for everyone; (ii) identification of people who work little or not at all as going against the interests of the community as a whole and as unworthy of being members of it; and (iii) determination of the worker being to blame for each of his own success and failure.

The semantic change of work ethic is related to the transformation from the work-based society to the knowledge-based society. Gorz (1989:42) writes about the crisis of the work ethic:

> "In actual fact the work ethic has become obsolete. It is no longer true that producing more means working more, or that producing more will lead to a better way of life. The connection between more and better has been broken; our needs for many products and services are already more than adequately met, and many of our as-yet-unsatisfied needs will be met not by producing more, but by producing differently, producing other things, or even producing less. This is especially true in regards to our needs for air, water, space, silence, beauty, time and human contact. Neither is it true any longer that the more each individual works, the better off everyone will be. The present crisis has stimulated technological change of an unprecedented scale and speed: 'the micro-chip revolution'. The object and indeed the effect of this revolution have been to make rapidly increasing savings in labour, in the industrial, administrative and service sectors. Increasing production is secured in these sectors by decreasing amounts of labour. As a result, the social process of production no longer needs everyone to work in it on a full-time basis. The work ethic ceases to be viable in such a situation and work-based society is thrown into crisis."[143]

Not only is ICT expertise essential in the core occupations of the "knowledge-based society", but it also intersects nearly all-economic sectors. As a consequence, ICT specialists are necessitated, privileged, and welcomed in the global labor market. It is believed that migrants in the 1990s accounted for about one-third of the increase in employment among computer engineers, systems analysts, and computer programmers. One can argue that the labor market has been internationalized for the ICT specialists.

Highly skilled workers differ only slightly from un- or semi-skilled workers if we think of projects as assembly lines.[144] In the context of spatial-temporal dimensions, there is no necessity to stand in the

---

[143] Ibid.

[144] Specialization of HSL correlates to specialized tasks in the assembly line by using the ideas of division of labor and interchangeable parts to create assemblies from parts in a repetitive manner. Assembly lines do not increase the speed of producing a single unit, but only increases the rate when there is a stream of units to be produced. This is mass production. While the assembly line is flowing, workers have to stand in the same place in line for hours and repeat the same motion hundreds of times per day. Moreover, these semi-skilled workers have only seconds or minutes to do their task. The workers are, in due course, replaced with machines which have ability to do some of these specialized tasks together.

same place for highly skilled workers but it is still important to stand in the right place at the right time.

3.4. Gender Gap in the ICT sector

The male dominance in the labor market is not disputable in any country. On the one hand, female labor power is concentrated in domestic and care labor fields, while men dominate in applied science and engineering. Women are more likely to enroll in fields related to health care professions, education, and in the social and behavioral sciences, while they are less likely to enroll in natural sciences and in industrial and engineering fields. The leading positions in any sector, on the other hand, seem to be allocated for men. Teachers are often women, but school directors and principals are more often men. Most assistants and secretaries in universities are women, but professors are generally men. Women usually work as nurses and pharmacists, however doctors are mostly men.

Turkey and Germany have significantly different pictures of the participation of the female workforce into the labor market and labor distribution between the sexes. The comparison between these two countries in this context enables observations and experiences of the HSL migrants from Turkey in Germany, especially female ones.

Looking at the "formal" numbers, women in Germany take part in the labor market more than in Turkey. The overall employment ratio in the population between 15 and 64 years old in 2003 was only about 26 percent among women in Turkey. In the same year, 59 percent of women between 15 and 64 in Germany were employed.[145] Although Turkey has a lower proportion of female students and graduates than any EU member country, the gender balance is less entrenched, with relatively more female representatives in the natural sciences and in industrial and engineering fields.[146] In fact, it is clear that women have a relatively high representation in

---

[145] Source: European Commission 2004. http://www.bmfsfj.de/bmfsfj/generator/Publikationen/genderreport/2-Erwerbstaetigkeit-arbeitsmarktintegration-von-frauen-und-maenner/2-2-europaeischer-vergleich.html

[146] This is supported by OECD Education Database 1995 and Eurostat 2004.

sciences and engineering in Turkey in comparison with the West Europe. In 1998, the percentage of female students in engineering departments was 25 percent in Turkey, while it was just 19 percent in Germany (Zengin-Arslan, 2002). The female academic rate is about 36 percent in Turkey, female lecturers in the natural sciences in tertiary education make up 40 percent of the total (20 percent in Germany), and female lecturers in the engineering departments constitute 29 percent of the whole (13 percent in Germany) according to TÜBİTAK.[147] In Turkey, men dominate the departments of mechanical, electric and electronic engineering, while the gender distribution in departments of computer engineering, industrial engineering, and other scientific fields related with the ICT sector is comparable.[148]

The same proportions are reflected in the labor market of the ICT sector. In Turkey, despite the absence of formal statistics of this manner, media analyses estimate that female employment ratio in the ICT sector is dramatically high in comparison with other sectors – about 40 percent.[149] According to the statistics about the gender balance in Germany from the Federal Statistical Office, the overall rate of female workers in the ICT sector is near 26 percent and the rate of women among ICT-Specialists is only about 15 percent in 971,000 in Germany.[150]

---

[147] www.empoweringwomantr.org/tr/calismalarimiz/calisankadinlar.ppt See also Kalkan, 2002.

[148] For information, see also http://www.sas.com/offices/europe/turkey/news/basindasas/inthenews_new_010706.htm

[149] http://www.kadinhayat.com/reader.php?cat_id=8&id=2614

[150] www.netzwerk-fit.de/tools/statistiken/arbeit/Erwerbstaetige_in_IuK-Berufen_nach_geschlecht.pdf

CHAPTER 6. TYPOLOGY OF HSLM

In the following, under five dimensions, I will reevaluate the common and distinct attributes derived from the theoretical sample. They will be examined within the whole data framework which consists of 33 interviews in the study. In doing so, interpretations and contextualizations will be brought together in order to present the typology of HSLM from Turkey to Germany.

Before introducing the developed typology of HSLM, I would like to underline one point. Geographical mobility and immobility in Turkey before international labor migration provides important clues to answer the question of who HSL migrants are. Although it is not used as a dimension in itself, geographical mobility crosscuts all five dimensions of the typology to some degree. In order to explain geographical mobility in Turkey, I roughly clustered the cities into four modified regions: (i) *Istanbul*; (ii) *Ankara;* (iii) *West* (of Ankara); and (iv) *East* (of Ankara). As such neither the classical seven regions determined by climate geography nor more the complex twelve regions coded by the nomenclature of territorial units for statistics (NUTS)[1] are employed in my study. It is not surprising that Istanbul and Ankara, as the two biggest metropolitan areas of Turkey, have distinguishing properties[2] according to the social and economic development indicators in education and labor market. Furthermore, since the urban versus rural distinction is quite meaningful for West and East Regions, the regions referred to in-

[1] Turkey is typically divided into seven regions: Marmara, Aegean, Black Sea, Central Anatolia, Eastern Anatolia, Southeastern Anatolia, and the Mediterranean. To the hierechical list of NUTS, Turkey is divided into twelve regions: Istanbul (TR1), West Marmara (TR2), Aegean (TR3), East Marmara (TR4), West Anatolia (TR5), Mediterranean (TR6), Central Anatolia (TR7), West Black Sea (TR8), East Black Sea (TR9), Northeast Anatolia (TRA), Middle East Anatolia (TRB), and Southeast Anatolia (TRC). See http://ec.europa.eu/eurostat/ramon/nuts/codelist_en.cfm?list=cec

[2] There are eventually a total of sixteen metropol municipalities in Turkey.

crease to six: (i) Istanbul; (ii) Ankara; (iii) Urban-West; (iv) Urban-East; (v) Rural-West; and (vi) Rural-East. This division reveals more explanatory statements regarding highly educated people and their origins in Turkey, and as such it is the geographical terminology used in the current thesis.

1. Family Background

The empirical study shows that the HSL migrants come from nuclear families in Turkey and their family size ranges between three and five individuals. Most families have an internal migration background. Some even have emigrant roots. Two of them are especially interesting, since they moved to Germany to work and came back to Turkey after a while in the 1970s. In other words, these two are return guest worker families.

1.1. Difference in Family Models: Cultural Capital of the Mother

As shown in TABLE 7, the educational attainment of the parents in the case study are much higher than average in Turkey.[3] It can still be claimed, however, that there are two similarities of the sample to the whole picture of Turkey: parents having lower educational position come predominantly from rural areas, more particularly Rural-East and the gender gap in the education level is still present, albeit fairly smaller. Also, gendered labor division between the parents is noticeable in the case of some families. In other words, the father appears as breadwinner of the family, the mother as housekeeper. As discussed in the interpretation reviews, there is a phenomenon whereby educated mothers in elite families do not work outside home, that is they should be considered housewives rather than unemployed women.

[3] In 15-64 age interval, people in Turkey having education higher than senior high school graduation consists of 1.4 percent in 1970, 3.2 percent in 1980, and 3.7 percent in 1990.

TABLE 7. PARENTS: EDUCATIONAL AND OCCUPATIONAL POSITIONS

Interviewees	Educational Position		Occupational Position	
	Mother	Father	Mother	Father
Prunus	Primary School	Primary School	Housewife	Skilled Worker
Buxus	University	University	White-Collar Worker	Professional
Magnolia	Vocational Tertiary	University	Housewife	Entrepreneur
Juglans	Primary School	Senior High School	Housewife	White-Collar Worker
Sorbus	Senior High School	Senior High School	White-Collar Worker	Skilled Worker
Salix	Vocational Tertiary	Vocational Tertiary	Worker	Skilled Worker
Rhus	Junior High School	Junior High School	Housewife	Entrepreneur
Castanea	University	University	Professional	Professional
Acer	Senior High School	Senior High School	Housewife	White-Collar Worker
Populus	University	University	Professional	Professional
Tilia	Primary School	Primary School	Housewife	Worker
Cercis	Senior High School	Senior High School	White-Collar Worker	White-Collar Worker
Fraxinus	Primary School	Vocational Tertiary	Housewife	Skilled Worker
Abies	Primary School	Senior High School	Housewife	White-Collar Worker
Fagus	Primary School	Senior High School	Housewife	Professional
Ailanthus	Senior High School	Junior High School	Housewife	Entrepreneur

Laburnum	Senior High School	University	White-Collar Worker	Professional
Sambucus	University	University	White-Collar Worker	White-Collar Worker
Juniperus	University	University	White-Collar Worker	White-Collar Worker
Rhamnus	Literate	Vocational Tertiary	Housewife	Professional
Syringa	Primary School	Primary School	Housewife	Worker
Hippophae	Senior High School	University	White-Collar Worker	Professional
Quercus	Primary School	Senior High School	Housewife	Skilled Worker
Mespilus	Senior High School	Senior High School	Housewife	Professional
Picea	University	University	Professional	Professional
Euonymus	University	University	Professional	Professional
Betula	Primary School	Primary School	Housewife	Skilled Worker
Morus	Senior High School	University	Housewife	Professional
Platanus	University	University	White-Collar Worker	Professional
Robinia	University	University	Professional	Professional
Celtis	Primary School	Primary School	Housewife	Skilled Worker
Pinus	Senior High School	University	Entrepreneur	Professional
Carpinus	Illiterate	Junior High School	Housewife	Skilled Worker

The existence of state-feminism in Turkey, which was explained in the chapter on the education system in Turkey, attempted to create gender role models and encourage women to be educated. State-feminism and its influences bring about the new mother model, that is, the educated housekeeper for middle and upper middle class families. If the father is able to provide high enough financial status for the family the mother likely would not work; it is also common to stop working after marriage. This pattern often changes if the wife has her own profession based on tertiary education, or if she is a white-collar worker. Apart from the mother being the "housewife" regardless of educational attainment, there are in fact a significant number of the mothers in this case study who have a professional life in the labor market.

The role model for Republican women in Turkey covers female careerists who are held in high esteem and remembered with respect in public, *persona grata*, even though they still try to comply with the patriarchal family model.

It is obvious that family background establishes the basis of the capital resources of HSL migrants and their aspirations. Taking all of the above into consideration, I implicitly argue that middle class fathers drive their children to education and prepare the necessary economic infrastructure; mothers educate the child by means of socio-cultural resources. I divide in TABLE 7 the occupational positions of the parents of HSL migrants into six categories: entrepreneurs, professionals, white-collar workers, skilled workers, and workers, in addition to housewives.[4] Furthermore, I propose a family background typology with two components. The first component is based on the mother's educational and working position in order to display the cultural status of the family, and the second is related to the socio-economic status of the whole family. As seen in FIGURE 8, by correlating the components, seven parent types emerged.

---

[4] The category of skilled workers mostly covers technicians. Artisans/craftsmen are also evaluated under this category. Low-level civil servants and teachers are attached into the white-collar workers. High-level civil servants and academicians are attached into the category of professional, which covers engineers, medical doctors, lawyers, and pharmacists.

FIGURE 8. CULTURAL STATUS REGARDING THE MOTHERS AND THEIR CORRELATION WITH SOCIO-ECONOMIC STATUS

Mother		**Work**	
		+	-
Education	+	2. Model	1. Model
	-		3. Model

Cultural Status	**Socio-Economic Status***		
	A	**B**	**C/D**
1.Model	+	+	- -
2.Model	+	+	- -
3.Model	-	+	+ +

*In terms of economic status, A is the highest quantile, B is the second highest quantile, C and D are the next quantiles by household income.

Musgrave (1979:71) said that the family "not only transmits material benefits to its offspring, but also passes on some of the more indefinable and immaterial aspects of social class." The current study supports this argument, by understanding immaterial benefits of the family as cultural capital. The educational attainment and employment situation of the mother are used as the main indicator to explain such phenomena.

1.2. Family Background Typology

Due to the family background typology, I categorized all interviewees, excluding Salix whose parents migrated from Bulgaria to Turkey via Russia.[5]

[5] His mother in spite of being educated works as a worker in Turkey, however this downward mobility dealing with their migration experience differs from the general parents picture of Turkey and I decided this case is exceptional.

1. **1A** refers to having an entrepreneur father and an educated housewife mother.
2. **1B** refers to having a professional/white-collar worker father and an educated housewife mother.
3. **2A** refers to having a professional father and an entrepreneur/professional/ white-collar worker mother.
4. **2B** refers to having a white-collar/skilled worker father and a white-collar worker mother.
5. **3B** refers to having a professional/white-collar worker father and an uneducated housewife mother.
6. **3C** refers to having a skilled worker father and an uneducated housewife mother.
7. **3D** refers to having a worker father and an uneducated housewife mother.

Among the family types, only 3D represents a working class family background. It is impressive, however, that this family type exists if and only if there is a migratory relation with Germany as "return guest worker". Another distinguishing factor is the lack of daughters in the family types 3C and 3D. The family types 3B/2B/2A/1B/1A live in urban areas, while the family type 3C is encountered mostly in rural areas. The family mobility, which depends on the occupational appointments of the parents, is seen in the family types 2B and 2A. Urban families are more mobile (urban-urban movements) than rural families. It is interesting to observe that the family type 1A tends to be sedentary. Moreover, among the parents there is the tendency to live on the coast after their retirement, which often coincides with the university graduation of their children. It is also common to oscillate between a metropolitan area and a smaller city. These points correspond to middle class status of the family.

1.3. Triviality of Kinship Network in the Host Country for HSLM

It is believed that most people in Turkey have at least one somewhat close relative in Germany. It is also generally argued that migration channels provided by the family network in Germany cause subsequent migrations from Turkey. This argument is not verified by the data of highly educated people. 28 out of 33 interviewees underline that they do not have any relatives in Germany, whereas only five cases mention the existence of their relatives in Germany. Two of them, Tilia and Syringa, who are the sole examples of family type 3D, differ from the others in having a returning guest worker family background. Their parents currently do not live in Germany but in Turkey, while the new generation has a propensity to live in Germany. This indicates that return German guest worker families' descendents have the potential for HSLM to Germany. Their kinship network in Germany facilitates the beginning period of their HSLM career. However, this network does not play a significant role after the stabilization of the migration. Moreover, Hippophae's father went to Germany for university education in the 1970s with his wife, but they then divorced and she returned to Turkey with their six-month-old child. Hippophae then visited Germany to see his father for the first time when he was 16 years old, because his father had had entry problems to Turkey due to political and military service issues. His father is currently a German citizen and works as a professional filmmaker. Except from these three generic cases, the other two participants are Rhus and Euonymusm, whose family background types are 1A and 2A, respectively. Both have relatively distant relatives in Germany in comparison with the previous three, but they have remained distant from their kinship network apart from Euonymus' taking advantage of it during her first internship period in Germany.

The rest of the interviewees do not have relatives in Germany. In addition, Fraxinus, Acer, and Quercus lived as HSL migrants in different countries before Germany, but they did not have any relatives in those host countries either. Clearly, there is not an important role of the kinship network in the host country in the context of HSLM.

Taking all interviews into consideration, it seems that the parents do not have any effect on the decision to migration of their highly educated children, or on their decision to return. This result contradicts some studies that argue for the role of family on the decision to return Turkey. This does not mean that HSL migrants do not have close family ties.[6] Family/kin networks in Turkey are still very strong, not only in rural life but in also urban life. With advances in ICT and transportation, HSL migrants are, however, able to maintain closer links with their home countries than ever before, and have the opportunity to travel between host and home countries. Almost all interviewees state that they have regular contact with their family and visit the family residence three to ten times per year. Their family members sometimes visit them as well. The important point here is that they mostly prefer constant and regular relations with their relatives, who have still hardly direct social control on their life in Germany.[7]

Moreover, it is obvious for HSL migrants from Turkey that leaving home is inevitable in order to be able to create their own lives. Relatedly, they figure that where they work – be it in Turkey or abroad - makes no difference regarding their relations with family. As a matter of fact, these migrants approach "being away" different than the idiom "out of sight, out of mind". To illustrate,

> "Because I studied at the university in Ankara, I have been far away from home for a long time. Therefore, they always know that I am fine. I do not call them often." (Laburnum, Family Background 2A)

> "I am from Ankara because that is my birthplace and where I grew up. However, I have been out of Ankara for seven-eight years and then I was based in Istanbul. It means again being far away from home, so it does not make any difference… We worked with technology. It was also impossible to go from Istanbul to Ankara every week, and hence you could talk on telephone, so there was no difference between a call from Istanbul and a call from Frankfurt." (Acer, Family Background 1B)

---

[6] Ritterberger-Tılıç and Kalaycıoğlu (1998:78-9) argue that family/kin networks in the context of Turkey can be seen as "alternative means of social control and organization" which "should not be understood as resistance to the goals of the constructed model of modernity and Westernization, but are perceived by the members of society as more efficient mechanisms to gain access to such goals", because of the limited state welfare agencies that are "not capable of offering solutions to their problems".

[7] I will explain more about freedom from societal pressure in the context of individuation in migration experience.

It is clear that highly-educated people, independent of their international migration experience, often establish their life with the presence of a spatial distance to their core family. They see this as a life imperative. They again underline their indifference to the kinship network, and even of the nuclear family. Their being distant from the family network is not unexpected and the spatial distance is even preferential for them, since it is similar to the conditions they had while in Turkey.

2. Educational Background

2.1. Importance of Geographical Mobility in Education

The common characteristic of the families of HSL migrants is the protection of their children from the disadvantages of their im/mobility. In other words, the parents stay in the current city, move to another city, or send their child there to provide better education for him/her. Some families take advantage of state-boarding schools, and some others prefer private schools to educate their children. It is also clear that families, if they live in a small city, often send their child to a bigger city in order to let them attend a better high school or university, or they even move explicitly for this purpose. These points indicate a feature of middle class family, which is very children-oriented.[8] In other words, the parents live in dependence of their children, they are very interested in them, move and behave according to their educational career. At the same token, these middle class parents' attitudes intermingle with the competitive market of the Turkish educational system. In order to see the educational background of HSL migrants, it is therefore important to look at their mobility before the start of their migration career.

As shown with the theoretical sample in TABLE 8, migrants' individual geographical mobility in Turkey comes about by two main route patterns: (i) rural to urban movement to attend secondary education; and (ii) of course along East-West-Ankara-Istanbul.

---

[8] This is also one of modernity indicators. The more traditional family model does not follow their children educational and professional career.

Both geographical movement directions in Turkey form an ordered, gradual, chosen career path toward becoming the HSL migrant. This geographical mobility model is also verified by other interviews (full data not shown).

TABLE 8. GEOGRAPHICAL MOBILITY IN TURKEY BEFORE HSLM

Interviewees	Origin*	Secondary Education	Tertiary Education	Working Experience in Turkey
Rhus	Istanbul	Istanbul	Ankara	Istanbul
Euonymus	Urban-West	Urban-West	Istanbul	None
Fraxinus	Rural-East	Urban-West	Istanbul	Urban-West, Istanbul
Syringa	Urban-East	Urban-East	Ankara	Ankara, Istanbul
Mespilus	Istanbul	Istanbul	Istanbul	Istanbul
Acer	Ankara	Ankara	Ankara	Istanbul
Ailanthus	Istanbul	Istanbul	Istanbul	None
Juglans	Ankara	Ankara	Ankara	Istanbul
Sorbus	Urban-West	Urban-West	Istanbul	None
Prunus	Rural-East	Urban-East	Urban-West	Urban-West
Magnolia	Urban-East	Urban-East	Ankara	Ankara, Urban-West, Istanbul
Quercus	Rural-West	Urban-West	Ankara	Ankara, Urban-West
Laburnum	Urban-West	Urban-West	Ankara	Istanbul
Sambucus	Urban-East	Ankara	Ankara	Ankara
Rhamnus	Rural-East	Urban-East	Ankara	Ankara, Istanbul

* Origin refers to the birth of place, except for Syringa born in Germany and Juglans in Istanbul, but they had then moved to the modified region of origin in the first years of their life.

As shown in FIGURE 9, the second direction followed in order to be a HSL migrant shows an ascending hierarchy between the above-defined four regions. If any HSL migrant was from East, they inevitably moved to Istanbul via first the West and then Ankara. If they were from the West, they necessarily move to Ankara and then Istanbul, or directly to Istanbul. If they were from Ankara, they stay there or move to Istanbul. Istanbulers were not in need of any movement before HSLM. The study displays that one hardly sets off in the opposite direction.

FIGURE 9. PATTERN OF GEOGRAPHICAL MOBILITY IN TURKEY BEFORE HSLM

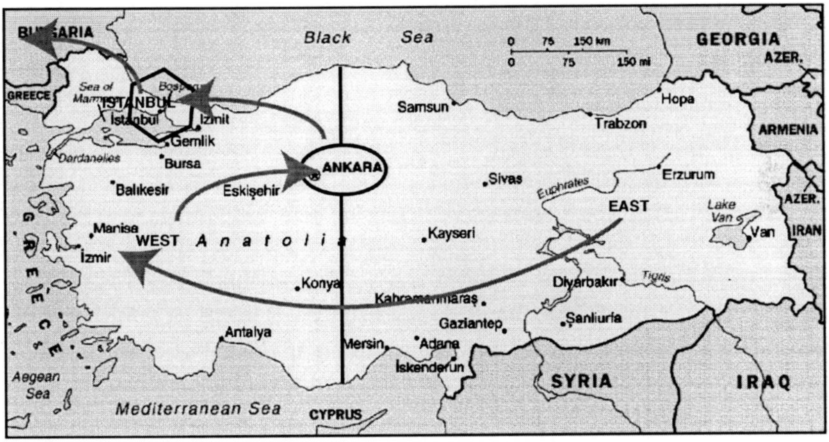

The second phase of mobility occurs at the time of tertiary education, while the third coincides with the start of professional life. The Istanbul and Ankara regions are the main destinations for the university years and thereafter. The majority prefers Ankara for tertiary education. This is verified by the entire data framework.[9] The reasons include having competent and competitive universities comparable to Istanbul, being a more secure city relative to Istanbul, and its geographical proximity to other locations in Turkey.

[9] Most of people who bring up in Istanbul have no need for mobility before Germany. There are however some who went from Istanbul to Ankara for tertiary education (See Rhus). As shown in Table 9c, their universities are METU, ITU, BU, MU, EU, AU, HU, BILKENT, and ERCU. Their departments are computer engineering, electric and electronic engineering, industrial engineering, mathematical engineering, mechanical engineering, management, economy, computer programming, and mathematics.

After graduation, however, highly educated laborers mostly prefer Istanbul. Another significant portion shifts to the Urban-West Region, as clearly seen in TABLE 9.

TABLE 9. CORRESPONDENCE OF GEOGRAPHICAL MOBILITY WITH CAREER STAGES

Modified Regions	Rural		Urban		Ankara	Istanbul
	East	West	East	West		
Origin	3	1	3	3	2	3
Secondary Education	-	-	4	5	3	3
Tertiary Education	-	-	-	1	9	5
Working Experience*	-	-	-	*4*	*5*	*9*

* Not one-to-one correspondence.

Among the interviewees of the theoretical sample, Rhus, Mespilus, and Ailanthus are from Istanbul. Euonymus, Fraxinus, and Sorbus are not originally from Istanbul, but lived in Istanbul during their university years. Syringa, Acer, Juglans, Magnolia, Laburnum, and Rhamnus worked for a while in Istanbul. There are a few cases that came to Germany without a previous stay in Istanbul,[10] But Istanbul has a significant meaning for all migrants as the city of origin, the city of transit for migration, or for many, as the only option for their return.

2.2. High School Preferences: Capital Transformation and Reproduction due to Family Resources

The selection of a high school corresponds to the first move in many migrants' biographies. Urban migration for the purpose of secondary education is a prerequisite of access to the HSLM status if the population under consideration comes from a rural background. In other words, living in the city, at the latest during secondary education period, is *sine qua non*. Those who were brought

[10] These cases go abroad through Ankara or Urban-West, mainly Izmir.

up in cities went to the high schools in the city where they lived together with their family. These individuals first moved to another city and left their family when beginning their university studies or when finding work. Including the selection of university, none of the educational choices and related migration is the individual decision of the student. Minor or major, implicit or explicit, the role of the whole family is always apparent, since this process, without exception, depends on family capital resources, and is hence a household decision. As a result, these concerns are substantially explained through the family background typology.

There is a pretty obvious correlation between expenditures on education and household incomes in Turkey, which was examined in the contextualization chapter. The higher the economic quantile of the family, the more expenditure for education it has. Family types 1A and 2A spend more in the stage of secondary education because the families with the A socio-economic status prefer to send their children to private elite high schools, as seen in TABLE 10. As previously mentioned, I restricted my study with the criterion that Bachelor's of Science degree must have been earned from a university in Turkey. I noticed that this excluded most graduates from the elite high schools of Turkey, especially private old-established "foreign" high schools mentioned in the contextualization of the education system, because their graduates prefer going abroad to study.

Interestingly the family type 2A tends to send their children, especially their daughters, to public elite high schools, namely Anatolian high schools. Similarly to family type 2A, the parents of family type 2B often make school decisions for the secondary education of their children and meet requirements through cultural capital reproduction. Furthermore, the B and C socio-economic quantiles are relatively more interested in expenditures outside of formal secondary education, since they aim to send their children to public elite high schools and universities. In order to prepare their children for the entry exams to such institutions, they attempt to afford private lectures and lessons which lay outside of formal education. The term "public elite high schools" refers mainly to Anatolian and Science High Schools, outside of a few prominent General High Schools. As mentioned before, interviewees moved to urban areas for secondary education if they came from a rural background. It is noticeable that all of them with family type 3C, attend the successful state-boarding public high schools, as noted in TABLE 10.

TABLE 10. CORRELATION BETWEEN FAMILY TYPOLOGY AND SECONDARY EDUCATION

Family Background Type	Amount	Gender	
		Male	**Female**
1A	3	Private	
2A	10	Private	Anatolian
2B	4	Anatolian, Science, Private with grant	
1B	3	Anatolian, Special Public, Anatolian Vocational-Technical	
3B	4	Anatolian, Special Public	
3C	6	Science, Anatolian, Anatolian Technical-Vocational State-Boarding	
3D	2	Public	

The absence of female HSL migrants from the family type 3D is also remarkable. Family type 3D actually indicates a return guest worker family background. This shows that it is hard to find a highly educated migrant from the working class. At the same time, however, it implies that women have higher chance to be HSL migrants if their family has more cultural and economic capital.

By confirming Bourdieuan approach to the capital forms, I hence suggest that the child's attendance at public elite schools indicates reproduction of cultural capital in the family and the attendance at private schools indicates transformation from economic capital to cultural capital. Furthermore, both provide social capital by product.

2.3. Tertiary Education as Inevitable Consequence

It is evident that educational attainment and navigation are related to family background explained by cultural and socio-economic status. In other words, there is a necessary relationship between the family and the educational system. Education is an investment in the family's future by transforming and reproducing capital. Secondary education appears as a milestone for the educational backgrounds of HSL migrants. Their preferences for high schools seem like a family institution strategy which is shaped by capital resources. Afterwards, they earn high scores in the entrance exam and they are placed into the best universities of Turkey. The opportunity for an advantageous tertiary education can be seen as a consequence of graduation from an elite high school. Rather than attaining tertiary education, middle class families are in particular interested in secondary education of their child. Moreover, most HSL migrants from Turkey come from a child-oriented family which attaches importance to education. Of the subjects of this case study, not one had a sibling who did not attempt to complete a university degree (data not shown). It is clear that tertiary education appears as one mostly predictable consequence of their family environment. Additionally, it can be said that Alevi families show special care to their children's study (See Prunus and Rhamnus in interpretations of the theoretical sample).

2.4. Educational Background Typology

Clearly, the individuals relevant for the current thesis have an esteemed educational career in Turkey. This internationally valued educational background appears as a key for HSLM. By forming an educational background typology, the distinction without a difference can be observed in the attainments that later influence migration. These educational achievements contribute to an acquaintanceship with the migratory destination. In this regard, language competence, familiarity with the future destination of HSLM, and scholarly achievement are important factors in migration.

Many are taught English in the Turkish educational system. Some of those in this study learned German as a second foreign language during their secondary education, whereas Fraxinus (Balıkesir Anatolian Vocational-Technical State-Boarding), Juniperus (German Private with grant), Hippophae (Bornova Anatolian), and Celtis (Istanbul Anatolian) started learning German as thier first foreign language in their high schools. A clear majority of subjects followed lectures in English at their universities except for Ailanthus and Betula (Marmara, Informatik), whose university courses were held in German.[11] Graduation from high schools and/or universities in Turkey whose classroom language is German can be read as full preparation for life in Germany. Moreover, attendance at these schools correlates to having more institutionalized opportunities for HSLM to Germany.

More than two thirds of my theoretical sample had experiences abroad before becoming migrant laborers in Germany. Comparing this fact to TABLE 8, it can be seen that the remaining one third have already working experience in Turkey. The former group consist of people who first go abroad for the purpose of graduate studies, internships, summer school, or language courses, practices which I call "warm-up exercises" to HSLM.[12] Warm-up exercises display the internationalization of university education, and make the host country where such exercises took place the most likely destination of HSLM. It can be said that the people who have warm-up exercises in Germany are well-trained to emigrate to Germany.

In summary, I present an educational background typology with respect to five related components: education in English, education in German, German language course attendance, internship in Germany, and Master's degree in Germany. These factors reveal four highly educated types as follow:

1. **Fully-Prepared for Germany** This requires education in Turkey with German as the teaching language. This basis mostly leads to warm-up

[11] Acer, Tilia, Abies, and Rhamnus used only Turkish as the teaching language.

[12] Attendance at German language courses seems as a slightly different position from other warm-up exercises to HSLM, since almost all of the people follow language courses after coming to Germany, if they do not learn German before.

exercises for in Germany. The first choice of a fully-prepared HSL migrant is Germany.

2. **Well-Trained for Germany** This type requires warm-up exercise, a German language course in Turkey, or an internship and/or graduate study in Germany. This type of HSL migrants explicitly or implicitly intents for HSLM to Germany as the host country. Being well-trained for Germany, just like in the case of full-preparation for Germany, gives this country precedence among the possible destination countries.
3. **Well-Trained** This requires education in Turkey with English as the teaching language. They are professionally ready for HSLM career in any host country. The potential host countries in their mind are one of the Anglo-American countries.
4. **Root-Trained** The family of the to-be the HSL migrant has previous migration background in Germany, which renders Germany the most likely country as destination. The 'root-trained' is a type whose parents worked in Germany once in their life. This working experience influences educational motivations of their children such as learning German as first foreign language and school preferences.

A successful educational background is imperative for HSLM decision. Around half of the HSL migrants, 17 out of 33 interviewees in my case, are *well-trained* for the internationalized labor market. This common type mostly aims at Anglo-American countries as the destination country of their migration. Choosing Germany appears coincidental to the well-trained, however the main reason is actually the "success" of German Green Card program, which will be explained in the next section. Nine participants in my study are *well-trained for Germany*. That is, they have warm-up exercises for HSLM, specifically to Germany, in contrast to the well-trained type. Five participants are *fully-prepared for Germany*. In other words, their educational background covers either a high school or a university department with German as the teaching language. The other two participants, are *root-trained type*, differ from the others because of their return guest worker family background. Their HSLM decision in favor of Germany and not to a different destination country is not directly related with their "success" in formal education system in Turkey, but rather their familiarity with Germany and the accessibility of institutionalized networks.

3. Migration Story

"A man does not 'by nature' wish to earn more and more money, but simply to live as he is accustomed to live and to earn as much as is necessary for that purpose." (Weber, 2003:60)

"[…] To live like a tree single and at liberty
and brotherly like the trees of a forest,
this yearning is ours."[13]

3.1. Advanced Cultural Capital

The case study shows that HSLM is recognized by its embodied actors, *Dasein*, as (i) culturally ideal, (ii) necessary, and (iii) individual. Firstly, for highly educated people, migration from Turkey to Germany represents primarily not financial improvement but actually an increase in cultural and symbolic capital. In fact, most argue that they are able to earn in Turkey as much as in Germany.

> "When looking from Turkey at us here in Germany, some said to me, 'Oh, Germany! Sure, you also work for Falcon, definitely, you earn a lot.' Nevertheless, that is a mistake; we earn more-or-less the same as the standard employee in Turkey. If you also want to have a social environment here, then your income remains the same amount as the standard income in Turkey. Maybe there are some people who come here in order to save money but I am not like them since I am trying to protect the level of my living standard in Turkey." (Rhus, Family Background 1A, Well-trained)

> "Well, about that I don't really know what to do. I didn't save much money. Now I have to save some, but it seems the money we get here is not that different, I do my best…[…]" (Magnolia, Family Background 1A, Well-trained for Germany)

> "My wage in Turkey was the same as it is here. This is an enormous amount for Turkey. Through my migration I was not aiming at a better salary. I did not come to Germany in order to earn more. […] Accordingly, it was not like I came to Germany to earn more or so. […]" (Rhamnus, Family Background 3B, Well-trained)

They explicitly question their advantage in the manner of economic capital but they acknowledge their favorable position with regard to

[13] Quotted from the poem *Davet* (Invitation) by Nazım Hikmet tr. by Fuat Engin.

cultural and symbolic capital.[14] This position associated with HSLM careers is a result of the immaterial acquisitions such as the learning of new cultures, seeing different places, and becoming acquainted with people from different societies. I name this advanced cultural capital. Like the other forms of capital, this can be transformed to others. This kind of capital additionally provides an increase in status for professional careers. In this context, the migrants with the family background type 1A and 2A formulate their migration as *investment*, in natural discourse.[15] As a matter of fact, all consider their migration *culturally ideal*, and not purely economicly ideal. Economic advantage is seen as a by-product, whereas cultural and political benefits appear to be the main reasons for HSLM. It is obvious that, at least from Turkey, HSLM is not simply economic migration but is also a profound cultural transition.

Secondly, most HSL migrants from Turkey in Germany perceive their migration as *necessary*. The compulsion for this kind of migration is, on the one hand, related to internationalization of the ICT labor market. This is verified by the emergence of internationalization in education and recruitment systems, notably opportunities of internships abroad and the existence of headhunters. On the other hand, highly educated people are exposed to *socio-political pressure to leave Turkey* (the "pushing factors") and *cultural-political pressure from the destination country* (the "pulling factors").

The HSL migrants do not receive any discouragement about living abroad from their families who, on the contrary, mostly encourage the decision to migrate. The parents mostly support their children materially in the warm-up period to HSLM. I argue that the education system and the parents' approaches within their social environment create an *emigration disposition* for the youth of Turkey,

[14] I will interpret the difference in their social capital under the dimension of social relations.

[15] Pinus at the beginning of her interview even criticized the term migration. According to her, their movement should not be called as migration, in spite of five-year living and working experience in Germany.

aimed primarily at the West. All interviewees say they have a disposition to go abroad in order to study or work for a while before coming to Germany. There is actually a clear socially-constructed "achievement path" consisting of both educational and occupational achievements: attendance at one of the best high schools, acquiring acceptance from one of the best departments in one of the best universities, and then at least short-term educational and professional experience abroad. In other words, working abroad is required for the career of highly educated people. They follow this path and finally migrate to Germany. This pattern exposes the careerists in my study. There are also some among them whose migration also means release from the societal pressure or from a society subdued by military coup. The distinctive point between these and the pure careerists is their motivation for migration, which is much more affected by the socio-political pushing factors of Turkey than socio-cultural influence from abroad.

Last but not least, HSLM is realized and perceived as a solo experience. Migration is not an end but a means to an end, it is not a purpose but a medium for any highly educated person, since it is used for individualist political strategy for "living alone and free like a tree". As mentioned in the analysis of the interviews, migration clearly brings about a process of self-discovery due to the absence of socio-political intervention. Revelations of ethnicity, sexual orientation, and religious beliefs, as well as a newfound freedom of expression, can be results of migration. Furthermore, as mentioned above, no clear impact of the family network on HSLM has been found. Highly educated people therefore gain independence from social control thanks to their migration experience. Almost all migrants and, interestingly, all female migrants even talked about their self-reconstruction through migration. Although HSL migrants, especially single ones, declared their suffering from loneliness throughout the process, most felt they had been changed themselves positively by the experience.

They attributed their loneliness in part to their maturity, reasoning that they simply had more time for themselves. Even though their migratory experience appears highly individualized, in the most common concern was integration in the host country. This characteristic of the HSL migrants is significantly different from the typical labor migrants.

3.2. Military Service Problem: Institutionalized Expulsion

After analyzing the interviews, I am certain that HSLM from Turkey carries a strong association with flight from obligatory military service. It becomes the main tangible and intelligible reason to leave Turkey for young professional men. Additionally, it is an indirect reason for some young married expert women such as Mespilus, in addition to the second order migrants. A significant amount of young highly educated men from Turkey work abroad for at least three years and pay a significant sum in order to reduce their compulsory military service to three weeks. This kind of military service does not result in any discontinuity in their careers, since they can perform their draft in vacation time. This motivation "legalizes" their movement not only in their eyes but also, curiously, in the public opinion of Turkey. Labor migration is seen as a respectable option and is often recommended to young men. I hence argue that a significant amount of HSLM from Turkey occurs to avoid a full-term military service. This not only refers to a personal political strategy but also displays silent societal resistance. In this context, Sorbus' question to his professor after his graduation in Turkey is meaningful: "I have not done military service yet. What can I do?" At the advice of his professor, he carried out a graduate study in Germany and then remained in Germany to work. He declared in the interview he was going to 'draft by payment', using part of his next vacation. In addition, Rhus, Prunus, and Quercus already fulfilled the military service by payment, which was their main motivation for going abroad. Rhus appears keen to return, although all of them including Rhus did not return after exercising their right to complete military service rapidly. The problem of Turkish military service is enough to explain at least temporary (three year) HSLM. However, it is not the sole reason and the reasons for remaining in Germany include advanced cultural capital and the furtherance of a professional career. This may in fact become permanent migration when compounded with challenges in labor and social relations.

As ascertained in Quercus' interview, the required time for working abroad in the 1980s to acquire the right for draft by payment was only one year and the duration of service was two months. The required time has since been extended while the duration of the conscription has been shortened and scaled to fit annual leave. Now, the required time abroad is three years and service duration is three weeks. This shift indicates the political readiness of Turkey to send its highly educated labor power abroad. During labor emigration from Turkey in the 1960s and 1970s, the Republic of Turkey first made a point of the importance of remittances. As Abadan-Unat (1976:24-5) describes, there are two effects of remittances for the sending country: a rise in potential purchasing power and a rise in hard foreign currency at the disposal of the state organs. She also stresses the existence of the "boomerang effect": the re-export of remittances to the host country. On the other hand, it is known that highly skilled workers are less likely to send remittances.[16] As I specified in the chapter of contextualization, the whole title of the above-mentioned drafting is "military service by payment with foreign currency". In other words, the payments are made in foreign currency, currently 5,112 Euros. This system can be described as a collection of imperative remittances and, moreover, this system disallows the boomerang effect.

Approaches to the military service problem vary among highly educated people of Turkey. Six out of ten men, and one woman out of five in my theoretical sample explicitly talk about the issue of military service in Turkey as one of main pushing factors in their migration, as can be seen in the quoted passages from the interviews below. Only one out of the remaining four men performed military service before becoming a labor migrant. Three who did

[16] Some research indicates that unskilled workers are much more likely to make remittances to families at home and plan to return to their country of origin than skilled workers. For example, an economic survey in 2001 shows that skilled migrants from India in the USA earn 10 per cent of India's GDP, but none of this income goes back to India (Jorgensen, 2003:8).

not mention the military service issue in the interviews would still presumably have this issue in their life agenda, since they remain under the obligation of military service as long as they are male citizens of the Republic of Turkey.

> "There was a problem dealing with the military service. The explicit reason of my decision to work abroad is to solve this problem… Most of the people coming who are male candidates think of escaping from the military service (*kaçmak, yırtmak*). My first main purpose of coming here was escaping from the military service. I considered returning after completing the three-week-military service. Although I made the conscription by payment, I have not yet returned (he smiled)." (Rhus, Family Background 1A, Well-trained)

> "I always had the idea to go to Germany in order to work, especially because of the Turkish military service. This was the main reason. I escaped in the last 20 days before my obligatory military service took effect." (Syringa, Family Background 3D, Root-Trained)

> "[…] My husband (Salix) had a military service issue and we decided to come." (Mespilus, Family Background 1B, Well-trained)

> "I did not want to serve in the military. I find it unnecessary. It is not losing time when you are in the most productive age. We are always productive every age. You have a profession in a certain field. You have perfection. You can use it every time in your life period. Every age has its own perfection. I do not believe in the protest like 'we should not go to the military service in our most productive ages.' According to me, the military service is unnecessary anyway. Perhaps, it is not unnecessary, but it should be done as a professional in this era. Wasting 15 months for the military service is totally unnecessary. It is okay, the military service can be needed, and hence professional military is also possible. What is the meaning of imprisoning (locking in) hundreds of thousands of people? Anyway, there will not be a function of these people in war. Wars come technologically into force. Wars are already not dependent on the quantity of soldiers. Moreover, the soldiers' condition is definite. To force a person struggling to make a living in this condition… I do not know, but I believe that nobody makes the military service willingly. Perhaps, there are some, called 'patriotic' (*vatansever*), but everybody loves his/her homeland (*vatan*)." (Sorbus, Family Background 2B, Well-trained for Germany)

> "The reason I looked for job opportunities abroad was related to escaping from the military service as soon as possible, because I did not want to serve in the military. That is obligatory and I did not want to do it." (Prunus, Family Background 3C, Well-trained)

> "It is like this: military service,,, it is not something to be afraid of actually. So why did I,,, it was not like I was afraid, but I preferred to do it in two months, instead of 18. I thought like, I after working one year abroad, even if you subtract the payment for the military, I had more money than I would have if I had stayed in Turkey and worked there. Seeing a different country and working in research were appealing too. So the time abroad was going to be useful both from technical and economical aspects. The time I was going to lose during military service,,, well, let's don't say lose but, the time was going to be used suboptimal, instead of optimal. Furthermore I was going to be able to see how a foreign company functions. And additionally I would make some money. But if the conditions wouldn't be like that, for instance some friends will have to work for five years in order to make that amount of money, because the conditions are not so good anymore. The conditions back then were good, with the money earned in a year, we were able to pay for military service, and some money was even left over. Given those conditions, I found it logical. But now we see, some friends are coming, they will earn the necessary amount in five years or more,,, difficult. So if it would be like that, I wouldn't come. On the other hand, now after all that it is easy to say this (I laugh). It is like this for me, I assess my situation back then rationally, and if the same conditions would hold now, I would do the same." (Quercus, Family Background 3C, Well-trained)

> "[Military service] has a big influence on [my migration]. […] For instance in case I had gone to the military service. I am one hundred percent sure that I couldn't have finished it duly on time. [I asked if he would consider doing it by payment.] No. Why should I pay for weapons?" (Rhamnus, Family Background 3B, Well-trained)

Military service is the underlying reason for labor migration for most young men of Turkey. It is seen as a problem, a reason to migrate, unwanted, unnecessary, dreaded, lost time, a condemnation and an obligation, irrational, suboptimal, unproductive, and supportive of the military and, therefore, of war.

I consequently claim that there are four ideal types of male migrants, in relation to military service. The first type does not pay attention to military service regarding his migration, it is either irrelevant to his migration (if he has already completed it) or it is an accidental by-product of his migration, and he does not show any interest in this topic (*becoming migrant for unintended consequence*). The second type organizes his migration specifically with the intention of earning the right to reduced military service. He saves money to pay the military while working abroad. Having enough money and the required amount of time abroad, he performs the three-week draft by payment in his vacation. He then easily decides to either return or to continue working abroad (*becoming migrant for intended consequence*). The third type initiates his migration as an emergent plan to escape from this compulsory duty but he has no certain plan about his future (*becoming migrant as a last resort*). Through the challenges of his migration experience, he converts into the second or the fourth type. The fourth type, like the second and third, goes abroad without the intention to return in the near future since he is against military service by payment (*becoming migrant without absolute solution*). He may then solve this problem simply by giving up his citizenship, or becoming a dual citizen, or he may be reclassified as the second type, if he does not want to totally abandon his country of origin.

The prevalent type is apparently the second. This type of male migrant is socially and institutionally constructed. It remains dangerous to cry "the king is naked", in a society which has seen so much trouble with military governments and has apparent but silent strategies of resistance to military service. Article 318 of the penal code of the Republic of Turkey prescribes punishment for people speaking negatively about military service. Questioning the military is also risky since it may be evaluated as an insult to the Turkish nation and its institutions and thus, through Article 301, a crime. These circumstances create a paranoia that often silences the first type: Iwazaru among the three monkeys: "speak no evil".

3.3. Programs for HSLM (Green Card to Blue Card): Institutionalized Attractors

If any person has neither adequate educational attainments specially for Germany (the types 'full-prepared for Germany' and 'well-trained for Germany') nor any migratory history with Germany in their family (the type 'root-trained'), the first country of choice for working abroad for ordinary 'well-trained' persons from Turkey is an Anglo-American country, notably the USA and the UK. In interviews, almost all HSL migrants explicitly mentioned their first preferences for these countries. Moreover, the image of Germany in the mind of people in Turkey has changed since labor migration from Turkey to Germany in the late 1960s and the 1970s. This image has been reinforced in the three decades since the 1970s with many works of art including literature, cinema, and music relating experiences of the "guest worker" generation. According to this image, Germany is often connected with *welfare* (economical richness) and *pain* (alienation and homesickness). To illustrate these two associations, I present two quoted passages as follows:

> "Everybody has an idea to work abroad in his/her mind. At least, everybody sees an *Alamancı* in his/her environment! Everybody feels an admiration for their high quality of life! There is a common opinion that everything is better abroad!" (Fraxinus, Family Background 3C, Well-trained)

> "[...] I had not considered coming to Germany before. Actually, I did not want to come here, because Germany is always seen in 'our' eyes as having a negative image, such as a 'bitter land' (*'acı vatan'*). At least according to me, Germany was a "bitter land" and did not have any attractive side. In other words, I did not want to come here as a tourist. People come here only in order to work. However, if I would have had this kind of intention, I could have selected to go to another country, another European country or America (he addresses the USA)." (Sambucus, Family Background 2B, Well-trained)

The contrast between these two associations concerning Germany in the collective memory of Turkey is evident. In the general perception of HSL migrants, who do not have any specific preparation for Germany as the country of destination but are 'well-trained', the dominance of the latter association over the former before coming to Germany is noticeable. The HSL migrants with full preparation and appropriate training for Germany differ from the others in that they are less dependent on the doxa.

Besides the traditionally known HSL receiving countries of the USA, Canada, Australia, Japan, and New Zealand, European countries such as Germany, the Netherlands, and the UK began in the late 1990s to compete openly for foreign skills, with varying degrees of success. Germany executed a "Temporary IT-Specialist Relief Program", generally known as the "Green Card" scheme, in August 2000, which was designed particularly to attract ICT specialists from non-EU countries. Also, the Netherlands set up a fast-track scheme in July 2001, reducing the bureaucracy related to work visas for ICT specialists, and research and development staff. In addition, the UK has run both a "Work Permit System" and a "Sectors Based Scheme", and also initiated a "Highly Skilled Migrant Program", especially to allow ICT specialists to come to the UK to look for work since the beginning of 2002. It can be seen that there is a huge competition for ICT specialists from non-EU countries. However, at the beginning of 2009, the EU attempted to eliminate the competition with a new program, "Blue Card", designed to attract foreign highly valued skills into the European labor market. The relevant point here is that the Green Card program first underlined demand for temporary HSLM. However, it was then itself made temporary with the new German immigration law in 2005 after which the Blue Card program was extended by the EU.

Between 2000 and 2005, the German Green Card Program increased the exposure to HSL possibilities in countries outside the EU and streamlined the procedures. Still, most argued that the program was not successful, focusing on failure to fulfill target numbers. My study explicitly demonstrates that the program created *activation of HSLM disposition* in Turkey towards Germany in the context of the engineering profession, a demographic which usually migrates to the USA and other English-speaking countries. The fieldwork of the present thesis shows that almost all ICT specialists from Turkey in the early 2000s select Germany as the country of destination because of the emergence of the Green Card Program and proximity to Turkey. The program was effective particularly with the ICT specialists who had not previously considered this country. Therefore, the relative attractiveness of Germany as a destination country was boosted for the 'well-trained' type.

In my sample, the vast majority of Green Card holders easily received a permanent residency permit as a standard consequence of working for five years. Still, to avoid losing rights in Turkey, none chose to become German citizens. Since German citizenship does not allow dual citizenship, all HSL migrants from Turkey in the whole data framework, excluding Fagus, find naturalization undesirable.[17] Although the Republic of Turkey offers a Blue Card, the newly revised Pink Card, for previous citizens who have sacrificed their citizenship for another, these cards have not yet assured and convinced migrants of their rights, specifically regarding heritage and pension.[18]

3.4. Typology based on Migration Stories

The migration story for those under consideration covers, on average, a five-year working experience in Germany. However, any evaluation of this migration must consider the periods before and after the time abroad. The supposition of a history of unemployment in Turkey for the HSL migrants is not supportable in my study. In other words, in no case was the decision to depart from Turkey to Germany made after a long period of unemployment. Moreover, the driving force behind HSLM is not purely better pay, as mentioned before. In summary, the relevant migration is not dependent on different wage and unemployment situations in Turkey and Germany. As a matter of fact, the migrants seek to build careers. That is to say, migration is chiefly and importantly a life

[17] Fagus (Family Background 3B, Well-trained) considers application for German citizenship; accordingly he plans not to perform the military service in Turkey, even though he explicitly said this obligation was not among his reasons to leave Turkey (His type related with military service is 1).
[18] This Blue Card is not the EU Blue Card.

stage devoted to career construction. This endeavor subjects the migrants not only to work but also to social interaction. It explains their interest in adaptation to the current society, notwithstanding their calculation and concerns for their coming life stages, such as setting up a family and/or having a child.

Most began their migratory project within temporary conditions that were legally determined, for example under the Green Card Program. Taking their age (late 20s and early 30s) into account, they are already in the transitional period of their life. After reading all interviews about their plans for the future, almost none of the interviewees say, "I will certainly return to Turkey", or "I will certainly stay in Germany", or "I will certainly go to another country". Some form of indecision to stay or to move is the prevailing attitude and is exhibited by all. In the theoretical sample, there are two distinctive examples constituting two opposing positions. Rhus made the decision to return, whereas Mespilus decided to stay in Germany. Most of the adventurers in HSLM say they are open to move if required by their career. It is obvious that holding a permanent residency permit is not a reason to stay in Germany but it removes the barriers to a migratory career. Briefly, I found two ideal types evident in the migration stories:

1. **Adventurer** This type takes risks. Their actions, regarded as daring or reckless, are the result of socio-political influences in Turkey and cultural-political influences from the core countries in globalization. This type includes people who seek release from the pressures on them to solve the over-whelming problems facing the society. Also included are careerists who declare they move for their profession. The intention to work abroad was shaped, in the minds of these people, during the years of their education.

2. **Attached** This type comes to Germany to be with their German partners.

4. Labor Relations

The analyses indicate that there are five main characteristics of the environment relevant to the HSL migrants: (1) the existence of the social state as an intervening factor representing an unexpected benefit, (2) the insignificance to the migrants of the inevitable devaluation in prestige of their educational background, (3) the crowding phenomenon as a threatening interference, (4) the gender gap difference in the ICT sector between Turkey and Germany, and (5) the flexible work ethic and shifting meaning of leisure time.

4.1. Social State as Unexpected Benefit[19]

Almost all interviewees appreciate the social state of the Federal Republic of Germany, notably in the context of worker rights and social security benefits. The only critic came from Juglans who has more working experience in Germany than the Green Card holders. She has observed the decreasing role of the social state in recent years.

Even though both nation-states declare their social character at the constitutional level, the pragmatic difference between the two is remarkable for the HSL migrants. They do not, however, migrate for this purpose. It seems to be an unexpected benefit, rather than a pulling factor. Although this does not pull people, it keeps them, and in this manner stabilizes migration. The benefit of the social state resists further migration away from Germany. In fact, worker rights in Germany are better not only in comparison with Turkey, but also with the other potential destination countries, like the USA and the UK. In particular, the biggest advantage of working in Germany is commonly considered to be the relatively large amount of leisure time available. It can be argued that the social state, as a response to the inequality problem, relieves not only the disadvantaged but also the privileged – potentially alleviating the financial burden of those with higher income such as the highly skilled workers, who are often referred to as the "new petite bourgeoisie".

The study additionally argues, by exposing over-time working conditions in Turkey, that the lack of *Betriebsrat* (work council) in labor relations is an implicit disadvantage of working there.[20] In some European countries there is a long tradition of work coun-

[19] In some literature such an unexpected benefit is referred to as an Intervening Opportunity.

[20] The *Betriebsorganisatorisch Eigenständige Einheit* is also an item of the social state postulates in Federal Republic of Germany.

cils.[21] The *Betriebsrat* in Germany has arguably been the most successful implementation among them. It is based on the Work Constitution Act (*Betriebsverfassungsgesetz*), represents employees, and functions as a local, company-level complement to national labor negotiations. Work councils fill the agreement-practice gap in the labor market. The model comprises essentially two stages in which general labor agreements are first made at the national level by labor unions and employer associations, after which companies meet with work councils to adjust these agreements to local circumstances. This integrated structure allows the application of regulation from the national to local level, and also significantly the administration and enforcement of these regulations to be fed back from the local to the national level. Highly skilled employees in general appear discontent with the intervention of work councils to individual salary bargaining with HR departments but glad for their control related to working time limits. Probably the reverse is valid for the employer.

4.2. Insignificance of Devaluation in Educational Prestige

All highly educated people notice a form of devaluation of their educational qualifications after migration. However, they do not consider this decreased prestige to be important. Their lack of concern for this devaluation is grounded in their belief that they will be given opportunity to demonstrate their skills and previous occupational background in a working environment, and their confidence in their capability of doing so. Moreover, having the warm-up exercises in Germany is not only effective to overcome their prospective migration problems but also to assist their career presentation to the German labor market. In this context, it is especially the 'attached type' who experienced difficulty during the initial stages of their migration.

[21] They are called *Betriebsrat* in Germany, Austria, and Switzerland, *Ondernemingsraad* in the Netherlands and Belgium, *Comité d'Entreprise* in France, *Conseil d'Entreprise* in Belgium, and *Comité de empresa* in Spain.

4.3. Crowding Phenomenon as Threatening Interference

The concept of crowding phenomenon in relation to migration was explained beforehand. The crowding phenomenon causes prejudices in the labor market. Almost all interviewees talked about encountering among their colleagues disbelief that someone with such a national background were qualified for a professional career. Because of this, the HSL migrants made an extra effort to display their technical skills and general aptitude for work in order to counter the existing prejudices. Their acceptance as a professional by their coworkers is therefore grudgingly given, as would not be expected, for example, in the case of a transferring football player. Nevertheless, the effect of the crowding phenomenon on the new migrants is explicit in social relations. This will be further examined a following section titled "Black Swan Phenomenon".

4.4. Migrant Women Dealing with Gender Gap in German ICT sector

In my case study, all women talked about the presence of more female specialists in the ICT sector in Turkey than in Germany. As shown in the statistics of the previous chapter, there is a significant gendered division of labor and gender gap in the ICT sector in Germany. The female ICT specialists from Turkey are necessary to fill this gap. They acknowledge their own *rara avis* position in the German labor market.

A further point relevant to female migrants is the relative abundance of possibilities for self-improvement in Germany. As a consequence of heavy local traffic and longer working hours in Istanbul, all experts from Turkey enjoy more recreation time in Germany. This restructuring of time is more noticeable for women, when the gendered division of domestic labor is taken into account. In addition to the comfort of being distant from the societal pressures of their homeland as well as having a more secure everyday life, the longer time afforded them for leisure is a powerful stabilizing factor for female HSL migrants. In other words, the migrant women have stronger reasons to stay in Germany than the men. It is noticeable that four out of the five female migrants in the theoretical sample prefer to work for German-based large-scale companies, use German as the business language, and show a better capability to reorganize their leisure time in Germany, in comparison with the male migrants.

Female HSL migrants from Turkey in Germany experience more problems in labor relations because of the gender gap, whereas males encounter more problems in social relations. They observe discrimination based on nationalized gender. The women migrants (excluding the 'attached') are more successful than the men in reorganizing their leisure time.

4.5. Flexible Work Ethic and Shifting Meaning of Leisure Time

Flexible labor relations give rise to new mechanisms for recruitment, as mentioned. The current study demonstrates that the HSL migrants are mostly recruited through private employment agencies. It shows that the internet has become the most common job search medium for employment. Internet platforms have emerged as the biggest headhunters in recruitment in Europe; specifically, London-based headhunters play a disproportionately important role. They recruit people for international large-scale companies located in Germany.

Through the so-called German Green Card Program, the recruitment process in Germany for the migrant ICT specialists was made significantly easier. In the first years of this century, some large-scale international firms announced job opportunities for ICT consulting in Germany in Turkish newspapers and the job interviews for these even took place in Istanbul. In the auspices of the program, the applicants passed through the formal migration procedures without great effort. A clear majority of them mentioned the ease of these procedures in the interviews. However, the previous HSL migrants (Juglans) and some outside the program (Sambucus) experienced relatively more difficulty during the first recruitment period in Germany. Like these two migrants, interestingly of the 'attached' type, the 'root-trained' type of migrants (Syringa) experience problems in employment, despite being Green Card holders. This uneasy position for the 'root-trained' type stresses that the role of facilitation played by the family network is not critical for the highly skilled people embarking on a career determined by migration.

The ICT specialists mostly work under more flexible conditions than previously experienced, leading to a change in career structure. The HSL migrants certainly recognize the absence of a lifelong job guarantee in the current working conditions. As seen in the interview with Quercus, the subject with the longest foreign working experience, the insecurity of these labor relations increases over time. In fact, he underlined that flexible working implied both increased income but also increased risk in comparison to that experienced by the typical employee. The recent labor relations appear insecure and transitional, a consequence of their flexibility. The HSL migrants declare they always maintain a second option lest they lose their job. Thus, most are not afraid by the possibility of losing their job. They consider that this could happen and that it would not necessarily be a consequence of their failure. For instance, they consider economic crises to be a comprehensible reason for dismissal. They believe in the existence of institutionalized labor relations, which are very similar regardless of the country. It is significantly correlated with their lack of membership of labor unions. This study supports Sennett's argument about the current apprehension towards labor relations: the attitude that none are guilty and that "we are all victims of time and place". The important value according to the HSL migrants at this point is preparedness. As mentioned before, the study also demonstrates that HSL migrants do not have a long-term unemployment background in their occupational life in Turkey. In addition, all tend not to change the company they are working for in their career abroad unless necessary. In this context, Fraxinus, Acer, and Quercus in the theoretical sample partly differ from the others since they change their companies whenever they move country. These three, as single men (Quercus is now married), had a more flexible career than the others.[22]

Strategies of the migrants to cope with insecurity in the work environment vary with marital status. The couples are naturally better shielded from this by virtue of their partnership (Juglans, Ailanthus, Quercus, Sambucus), while the singles delay marriage until they have proved themselves in their career, because they see marriage as a form of risk (Rhus, Euonymus, Fraxinus, Acer, Sorbus, Prunus, Magnolia, Laburnum). It is of interest to note that being single is a financial benefit, and that divorce is relatively common among highly educated migrants (Syringa, Mespilus, and Rhamnus) due presumably to the reduction of responsibility that divorce entails, in addition to the friction created by challenges such as integration into a foreign society.

Other implications for the migrants of flexibility are project-based work and uncertain shift start and end times. Most of them commute often between work places, particularly those working for large-scale international companies. This mobility is dependent upon projects. This is defined as spatial or locational flexibility. Deadlines of projects, and meetings with coworkers or customers, determine their work schedule. Hence, although they refer to the absence of defined daily shifts as temporal flexibility, this is better termed variability. Although dependent on project demands, they are able on a daily basis to determine their own working hours and workload. It is not only the schedule that is variable but also their colleagues. The loss of a life-long position and the realities of working with transitional coworkers destroy the old work ethic and hamper solidarity. Instead, the emergence of life-long learning and new form of communicative skills for professional adaptation to every new work atmosphere shape the new work culture. This can be considered an indicator of transformation from a work-oriented society to a knowledge-oriented one.

---

[22] The other common attributes of those with more flexible careers were debated in the interpretation review of the interview with Quercus.

The new work culture comprises project-work and variable conditions for the workers. It is worth noting that variable work demands flexible life-style from the employees. Features of the new work culture include a diminishing of routine and increased risk for human beings in labor relations. There is a distinction between knowledge of repetitious, specialized tasks and knowledge of the whole process: the piecework vs. the overview. A project manager, like the control chief in a textile factory, is required to know the entire process of a single project, and not more than this. According to some interviewees, specialization in one field is common in the ICT sector of Germany, whereas an understanding of every step of a process is popular in Turkey regardless of the scale of the company. In fact, there is a difference in work culture between the country branches of the same international company.

For the HSL migrants, "flexibility" additionally implies working in an international atmosphere, speaking English predominantly, and cultural plurality of work habits. Complaints about the work ethic in Turkey and the difference in work ethic between Germany and Turkey are often voiced in the interviews. Some underlined their experiences and observations about differences in the working practices between people with different national backgrounds. The stricter hierarchy in the workplace in Turkey is the first thing to be criticized in comparison to Germany. The work culture in Germany has recently adopted the coaching of techniques for team working. The HSL migrants are very glad about this, but they notice alienation among their colleagues. In Turkey colleagues have more personal relations with each other, whereas they consider the maxim "colleague is colleague" to be dominant in Germany. Probably, the longer working hours in Turkey are the cause of the higher social interaction at the work place.

More apparently, the HSL migrants from Turkey enjoy more leisure time in Germany. They prefer Germany in this regard over Turkey and other destination countries of HSLM. On the one hand, an unexpected benefit of the social state is elevated recreation time. On the other hand, the "flexibility" introduced by decomposing working hours by project and meeting creates an illusion about recreation time. Leisure time is crucial for migrants in their adaptation to the host country. As mentioned under the migration story dimension, the main aim of migration appears to be to accumulate advanced cultural capital for building careers. This accumulation is realized in both work and leisure time. People can be classified regarding labor relations according to their adaptation to the flexible labor market. This professional integration into the labor market also partly includes leisure time. Their integration into German society is also determined by their integration into the social sphere, something taking place primarily during leisure time, and will be explained in the next section on social relations.

4.6. Typology based on Labor Relations

The main distinction in approaches towards work, in other words the degree of integration in the flexible labor market, are most prominently exhibited by three interviewees: Rhus (unitary integration), Acer (flexible integration), and Juglans (critical integration). It is recognizable in the interviews that a clear majority of highly educated migrant workers identify themselves by their capability to integrate into the flexible labor conditions, which are shaped by the current labor market. Types are:

1. **Unitarily integrated** This type, as if working under the old conditions, searches for job security until retirement by collaborating with the employer.
2. **Flexibly integrated** This type, aware of the change in work relations, tries to adapt to them by accepting a variable lifestyle oriented around work. They take risks in an attempt to find secure working conditions. The market offers them various job opportunities, based on the companies with which the HSL migrants are affiliated, but only until a certain age after which opportunities are scarce. They however consider themselves impotent to influence these labor relations.
3. **Critically integrated** This type, also aware of the difference in the working conditions, refuses to identify themselves by their work and makes use of labor unions to consolidate their position.

5. Social Relations

"I'm an alien, I'm a legal alien. / I'm an Englishman in New York"[23]

"There is no line defense, there is only zone defense. This zone is the whole homeland."[24]

Among the various social relations of the HSL migrants, four typical groups can be identified: (i) people having identical or similar migration experience; (ii) HSL migrants from other countries; (iii) non-migrants; and (iv) ethnic community except for HSL migrants.

5.1. Professional Ethnic Network

Biographical interviews were analyzed to reveal general information about the social networks of HSL migrants. In all respects, one social network, neither family nor purely ethnic, stands out in this study: the professional ethnic network. This network is appropriately defined as "collectively self-identified professional ethnic network".[25] Besides the aforementioned common usage of the internet, another mechanism of job-seeking is through a previous HSL migrant, often one who graduated from the same school or faculty in Turkey. This migrant channels relevant work opportunities to the seeker. This role of the network has repeatedly come into focus over the last decade. Migrants share their experiences with each other, concerning formal migratory processes, labor and social relations, and strategies for stabilizing their own life in the host country. Because of the variability of these processes and conditions in the host country, it is of capital importance that the migration experiences of the communicating migrants be temporally close. Therefore the professional ethnic network has two primary roles. Firstly, it plays an informative role, assisting in the preparation and initial stages of migration. Secondly, it plays a facilitative role, stabilizing current migration. It is this second role that is currently more important, although the informative role is increasing

---

[23] It is from the lyric "Englishman in New York" of Sting's song.

[24] In the course of the Battle of Sakarya in 1921 in the Greco-Turkish War (1919-1921) after the World War I, the commander-in-chief Mustafa Kemal articulated his warfare art to the soldiers with this phrase.

[25] See also Vertovec, 1999:449, Poros, 2001; Vertovec 2002.

in significance and will foreseeably become more important in coming years.

There is a recognizable trend in the attitude of migrants. At the beginning, the tendency is to consider themselves alone and to reject the network. Following this comes a phase of helplessness where they identify themselves as members of the migrant network, but requiring the help of others and with little to offer themselves. Later, however, there is a shift in perspective whereby they come to see themselves as being useful members of the group, capable of helping themselves, and also of helping others.

Despite the intended facilitative role of the network, which generally aids solidarity and assists with adaptation to the new environment, a few of the interviewees such as Mespilus, one of the network's key figures, complain about insufficient help from others. In Rhus' words: "We learned from ourselves for ourselves." This is the final stage in the trend that can fittingly be labeled "migrants-for-migrants". In fact, highly educated people who migrate at similar times have common problems and interests. Indeed, the existence of the professional ethnic network appears necessary, although most try to distance themselves from the network, especially in their first years. The reasons for this are: (i) integration with non-migrants (in spite of the migrants' anxiety for adaptation); (ii) accumulation of the aforementioned advanced cultural capital; and/or (iii) fear of resembling other migrant communities - including unrelated nationalities, but especially the preceding labor migrants from Turkey and their descendants. As is obvious in these three reasons, the focal point of this network is professionalism rather than ethnicity. As a matter of fact, almost all prefer not to live in Turkish districts. Absolute avoidance of the professional ethnic network is possible exclusively for the short visitors, people from Turkey who did not graduate there, and "sensitive trees" that broke all connections with Turkey for political reasons.

5.2. Virtual Communities

The professional ethnic network also maintains a systematically organized presence in cyber environments, primarily internet forums and mailing lists. These internet communication platforms provide archives containing knowledge of the formal procedures of migration, the migrants' experiences of managing these, exchanges about daily problems as well as job and house announcements. Additionally, they cover political debates and opinions on life in Germany and on the labor market.[26] Moreover, the people connected to these virtual communities arrange social meetings. The existence of several virtual communities based around the HSLM network highlights several aspects of the organizational and operational structure of the professional ethnic network. In the fieldwork conducted for this study, various "expatriate" (virtual) communities, of differing sizes, of the professional ethnic network were encountered. These can be categorized into seven main types. In decreasing order of size, they are: (1) "*almanya'dayız*" ("We, from Turkey, are in Germany") covering the majority of the recent highly educated labor migrants; (2) networks oriented around the Green Card program (currently disappearing but showing signs of morphing into a sector-based professional ethnic network); (3) the alma-mater networks (the most durable); (4) the like-minded networks, distinguished by their political points of view (the most active); (5) networks covering all professional migrants from different countries in Germany; (6) company-based networks (where a company employs a significant number of people from Turkey); and (7) networks comprising highly-educated second and/or third generations of the previous labor migrants from Turkey.

On internet communication platforms the professional ethnic network can be decomposed into several different groups. Nevertheless, one virtual community, established in 2002 and now the biggest, plays a dominant role in the present professional ethnic network. It had more than 1,000 members at the beginning of 2007

[26] Computer-mediated communication platforms, or online discussion platforms, can be separated into intranet communication platforms and internet communication platforms. The former platforms, like homepages and web blogs, are increasing in importance and have personal features. These platforms are attuned to the latter platforms. Internet communication platforms aiming at socialization are cyber fields which provide to share information among a certain group of people, virtual community.

with approximately 10,000 accumulated e-mails.[27] The continuously increasing quantity of mails, the rich archive and databases, various polls, assigned sub-groups, and the prolific sharing of professional knowledge with other groups underline the importance of this community. In the group description, it is emphasized that people who send e-mails provoking or participating in political debates or exclusive dialogue are expelled without warning. For political debates and personal conversations, the like-minded networks, as sub-groups, are offered by the moderators. This fact, belied by the ease of registering, highlights the moderators' role in the largest virtual community and indicates a preference for maintaining an apolitical atmosphere and remaining a purpose-oriented network covering all possible highly educated labor migrants from Turkey in Germany. Commonly encountered problems are easily identified on the different platforms. Although most prefer passive participation in this virtual community, over time a selection of the above-mentioned networks, particularly the like-minded and alma-mater networks, have become more active not only in cyber space but also in real life. Moreover, both potential and return migrants are beginning to concede the consequence of these virtual communities as a means of obtaining information. This increased attention exposes "brain circulation", and clearly shows the future of institutionalized HSLM.

Another attraction of the professional ethnic network for the migrants is assistance in dealing with the common problem of prejudice in Germany. The network can provide the member with additional meaning to their self-identification as a "grounded cosmopolitan". Some emphasize their disposition to be free from nationalist aspirations, although they still express a desire for a "port of

---

[27] When its message history is evaluated, the monthly average (mean) e-mails is about 155, the standard deviation is about 68, the median is about 149, the maximum e-mails (389) came in July 2003, the minimum e-mails (49) came in December 2006, August is the month of coming maximum e-mails (234), January is the month of coming minimum e-mails (114), 2003 is the year of coming maximum e-mails (monthly average: 201), 2002 is the year of coming minimum e-mails (monthly average: 145), the highly-intensive quarter period is June-July-August, the low-intensive quarter period is December-January-February.

refuge" in which they can, in a sense, drop their defenses, thanks to the similar social background of their co-members.

5.3. Relations with HSL Migrants from Other Countries

Neighborhood has very little significance for employees in both Germany and urban Turkey, according to HSL migrants. The absence of their family network, though, is remarkable, and even though some have kin in Germany, they are also reluctant to associate often with them, as mentioned before. Most do not show any interest for social contact with ethnic people, the so-called "German-Turks". The presence of the ethnic network implicitly provides entertainment and leisure opportunities, such as markets and restaurants, and so for the labor migrants who avoid this network, the workplace is the main resource for social relations. Nevertheless, social relations of HSL migrants are under the influence of the attitude in Germany of "colleague is colleague". Non-migrant highly skilled employees, who are usually raised entirely in Germany, make a clear distinction between their work life and leisure. However, this separation is not easy for a newcomer. It can be here argued that even when work is not dramatically altered by migration, the recreation of migrants is. Consequently, some complain about the scarcity of their social relations with non-migrants, but some recognize it as an inevitable result of the fundamental ontological difference between a migrant and a non-migrant in any given society.

In fact, all highly educated labor migrants from Turkey in Germany have close and frequent contact with other HSL migrants from different countries in their free time, besides the professional ethnic network. They also have similar interests and problems to adapt their leisure to the new conditions. Moreover, they contribute to elevating each other's advanced cultural capital. This can be read as a signal of "skilled diaspora".

5.4. Conceptualizing Symbolic Interaction with the Newcomer

"'You don't understand me,' said the duckling.

'We don't understand you? Who can understand you, I wonder? Do you consider yourself more clever than the cat, or the old woman? I will say nothing of myself. Don't imagine such nonsense, child, and thank your good fortune that you have been received here. Are you not in a warm room, and in society from which you may learn something. But you are a chatterer, and your company is not very agreeable. Believe me, I speak only for your own good. I may tell you unpleasant truths, but that is a proof of my friendship. I advise you, therefore, to lay eggs, and learn to purr as quickly as possible.'

'I believe I must go out into the world again,' said the duckling." (Hans Christian Andersen, The Ugly Duckling, 1844)

In the analysis of the interviews, various experiences, observations, and perceptions regarding prejudice, stereotyping, and discrimination were found. This was especially evident in the analysis of labor relations and, notably, social relations. The majority of HSL migrants mention prejudices of the locals towards Turkey and people from Turkey. They underline that they encounter these prejudices despite the presence of class differences between the old migrants from Turkey (including their descendants) and themselves, despite differences between people from different backgrounds in Turkey, and despite the fact that many of those "Turks" who were born and brought up in Germany are far removed from the cultural heritage of Turkey and often do not even speak the language competently. In fact, they make the separation between "Turks in Turkey" and "Turks in Germany". Moreover, almost none identify themselves as "Turks in Germany". While introducing themselves as well-educated recent arrivals from Turkey, they see themselves as removed from "ordinary" migrants from the same country and their descendents. Most argue that the negative image in Germany about "Turks in Germany" and accordingly "Turks" and Turkey is a result of the first generation of unskilled labor migrants from Turkey; some read this image as a social product. Some declare that they acknowledge non-migrants' prejudices to be right, when they look at the people who came to Germany from rural Turkey in the 1960s and 1970s. They clearly recognize prejudices as a consequence of the migratory history. In order words, they believe that prejudices and stereotypes about them and their country of origin already existed in Germany before their arrival.

As explained in the section on the story of migration, HSL migrants attach the most importance to the integration issues in the host country. Encountering prejudices appears to be a significant challenge to their migratory path. These experiences fall into the category of the 'black swan phenomenon', illustrated in FIGURE 10. In Turkey, people of highly educated strata are seen by both others and themselves as "white swans". When they migrate to Germany, they appear as "black swans" in relation to the rest of the "Turks in Germany".

FIGURE 10. BLACK SWAN PHENOMENON

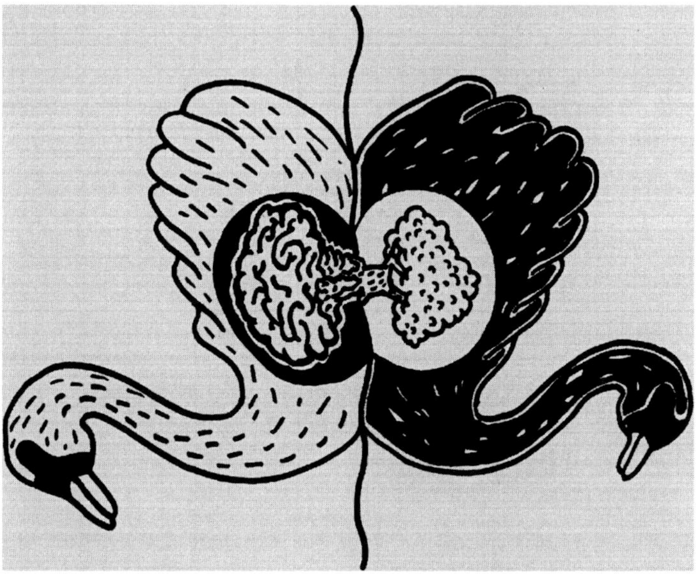

The 'black swan phenomenon' corresponds to the situation when a non-migrant comes across a counterexample of their paradigmatic prejudice. Upon meeting the counterexample, that is, the unexpected entity, contradiction appears in the current epistemology. 'Black swan phenomenon' evokes communication and symbolic interaction including symbolic violence.[28] Locals tend not to question their paradigms but they interrogate and have suspicions about the migrants: "you cannot be Turkish". Non-migrants are therefore likely to regard "black swans" as exceptional, the perception being: "you are different". In practice, locals are interrogative and migrants are responsive in conversation. In the majority of cases all questions asked by the non-migrants are strange and new for migrants who try to answer.

FIGURE 11. COPING STRATEGIES TO BLACK SWAN PHENOMENON

	Liberal Strategy	**Conservative Strategy**	**Collectivist Strategy**
Generalized Other	Leading culture in the current country	Leading culture in the country of origin	Subcultures
Social Behavior	Will for individually acceptance	Effort for eliminating prejudices	Refusal of being exception

In fact, some, in order to counteract these prejudices, begin to introduce themselves and represent Turkey as they have experienced it. Therefore, they try to explain how they differ from the rest of the "Turks in Germany". As shown in FIGURE 11, coping mechanisms of HSL migrants with 'black swan phenomenon' can be collected in three main strategies: (i) liberal; (ii) conservative; and (iii) collectivist. These coping strategies are generally mutually inclusive.

[28] According to symbolic interactionism (George Herbert Mead and Herbert Blumer), people act based on meanings that are derived from social interaction and modified through interpretation.

As a result, HSL migrants cannot be categorized by these strategies, however they still provide some hints to comprehend their motives.

5.6. Typology based on Social Relations

As previously mentioned, all HSL migrants have close contact within the professional migrant network, covering highly educated migrants from Turkey and other countries. HSL migrants from Turkey in Germany can particularly be categorized according to their attitude toward two problematic groups of locals with whom they have social relations. These two groups are: (i) non-migrants; and (ii) their ethnic community excluding HSL migrants. Both of these groups make an issue of their "integration" in Germany.

Depending on their experiences and expectations, attitudes of HSL migrants concerning these two groups are formed on the basis of incomplete information. These attitudes are continuously shaped by every social interaction. HSL migrants are more empathetic toward the problematic group when they focus on common interests. If they feel the strong presence of "cultural difference", then they become more critical of the target group. In the context of non-migrants, the term "cultural difference" generally gives an account of prejudices, stereotyping, and discrimination. The corresponding term dealing with the ethnic community usually refers to class difference. There are four different types according to these attitudes:

1. **Fully integrated:** empathetic attitude toward both groups
2. **Elitist integrated:** empathetic attitude to non-migrants in Germany but critical toward the old labor migrants from Turkey and their descendents
3. **Collectively integrated:** critical toward non-migrants in Germany but empathetic toward the old labor migrants from Turkey and their descendents
4. **Selectively integrated:** critical toward both groups

There is a significant relationship between the future plans of the migrants (discussed under the migration story dimension) and state in social relations. Particularly, intention to stay in Germany is strongly correlated with the 'fully integrated' type.

CHAPTER 7. CONCLUSION

1. Primary Findings

This dissertation achieved its main aim – to develop a typology with regard to the embodied and situated agents in HSLM. First, the semi-structured interviews with the ICT specialists from Turkey, who have working experience in Germany, were interpreted by a hermeneutic reading in the framework of grounded theory. Later, the relevant contexts were explicated by using three essential components of HSLM (education, work, and migration). Interpretations and contextualizations brought to light five analytic dimensions of the typology (family background, educational background, migration story, labor relations, and social relations). Furthermore, the qualitative analysis revealed common and distinctive characters within the typology. The construction process of the typology uncovered the most important trends and patterns of HSLM.

The analysis on HSL migrants displays the relevance of capital resources inherited from their family. Two essential elements of resources, cultural capital and socio-economic capital, are utilized to explore their family background. In respect to cultural capital, the study exposes the crucial role of mothers. The mother is seen as the determinant figure in cultural capital reproduction for the family. In the case study, about two third of mothers obtained an educational level higher than secondary education; one third had completed tertiary education. Half of the educated mothers work as professionals; the other half are housewives. That means that there is a large number of HSL migrants who were brought up by educated mothers in Turkey. Moreover, both educated housewives and professional mothers live in cities, whereas uneducated mothers typically come from the rural areas. For that matter, the study assesses Alevi cultural capital as an affirmative value, in the context of the parents' encouraging approach to education of the child, in the rural-origin family (Prunus, Rhamnus, and Carpinus). The second element used to explore the family background of HSL migrants is defined by the socio-economic situation of the family. Thus, the family background dimension introduces capital resources which are passed down from the parents to their children. Most HSL migrants came from nuclear middle class families in urban Turkey. The working class background is only found in cases in which the parents spent time as workers in Germany (Tilia and Syringa). A clear majority of HSL migrants from Turkey does not have any relatives in Germany. In fact, the current study shows that the family network does not play an important role in the stabilization of HSLM.

The study demonstrates a significant relationship between family background and educational preferences. Indeed, the reproduction of cultural capital and the transformation of economic capital to cultural capital are conspicuous. Therefore, it is also necessary to underline that some kinds of public high schools offering free boarding are important for children with a rural family background. The study shows that rural-urban migration for secondary education is a prerequisite to become a (rural-origin) HSL migrant. Also, geographical movement routes in Turkey before HSLM form a pattern: starting from the East (of Ankara) to the West (of Ankara), from the West to Ankara, and finally from Ankara to Istanbul. This pattern appears to be a requirement for HSLM. Besides these attributes, the difference in education background results from having a "warm-up" experience specifically with Germany. German usage as a teaching language in secondary or tertiary education, summer school, graduate study, or an internship in Germany can be considered as warm-up exercises for HSLM. According to these criteria under the dimension of educational background, the migrants are divided into four ideal types.

The dimension of the migration story explains the grounds and implications of HSLM. Consequently, it covers not only the pre-migration (past) but also the post-migration period (future) of the embodied and situated actors of HSLM. Military service obligation in Turkey is seen as the main cause of HSLM among highly educated young men: institutionalized temporary expulsion without prejudice. They prefer to go abroad in order to obtain the right to three-week reduced military service. As seen in the example of Mespilus, it indirectly affects HSLM among young women as well. In addition, it can be underlined at this point that these men and women do not experience long-term unemployment in Turkey. Their selection of Germany as their destination country is comprehensible for the education background types 'fully-prepared for Germany' and 'root-trained'. The training for Germany by warm-up experiences also enriches the HSLM channels to Germany. The rest of HSL migrants belong to the biggest group of highly educated people in Turkey, the 'well-trained' ideal type. Their target to go abroad is limited to Anglo-American countries in the pre-HSLM period, since their language of instruction at school in Turkey is usually English. In this study, it is argued that the recent program in Germany for foreign ICT-expert labor, the publicly-presented German Green-Card Program, was successful in changing the preferences of HSLM workers from Turkey to Germany. Hence, it initiated a new period of HSLM history from Turkey to Germany. In other words, Germany became a more attractive destination country for 'well-trained' people in Turkey, targeting classical English-speaking HSLM receiving countries. The migration decision of the 'root-trained' type is influenced by their parents' migration experiences in Germany as "guest workers". According to the dimension of the migration story, the 'attached' type selects Germany due to their spouse. However, the 'adventurer' type has been the primary figure in the new era of labor relations. The 'adventurer' type does not aim for a better salary but protects her/his standard of living in the host country. They attempt to have a "successful" migration story as their life project. Unlike tourists, the 'adventurer' uses labor power as their institutionalized cultural capital in order to accumulate advanced cultural capital. The correlation of a "successful" HSLM experience to the amount of warm-up exercises and residence time in the host country is notable.

HSL migrants from Turkey, especially the 'adventurer', mostly appreciate the existence of the social state as an unexpected benefit of their migration career in Germany. They are glad to have more recreation time in Germany compared to Turkey and other possible destination countries. They do not consider working to be a burden; on the contrary, it is the main purpose of their residence abroad. According to those interviewed, flexible labor relations create working conditions that cannot guarantee a life-long career; they however accept this risky path. Moreover, continuous transitional work contracts lead to varying degrees/levels of integration into the labor market. The central role of projects in their work promotes this variability. In this context, they are no different from their counterparts, the non-migrant highly skilled workers.

The HSL migrant accumulates advanced cultural capital in both work and free time. Some have difficulties separating leisure time from work, since many used to have colleagues who become friends as a result of relatively longer working hours in Turkey, especially in Istanbul where the inner HSL migrants are situated. With migration to Germany, they have left not only their place of origin and family network but also less recreation time. For them, re-organization of their new leisure time – integration into leisure – is at least as important as labor market integration.

Under the dimension of social relations, the relevance of the professional ethnic network was elaborated by investigating its expressions in virtual communities. Having a simultaneous HSLM experience, and therefore more likely similar interests and problems, results in more social interactions in the professional ethnic network. The HSL migrants from Turkey also have well-established contacts with professionals from other countries in Germany. The analysis found the distinction in social relations to be correspond to either a empathetic or critical stance towards two reference groups: (i) non-migrants in Germany, and (ii) old migrants from Turkey and their descendants. The positions of the new migrants are shaped through their experiences and observations. Almost all mention prejudices about people from Turkey under the pressure of the 'crowding phenomenon'. In addition, the thesis explores all these with the newly developed concept: the 'black swan phenomenon'.

2. Secondary Finding: Black Swan Phenomenon

"'I will fly to those royal birds,' he exclaimed, 'and they will kill me, because I am so ugly, and dare to approach them; but it does not matter: better be killed by them than pecked by the ducks, beaten by the hens, pushed about by the maiden who feeds the poultry, or starved with hunger in the winter.' Then he flew to the water, and swam towards the beautiful swans. The moment they espied the stranger, they rushed to meet him with outstretched wings. 'Kill me,' said the poor bird; and he bent his head down to the surface of the water, and awaited death. But what did he see in the clear stream below? His own image; no longer a dark, gray bird, ugly and disagreeable to look at, but a graceful and beautiful swan." (Hans Christian Andersen, The Ugly Duckling, 1844)

Based on the principles of the state sovereignty, the nation-state has the right to control the flow of persons across its political boundaries, thus protecting itself against "unwanted migration". It implies that migrants are selected. Selective migration gives an incomplete picture of the country of origin. On the one hand, assigning any migrant as the representative of his/her country of origin – taking the migrant as information – is a primitive inductive approach. On the other hand, labeling or stigmatizing migrants according to a holistic picture of the country of origin or to the accumulated information is a primitive deductive approach. The study shows that these two approaches work together in developing and delivering judgments about migrants.

In the migrant-receiving countries, migrants and their descendants are usually labeled as their country of origin and identified with a paradigmatic group. Taking Germany as an example, the paradigmatic group is composed of people from Turkey. Even though neither kind of migration from Turkey to Germany is new, the massive un- and semiskilled labor migration in the 1960s and 1970s has created a crowding phenomenon. All Turkish people in Germany, despite having different backgrounds, are hence in danger of being stereotyped. The migrant stereotype in Germany is that of a rural-origin, uneducated, Muslim, Turkish, male "guest worker" in a patriarchal family situation.[1] Through this stereotype, a conven-

[1] They are even portrayed as "black sheep" as one from the migrant community failed in "integration".

tional image of Turkey is reproduced. Bommes (1993:67) explains „globaler Charakterisierungen *der* Türkei“ as follows:

> „klischees in soziologischer Form beherrschen den Alltag: *die* Türken stammen aus einer traditionallen Agrargesellschaft oder differenzierter einen Übergangsgesellschaft, in der sie aber häufig noch aus traditionallen Zusammenhängen stammen; *die* Türkei selbst hat kein ausgebautes Bildungssystem; die Menschen leben meist noch in bäuerlicher Subsistenz-wirtschaft und pflegen entsprecend bäuerliche Lebensgewohnheiten; der Islam bestimmt das Leben; das Patriarchat ist sehr ausgeprägt.“

A selective migration paradox from Turkey to Germany can be explicitly observed from a historical perspective.[2] Like the previous "guest workers", the current migrants from Turkey have also been "selected". Turkey is a demographically active country and its young, educated population has been increasing considerably. Unlike the previous dominant migrant type, HSL migrants, regardless of their sex, come from metropolises or big cities in Turkey and are highly educated and mostly non-religious. HSL migrants thus become visible as the new "Other" who are exposed to "irrelevant" prejudices of the locals. Furthermore, HSLM from Turkey to Germany brings about a different type of meeting between the new "Other" and the old "Other".

The 'black swan phenomenon' stems from the stress between ontology and epistemology.[3] Although "being" is difficult to define, humans as observers make linguistic statements in order to provide contexts for communication. These statements, despite their bias, are sources of episteme (paradigm) and implicitly form a basis for doxa.[4] The primitive episteme production, through avoidance of

---

[2] Remember the famous quote of Max Frisch "*Wir riefen Arbeitskräfte, es kamen Menschen*" (We wanted workers, but human beings were arriving). It can be updated under the current circumstances of migration: "*Wir rufen Fachkräfte, es kommen auch Menschen*" (We want workers, but human beings are coming too).

[3] The principle questions of ontology are "What entities exist?", "What can be said to exist?" and "Into what categories, if any, can we sort existing things?"

[4] For example, the phrase "This is a white swan" is an observation which corresponds to the statement "There is an X that is swan, and X is white" in logic. If this statement is treated as the premises of categorization, for which inductive reasoning and/or generalization are employed, we might reach the conclusion: "All swans we have seen are white,

further information gathering costs, is the primary reason of prejudices and stereotyping. The systematic accumulation of these episteme in human history creates apparatuses and results in discrimination (Otherization): reproduction and marginalization of the Other. Heidegger (1962) believes in the necessity of explicitly restating the question of "being" in order to destroy the history of ontology. Moreover, Gadamer (1991) underlines not only our "historically effected consciousness" (*wirkungsgeschichtliches Bewußtsein*) but also our embedment in a particular history and culture. Any attempt to re-define Being is bound to run into peculiar difficulties because of our a priori knowledge. We actually need the articulation of histories to understand the Other. In this direction, Levinas' ethics prioritize confronting the Other, since the face of the Other (as expression, not an object) speaks ("Do not kill me") and compels us to response.[5] To Levinas, the Other is ethically superior to the self. Following Heidegger, Levinas argues that the face-to-face encounter alters history or at least leaves a trace in it.[6]

Homi Bhabha (1990) describes immigrant communities as "the Other within", contesting the notion of a pure national identity and demanding to narrate the nation from the margins. From this perspective, Göktürk (2001) highlights the emergence of transnational motives in the Turkish-German scene, which are related to "speaking back" and address hybridity as a source of strength and pleas-

---

and therefore all swans are white." This inference is deductively invalid, since it is always possible that there is a non-white swan. Hume explains the problem of induction in his book *An Enquiry Concerning Human Understanding*: Given that every swan we have observed is white, what is the rational proof that the next swan will be white? Believing that science cannot be grounded on such a deductively invalid inference, Popper is also interested in the problem of induction and proposes a solution to the problem: falsification. All claims of knowledge could, in principle, be mistaken. The falsifiability criterion is that the singular existential observation of a black swan serves to show that the universal statement "All swans are white" is false. In logic this is called *modus tollens*. Whereas Popper is mainly concerned with the logic of science, Kuhn (*The Structure of Scientific Revolutions*) examines the history of science. According to Kuhn, scientists work within a conceptual paradigm that strongly influences the way in which they see data, and they go to great length to defend their paradigm against falsification by adding ad hoc hypotheses to existing theories.

[5] Derrida's ethics is founded on hospitality to the Other.

[6] This inflection leads to universality as ethical humanity, and not universality as politics.

ure, rather than lack and trouble. The study displays that HSL migrants coping with 'black swan phenomenon' contribute to this enrichment of transnational motives.

3. Contributions to Theoretical Discussions

The emphasis in the existing literature has most often been placed on the impact of HSLM on the economy. This one-sidedness leads to some blind spots by keeping the immigrant and her/his experience out of the center of sociological accounts. HSLM has thus been traditionally classified as an economic migration. This study introduced socio-structural grounds and influences of HSLM, rather than the economic cost-benefit analysis of such migration.

The departure of the "brains", for whose education state resources have even been spent, is accepted in Turkey as a by-product of globalization. By not working for their native country and not paying back the education that is granted them, those who migrate might even be accused of treason.[7] This is the most essential reason why HSLM became a hotly debated phenomenon in Turkey in the last decades, even though its history dates back long before than that. The history of HSLM from Turkey, which is assumed to have become institutionalized parallel to the non-qualified labor migration, can be traced back as far as Tanzimat, when, for the purpose of westernization, students were sent abroad, especially to Europe, where they received tertiary education with state support.

Going abroad is still a desired trend in Turkey, especially if it is temporary. In fact, on the educational path, studying abroad is one of the most yearned for elements of cultural capital. Since the establishment of the Republic of Turkey, the most preferred schools have been the ones teaching in a foreign language, with English,

[7] The fact that HSLM from Turkey was rendered more visible inside Turkey in the last years can be read as a new element in the nationalist discourses developing as a reaction to globalization. However, within this interpretation, the hurdle race of the Republic of Turkey on the way to the EU membership, the constant emphasis on national identity that grows under the guise of anti-imperialism and the fact that this emphasis, with its anti-American and anti-European wings, has now extended into anti-Westernism have to be underlined.

French, and German being the most popular. This has been true despite the adoption of the mono-lingual motto against the other languages present in the country. This fact is very telling regarding the attitudes of particularly the middle and upper-middle classes toward cultural capital. Long before the recent increase in the importance of learning a foreign language for the labor market, the teaching languages of the elite schools of Turkey were foreign languages. Attending these schools, together with its function in the reproduction of cultural capital, creates symbolic capital, and in fact, is regarded an upward mobility by itself. In addition to the cultural capital, these elite schools make attendees more prepared for the internationalized labor market.

Another way this dissertation contributes to existing literature is that it shows that HSLM should not be directly associated with unemployment and wage differentials, but as an element of career building. Unlike other migrants, the HSL migrants are more interested in integration problems, mostly to stabilize their career building process. They see HSLM as the buildup of advanced cultural capital. Being highly individualized, the HSL migrants are interested in "integration" in order to accumulate 'advanced cultural capital' which refers to valuation of experience abroad. The study also introduced a comprehensive explanation of "integration" on social relations with all locals (non-migrants and the people with a migration background from Turkey).

Work and leisure are intermingled with each other in flexible labor market conditions. Nyström (2005:24) determines two sides of the contractual labor relations for the workers. On the one hand, he sees the "reconciliation of work and family life", attached to temporal flexibility in work as its advantage. On the other hand, he interprets "discontinuity of social relations at the workplace" as its disadvantage. It is arguable that these two are more crucial phenomena for the migrant worker. The advantage of "reconciliation of work and family life" takes a different meaning for labor migrants since they mostly do not have a regular family life in the host country. Also, the migrants came single or perhaps married, and accordingly have different experiences of leisure time. The disadvantage of "discontinuity of social relations at the workplace" also creates more burdens for labor migrants since the work place is no longer a place to develop friendships. It is clear that both a flexible working model and social state opportunities have changed the organization of leisure. None of the previous studies have focused on the leisure reconstruction in the HSLM experience, i.e., integration into leisure in the current society rather than labor market integration.

The existing literature points to the relevance of the kinship networks and generally the ethnic network to migration. However, this study suggests an alternative approach to identifying the underlying mechanisms of HSLM in social networks. In particular, the result of the analyses indicates the triviality of both kinship and ethnic networks and importance of professional ethnic networks. This is particularly notable in the case of simultaneous migration under the same factual circumstances. Additionally, the study corrects the perception of the facilitative role of the professional ethnic network, and partly its informative role. The thesis clarifies the great importance of the network of HSL migrants from Turkey in Germany for the stabilization of the individual migration experiences. In regard to close relations between HSL migrants from different countries, the thesis affirms the validity of a "skilled diaspora" as well. Also, it seems to be difficult or uncommon for new highly educated migrants from Turkey to establish social relations with non-migrants and the old labor migrants from Turkey and their descendants in Germany. None of the exiting studies have touched on this issue. Although the main barrier to contact between these two groups is perceived by the HSL migrants as "cultural difference", this reason itself challenges the accumulation of advanced cultural capital that welcomes "cultural plurality" and makes signs of "cultural interactions" observable. In this context, "cultural difference" is constructed as a discourse of collective memory of the migration history. This discourse is revisited as the consequences of symbolic violence in the 'black swan phenomenon' under the impact of the crowding phenomenon. Nevertheless, it can be argued that it will gradually disappear as social interactions increase in the new era of

HSLM history from Turkey to Germany, which began with the Green Card program in 2000.

Furthermore, this study considers HSL migrants from Turkey to Germany as examples to illuminate the dynamics of international migration and thereby investigated the role of the nation-state, i.e., in particular its regulatory relevance for individual migration projects. The sending country of HSLM "bears the costs of raising and educating the emigrants in their unproductive years with limited benefits from its investment and the skills that those persons could contribute to the country", to the International Organization for Migration (1997:30). In spite of this reality, the study indicates institutionalized expulsion from the sending country and increasing numbers of attractors from the receiving country. Moreover, the analysis reveals not only new initiatives in Turkish nationality law but also changes in German migration politics which occurred as the consequences of internationalization of the flexible labor market making the socio-economic and political conditions relevant for the realization of HSLM. The study hence points out that nation-states, playing the role of receiver or sender, approve of HSLM to compete for graduated sovereignty, through "grounded cosmopolitan" migrants. The form of HSLM from Turkey to Germany, 'brain export', is more accurate than before.

REFERENCES

Abadan-Unat, Nermin. (1976). (Ed.), *Turkish Workers in Europe 1960-1975: A Socio-economic reappraisal*. Leiden: E.J.Brill.

Abadan-Unat, Nermin. (1976). Turkish Migration to Europe (1960-1975): A Balance Sheet of Achievements and Failures. In Nermin Abadan-Unat. (Ed.), *Turkish Workers in Europe 1960-1975: A Socio-economic reappraisal*. Leiden: E.J.Brill.

Adıvar, Halide Edib. (1972/c1926). *Memoirs of Halide Edib*. New York: Arno Press.

Akgün, Birol. (2000). The Turkish Diaspora in the United States and Its Role in Promoting Turkish-American Relations. *Turkish Yearbook of International Relations*, 31, 2.

Aktar, Ayhan. (2000). *Varlık Vergisi ve Türkleştirme Politikaları*. Istanbul: İletişim Yayınları.

Akyüz, Yahya. (1982). *Türk Eğitim Tarihi*. [History of Turkish Education]. Ankara: Ankara Üniversitesi, Eğitim Bilimleri Fakültesi Yayınları, #114.

Altınöz, Vuslat Devrim. (2003). *The Ottoman Women's Movement: Women's Press, Journals, Magazines And Newspapers from 1875 to 1923*. Unpublished MA Thesis. Miami University. Oxford, Ohio.

Altuğ, Sumru G., Alpay Filiztekin, and Şevket Pamuk. (2007). The Sources of Long-Term Economic Growth for Turkey, 1880-2005. *CEPR Discussion Paper 6463*.

AMAD. (1939). *Atatürk'ün Maarife Ait Direktifleri*. İstanbul: Milli Eğitim Basımı.

Andersen, Hans Christian. (1844). *The Ugly Duckling*.

APT. (2003). *Accession Partnership with Turkey-2003*. European Commission, Brussels, Council Decision of 19 May 2003 L145.

Atkinson, J. (1984). *Flexibility, Uncertainty and Manpower Management*. IMS Report No.89, Brighton: Institute of Manpower Studies.

Atkinson, J. and Meager, N.. (1986). *Changing Working Patterns: How companies achieve flexibility to meet new needs*. London: Institute of Manpower Studies, National Economic Development Office.

Aydin Senem, and Fuat Keyman. (2004). European Integration and the Transformation of Turkish Democracy. *CEPS: Turkey in Europe Monitor* 8: 1-12.

Aydınoğlu, İsmail Hakkı. (1976). Manpower and Employment Policies under the Five Years Plans and Emigration. In Nermin Abadan-Unat. (Ed.), *Turkish Workers in Europe 1960-1975: A Socio-economic reappraisal*. Leiden: E.J.Brill.

Bailey, Kenneth D.. (1987). *Methods of Social Research*. New York: Free Press; London:Collier Macmillan.

Bailey, Kenneth D.. (1994). *Typology and Taxonomies: An Introduction to Classification Techniques*. Sage University Paper Series on Quantitative Applications in the Social Sciences, Series No. 07-102. Thousand Oaks; London; New Delhi: Sage.

Bali, Rıfat N. (1999). *Cumhuriyet Yıllarında Türkiye Yahudileri: Bir Türkleştirme Serüveni (1923-1945)*. Istanbul: İletişim Yayınları.

Baltacıoğlu, İsmail Hakkı. (1943). *Türke Doğru*. Istanbul: Kültür Basımevi.

Barrere, Rudolfo, Lucas Luchilo and Julio Raffo. (2004). Highly Skilled Labour and International Mobility in South America. *STI Working Paper*, 10.

Berkes, Niyazi. (1959). (Ed.), *Turkish Nationalism and Western Civilization: Selected Essays of Ziya Gökalp*. Westport and Connecticut: Greenwood Press.

Berkes, Niyazi. (1964). *The Development of Secularism in Turkey*. Montreal: McGill University Press.

Bhabha, Homi K.. (1990). (Ed.), *Nation and Narration*. London and New York: Routledge.

Bhagwati, Jagdish N.. (1976). (Ed.), *The brain drain and taxation; theory and empirical analysis*. Amsterdam: North Holland Pub. Co..

Bolder, Axel, Stefan Naevecke, and Sylvia Schulte. (2005). *Türöffner Zeitarbeit? Kompetenz und Erwerbsverlauf in der Praxis der Leiharbeit*. Wiesbaden: VS Verlag für Sozialwissenschaften / GWV Fachverlag GmbH..

Bommes, Michael. (1993). *Migration und Sprachverhalten: eine ethnographisch - sprachwissenschaftlich Fallstudie*. Wiesbaden: Deutscher Universitäts Verlag.

Bommes, Michael. (2006). Migration and Migration Research in Germany. In Ellie Vasta and Vasoodeven Vuddamalay (Eds.), *International Migration and the Social Sciences. Confronting National Experiences in Australia, France and Germany*. Basingstoke.

Bourdieu, Pierre. (1983). Ökonomisches Kapital, kulturelles Kapital, soziales Kapital. In Reinhard Kreckel. (Ed.), *Soziale Ungleichheiten*. Göttingen, Soziale Welt, Sonderband 2: 183-198.

Bourdieu, Pierre. (1984). *Distinction: A Social Critique of the Judgement of Taste*. London: Routledge.

Bourdieu, Pierre. (1986). Forms of Capital. In John G. Richardson. (Ed.), *Handbook of Theory and Research for the Sociology of Education*. New York: Greenwood Press.

Bourdieu, Pierre. (1990). *The Logic of Practice*. Polity Press, Cambridge.

Bourdieu, Pierre. (1999). (Ed.), *The Weight of the World: Social Suffering in Contemporary Society*. Oxford: Polity Press.

Boyd, Monica. (1989). Family and Personal Networks in International Migration: Recent Developments and New Agendas. *International Migration Review* 23, 3: 638-670.

Burt, Ronald S.. (1982). *Towards a Structural Theory of Action: Network Models of Social Structure, Perceptions, and Action*. New York: Academic Press.

Carrington, William J., and Enrica Detragiache. (1998). *How big is the Brain Drain?* International Monetary Fund, Working Paper July 1998.

Castles, Stephen and Mark J. Miller. (1993). *The Age of Migration: International Population Movements in the Modern World.* London: Macmillan.

Choldin, H.M.. (1973). Kinship Networks in the Migration Process. *International Migration Review*, 163-175.

Chung, H. Kerkhofs, M. and Ester, P.. (2007). *Working Time Flexibility in European Companies. European Foundation for the Improvement of Living and Working Conditions.* Luxembourg: Office for Official Publications of the European Communities.

Coombs, Gary. (1978). Opportunities, Information Networks and the Migration-Distance Relationship. *Social Networks* 1: 257-276.

Copeaux, Etienne. (1998). (Trans.) *Tarih Ders Kitaplarında (1931-1993): Türk Tarih Tezinden Türk-İslam Sentezine.* By Ali Berktay. Istanbul: Tarih Vakfı Yurt Yayınları.

Crouch, Mira, and Heather McKenzie. (2006). The Logic of Small Samples in Interview-Based Qualitative Research. *Social*

Science Information 45 (4). London, Thousand Oaks, CA and New Delphi: Sage Publications.

Derviş, Kemal, Daniel Gros, Michael Emerson, and Sinan Ülgen. (2004). *The European Transformation of Modern Turkey*. Brussels: Center for European Policy Studies.

Devlet Planlama Teşkilatı. (1963). *Kalkınma Planı (Birinci Beş Yıl) 1963-1967*. Ankara: Başbakanlık Devlet Matbaası.

Dewey, John. (1915). *School and Society*. Chicago: The University of Chicago Press.

Dewey, John. (1939). *Türkiye Maarifi Hakkında Rapor*. İstanbul:Milli Eğitim Basımı.

Dobson, Janet, and John Salt. (2004). Review of Migration Statistics. *IMIS-Beiträge 25*. Special Issue: Organisational Recruitment and Patterns of Migration-Interdependencies in an Integrating Europe.

Durkheim, Emile. (1956). *Education and Sociology*. Glencoe: Free Press.

Düvell, Franck. (2004). Beyond Transnationalism: Globally Mobile Actors-empirical evidence from qualitative research. *International Migration Review*.

EARGED. (2005). *OECD PISA 2003 Projesi: Ulusal Nihai Rapor*. T.C. Milli Eğitim Bakanlığı, Eğitimi Araştırma ve Geliştirme Dairesi Başkanlığı. Ankara: EARGED.

Entwistle, N. (1997). Introduction: phenomenography in tertiary education. *Higher Education Research and Development 16*, 127-134.

Erickson, Charlotte. (1972). *Invisible Immigrants: the adaptation of English and Scottish immigrants in 19th century America*. London: Ebenezer Baylis and Son Ltd..

Erzan, Refik, Umut Kuzubaş and Nilüfer Yıldız. (2004). Büyüme ve Göç Senaryoları: Türkiye-AB. International Conference: Immigration Issues in EU-Turkish Relations - Determinants of Immigration and Integration. October, 2004. http://www.econ.boun.edu.tr/cee/gocturkiyeab.pdf

Esping-Andersen, Gøsta. (1999). *Social Foundations of Postindustrial Economies*. Oxford: Oxford University Press.

Eurostat. (2004). Science and Technology: Highest Proportion of Graduates in Science and Engineering in Sweden, Ireland and France. Press Release, 19 January 2004.

Faist, Thomas. (1997). The Crucial Meso-Level. In Hammar, T., G. Brochmann, K. Tamas and T. Faist. (Eds.), *International Migration, Immobility and Development*. Oxford: Berg.

Findlay, A.M.. (1995). Skilled Transients: the invisible phenomenon. In R. Cohen. (Ed.), *The Cambridge Survey of World Migration*. Cambridge: Cambridge University Press.

Findlay, Allan. (1990). A Migration Channel Approach to the Study of High Level Manpower Movements: A Theoretical Perspective. *International Migration* 28:15-22.

Flam, Harry. (2004). Turkey and the EU: politics and economics of accession. *CESifo Economic Studies 50, (1)*:171-210.

Franck, Peter Goswyn. (1970). "Brain Drain from Turkey" Committee on the International Migration of Talent. *The International Migration of High-Level Manpower: Its Impact on the Development Process*. New York: Praeger Publishers.

Friedrichs, Jürgen. (1983). *Methoden empirischer Sozialforschung*. Opladen: Westdeutscher Verlag.

Gadamer, Hans-Georg. (1991). *Truth and Method*. Second Revised Edition (First English edition, 1975). (Trans.) By Joel Weinsheimer and Donald G. Marshall. New York: Crossroad.

Gallagher, Shaun. (2005). *How the Body Shapes the Mind*. Oxford: Clarendon Press.

Gallagher, Shaun. (2008). *Philosophical Antecedents to Situated Cognition*. In Robbins P. and Aydede, M. (eds.) Cambridge

Handbook of Situated Cognitio., Cambridge: Cambridge University Press.

Gitmez, Ali S.. (1983). *Yurtdışına İşçi Göçü ve Geri Dönüşler*. İstanbul: Alan Yayıncılık.

Glaser, Barney. (1978). *Theoretical Sensitivity: Advances in the Methodology of Grounded Theory*. Mill Valley, Ca.: The Sociology Press.

Glaser, Barney. (1992). *Emergence vs. Forcing: Basics of Grounded Theory Analysis*. Mill Valley, Ca.: The Sociology Press.

Glick-Schiller, Nina, Linda Basch, and Cristina Szanton Blanc. (1997). From Immigrant to Transmigrant: theorizing transnational migration. In Ludger Priest. (Ed.), *Transnationale Migration*. Baden Baden: Nomos.

Gök, Fatma. (1999). 75 Yılda İnsan Yetiştirme Eğitim ve Devlet. In Fatma Gök. (Ed.), *75 Yılda Eğitim*. Istanbul: Tarih Vakfı Yayınları.

Goeke, Pascal. (2004). Transnational Migratory Identities between Nuremberg, Serbia, Crotia and Bosnia-Herzegovina. In Anita Böcker, Betty de Hart and Ines Michalowski. (Eds.), *IMIS-Beträge*. Heft 24. Special Issue: Migration and the Regulation of Social Integration.

Gökalp, Ziya. (1973). *Terbiyenin Sosyal ve Kültürel Temelleri*. (Ed.), Rıza Kardaş. Istanbul: Milli Eğitim Basımevi.

Göktürk, Deniz. (2001). Turkish Delight-German Fright: Migrant Identities in Transnational Cinema. In Deniz Derman, Karen Ross and Nevena Dakovic. (Eds.), *Mediated Identities*. Istanbul: Bilgi University Press.

Gorny, Agata, and Paolo Ruspini. (2004). (Eds.), *Migration in the New Europe: East-West Revisited*. U.K.: Palgavre Macmillan.

Gorz, André. (1989). (Trans.) *Critique of Economic Reason*. By Gillian Handyside and Chris Turner. London and New York: Verso.

Granovetter, Mark. (1973). The Strength of Weak Ties. *American Journal of Sociology 78*, (6): 1360-80.

Granovetter, Mark. (1974). *Getting a Job*. Cambridge: Mass.

Granovetter, Mark. (1978). Threshold Models of Collective Behavior. *American Journal of Sociology 83* (6): 1420-1443.

Güngör, Nil Demet, and Aysit Tansel. (2006). Brain Drain from Turkey: An Investigation of Students' Return Intentions. *IZA Discussion Paper* No. 2287, Bonn: IZA, September 2006.

Güven, Oğuz. (2007). *Zordur Zorda Gülmek*. Istanbul: Güncel.

Hanioğlu, M. Şükrü. (1995). *The Young Turks in Opposition*. New York, Oxford: Oxford University Press.

Hannerz, Ulf. (1996). *Transnational Connections: Culture, People, Places*. London: Routledge.

Hasselgren, B., and Beach, D.. (1997). Phenomenography: A good-for-nothing brother of phenomenology? Outline of an analysis. *Higher Education Research and Development, 16*, 191- 202.

Haug, Sonja. (2000). *Soziales Kapital und Kettenmigration: Italienische Migranten in Deutschland*. Wiesbaden: Leske und Budrich.

Haug, Sonja. (2004). Soziale Integration durch soziale Einbettung in Familie, Verwandtschafts- und Freundesnetzwerke. *Zeitschrift für Bevölkerungswissenschaft* 29 (2): 163-192.

Haug, Sonja. (2005). Migration Networks and Migration Decision Making. *Workshop: Interdisciplinary Approaches to Migration Theory*. Hamburgisches Welt Wirtschafts-Archiv.

Haupert, Bernhard. (1991). Vom narrativen Interview zur biographischen Typenbildung. In Detlef Garz and Klaus Kraimer. (Eds.), *Qualitativ-empirische Sozialforschung. Konzepte, Methoden, Analysen.* Opladen: Westdeutscher Verlag.

Hayhoe, Ruth, and Jurden Henze. (1984). Chinese Western Scholarly Exchange and the Danger of Dependency. *Comparative Education* 20, 2.

Heidegger, Martin. (1962). (Trans.) *Being and Time.* By John Macquarrie and Edward Robinson. London: SCM Press.

Hess, Barbara, and Lenore Sauer. (2007). *Migration von hoch Qualifizerten und hochrangig Beschaftigten aus Drittstaaten nach Deutschland.* Bundesamt für Migration und Flüchtlinge. Working Paper 9 der Forschungsgruppe des Bundesamtes.

Hume, David. (2000). *An Enquiry concerning Human Understanding.* (Ed.), Tom L. Beauchamp. Oxford: University Press.

Hunger, Uwe. (2003). *Vom Brain Drain zum Brain Gain: Die Auswirkungen der Migration von Hochqualifizierten auf Abgabe- und Aufnahmeländer.* Düsseldorf: Migration und Integration.

Hürriyet Newspaper on December 21, 1998. http://webarsiv.hurriyet.com.tr/1998/12/21/85584.asp [July 7, 2008 visited]

İçduygu, Ahmet. (2000). Socioeconomic Profiles. *Push and pull factors of international migration: country report – Turkey* (Eurostat Working Papers). European Commission, Statistical Office of the European Communities.

İçduygu, Ahmet. (2002). *International Migration and Turkey, 2002: the country Report for Turkey for the continuous Reporting System on Migration.* SOPEMI. Paris: OECD.

İçduygu, Ahmet. (2003). *Irregular Migration in Turkey.* Geneva: IOM.

Iqbal, Mahmood. (2000). *The Migration of High-Skilled Workers from Canada to the United States: emprical evidence and economic reasons*. The Center for Comparative Immigration Studies. Working Paper 20. San Diego: University of California.

Iredale, Robyn. (2001). The migration of professionals: theories and typologies. *International Migration* 39, (5):7-26.

Işığıçok, Özlem. (2003). Türkiye'de yaşanan son ekonomik krizlerin sosyo-ekonomik sonuçları: Kriz işsizliği ve beyin göçü. (The socioeconomic results of the last two economic crises in Turkey: Crisis unemployment and brain drain.) 03 June, 2003. www.isguc.org/calhay_beyingocu.php

Jedlicka, Davor. (1978). Opportunities, Information Networks and International Migration Streams. *Social Networks* 1: 211-284.

Joppke, Christian. (1999). *Immigration and the Nation-State: The United States, Germany, and Great Britain.* Oxford: Oxford University Press.

Jorgensen, Penny. (2003). *Report on the Eight International Metropolis Conference*. Vienna, Austria, September, 2003. www.metropolis2003.at

Kadıoğlu, Ayşe. (1996). The Paradox of Turkish Nationalism and the Construction of Official Identity. *Middle Eastern Studies* 32, (2).

Kalkan, Mine. (2002). Women engineers in Turkey: professional modernity in a traditional society. *Frontiers in Education 32* (3):S1C-16.

Kaya, Yahya Kemal. (1974). *İnsan Yetiştirme Düzenimiz: Politika, Eğitim, Kalkınma*. Ankara: Nüve Matbaası.

Kaya, Muammer. (2002). Beyin Göçü. (Brain Migration) Teknoloji Araştırma Merkezi. 27 March, 2002. http://ogu_tekam.sitemynet.com/yazilar2/TEKAM_24.htm.

Khadria, Binod. (1978a). Brain Drain – The Missing Perspective: A Comment. *Journal of Higher Education* 4, (1):101-5.

Khadria, Binod. (1978b). *Types of Brain Migrations: A Welfare Economic Classification with Implications for Brain Drain from LDCs*. Unpublished M. Phil. Dissertation. New Delphi: Jawarharlal Nehru University.

Khadria, Binod. (1999). *The Migration of Knowledge Workers: second-generation effects of India's brain drain*. New Delphi: Sage Publications.

Kim, Dae Sung. (2001). Modernization and Educational Reform in Ataturk's Period. *International Area Review* 4 (2): 97-110.

Kirişçi, Kemal. (2003). Turkey: A Transformation from Emigration to Immigration. *Migration Information Source*. Washington: Migration Policy Institute.

Kluge, Susann. (1999). *Empirisch begründete Typenbildung. Zur Konstruktion von Typen und Typologien in der qualitativen Sozialforschung*. Opladen: Leske und Budrich.

Kodaman, Bayram. (1991). *Abdülhamid Devri Egitim Sistemi*. Ankara: Türk Tarih Kurumu Basimevi.

Kolb, Holger, Susana Murteria, Joao Peixoto and Catarina Sabino. (2004). Recruitment and Migration in the ICT Sector. *IMIS-Beiträge* 2, Special Issue: Organisational Recruitment and Patterns of Migration-Interdependencies in an Integrating Europe.

Krishnadas, K. C.. (2001). U.N. Study: Brain Drain Costs India USD2b A Year. *Electronic Engineering Times* 1176: 24.

Kritz, Mary M., and Hania Zlotnik. (1992). Global Interactions: Migration Systems, Processes, and Policies. In Kritz, Mary M., Lin Lean Lim and Hania Zilotnik. (Eds.), *International Migration Systems: A Global Apprach*. Oxford: Clarendon Press.

Kuhn, Thomas. (1996). *The Structure of Scientific Revolutions*. Third Edition. Chicago: The University of Chicago Press.

Kurtuluş, Berrak. (1999). *Amerika Birleşik Devletleri'ne Türk göçü*. İstanbul: Alfa Yayınları.

Lewis, Bernard. (1968). *The Emergence of Modern Turkey*. London and New York: Oxford University Press.

Luhmann, Niklas. (2004/1996). Das Erziehungssystem und die Systeme seiner Umwelt. In Niklas Luhmann. In Dieter Lenzen. (Ed.), *Schriften zur Pädagogik*. Frankfurt a. M.: Suhrkamp Verlag.

Mabogunje, Akin L.. (1970). System Approach to a Theory of Rural-Urban Migration. *Geographical Analysis* 2:1-18.

MacDonald, Euan, and Ryszard Cholewinski. (2007). *The Migrant Workers Convention in Europe: Obstacles to the Ratification of the International Convention on the Protection of the Rights of All Migrant Workers and Members of their Families: EU/EEA Perspectives*. UNESCO Migration Studies Series, Vol.1.

Marton, Ference. (1981) Phenomenography – Describing Conceptions of the World Around Us. *Instructional Science* 10, 177-200.

Marton, Ference. (1986) Phenomenography: A Research Approach to Investigating Different Understandings of Reality. *Journal of Thought* 21, 28- 49.

Massey, Douglas S., Joaquin Arango, Graeme Hugo, Ali Kouaouci, Adela Pellegrino, and J. Edward Taylor. (1993). Theories of International Migration: A review and appraisal. *Population and Development Review* 19:431-66.

Massey, Douglas S.. (1988). Economic Development and International Migration in Comparative Perspective. *Population and Development* 14 (3):383-413.

McKenzie, Davis J.. (2006). Beyond Remittances: The Effects of Migration on Mexican Households. In Özden, Çağlar and Maurice Schiff. (Eds.), *International Migration, Remittances and the Brain Drain*. New York: World Bank and Palgrave Macmillan.

Mead, George Herbert. (1934). *Mind, Self, and Society*. In Charles W. Morris. (Ed.), Chicago: University of Chicago Press, 1934.

Süssmuth, Rita, Klaus J. Bade, Christoph Kannengiesser, Dr. Gerd Landsberg, Heinz Putzhammer, and Gert G. Wagner. *Migration und Integration–Erfahrungen nutzen, Neues wagen*. Jahresgutachten 2004 des Sachverständigenrates für Zuwanderung und Integration. Berlin: Sachverständigenrat für Zuwanderung und Integration, 2004.

Migration News. (2002). 9, 3. http://migration.ucdavis.edu/mn/Archive_MN/mar_2002-08mn.html.

Murthy, Narayana N.R.. (2003). India's experience in developing a vibrant software industry – lessons from Thailand. Speech delivered at the Thailand Science Park. 22.06.2003.

Musgrave, P.W.. (1979/1965). *The Sociology of Education*. London and NY: Methuen, (3rd edition).

Nohl, Arnd-Michael, Karin Schittenhelm, Oliver Schmidtke and Anja Weiss. (2006). Cultural Capital during Migration – A Multi-level Approach to the Emprical Analysis of Labor Market Integration amongst Highly Skilled Migrants. *Forum: Qualitative Social Research* 7, (3). Art. 14.

Nyström, Birgitta. (2005). The Legal Regulation of Employment Agencies and Employee Leasing Companies in Sweden". *Comp. Labor Law and Policy Journal* 23:173-210.

OECD. (2004). Learning for Tomorrow's World: First Results from PISA 2003.

O'Hara, Phillip Anthony. (1999). (Ed.), *Encyclopedia of Political Economy*. London and New York: Routledge.

Oğuzkan, Turhan. (1971). *Yurt dışında Çalışan Doktoralı Türkler: Türkiye'den başka ülkelere yüksek seviyede eleman göçü üzerine bir araştırma (The Migration of Persons with the Doctorate from Turkey to Other Nations.)*. Ankara: ODTÜ Fen ve Edebiyat Fak. Yay..

Oğuzkan, Turhan. (1976). The Scope and Nature of Brain Drain from Turkey In Nermin Abadan-Unat. (Ed.), Turkish *Workers in Europe 1960-1975: A Socio-economic reappraisal.* Leiden: E.J.Brill.

Ong, Aihwa. (1999). *Flexible Citizenship: The Cultural Logics of Transnationality*. Durham and London: Duke University Press.

Ong, Aihwa. (2000). Graduated Sovereignty in South-East Asia. *Theory, Culture and Society* 17, (4):55-75.

Özden, Çağlar. (2005). Educated Migrants: Is There Brain Waste? In Çağlar Özden and Maurice Schiff. (Eds.), *International Migration, Remittances and the Brain Drain*. World Bank Publications, Washington, DC.: The World Bank and Palgrave MacMillan.

Papastergiadis, Nikos. (2000). *The Turbulence of Migration: Globalization, Deterritorialization and Hybridity*. Cambridge: Polity Press.

Piore, Michael J.. (1979). *Birds of Passage: Migrant Labor in Industrial Societies*. Cambridge: Cambridge University Press.

Poros, M. (2001). The Role of Migrant Networks in Linking Local Labor Markets: the Case of Asian Indian Migration to New York and London. *Global Networks* 1, (3):243-59.

Pries, Ludger. (1997). (Ed.), *Transnationale Migration*. Baden-Baden: Nomos.

Pries, Ludger. (1999) (Ed.), *Migration and Transnational social spaces*. Aldershot: Ashgate.

Rao, Lakshmana. (1978), *Brain drain and foreign students: a study of the attitudes and intentions of foreign students in Australia, the USA, Canada, and France*. Queensland: The University of Queensland Press.

Reilly, P. (2001). *Flexibility at Work: Balancing the Interests of Employers and Employee*. Hampshire: Gower Publishing Limited.

Rice, James Mahmud; Robert E. Goodin, Antti Parpo. (2006). The Temporal Welfare State: A Crossnational Comparison. *Journal of Public Policy* 26 (3): 195-228.

Rittersberger-Tılıç, Helga and Sibel Kalaycıoğlu. (1998). The Nation State and the Individual: Alternative Strategies of Consent from Below. *Asian and African Studies* 7, (1): 69-79.

Robins, Kevin. (1997). Interrupting Identities: Turkey/Europe. In Stuart Hall and Paul Du Gay. (Eds.), *Questions of Cultural Identity*. London: Sage Publications.

Rouse, Roger. (1991). Mexican Migration and the Social Space of Postmodernism. *Diaspora* 1:12-4.

Sabour, M'hammed. (1997). The North African Intellectual Diaspora in the Nordic Countries: the Socio-Political Factors of Expatriation. In M. Sabour and K.S. Vikor. (Eds.), *Ethnic Encounter and Cultural Change*. London: Bergen.

Sassen, Saskia. (1998). *Globalization and Its Discontents: Essays on the Mobility of People and Money*. New York: Colombia University Press.

Sassen, Saskia. (2000). New Frontiers Facing Urban Sociology at the Millennium. *British Journal of Sociology* 51, (1):143-59.

Schüren, Peter. (2005). Employee Leasing in Germany: the Hiring out of an Employee as a Temporary Worker. *Comp. Labor Law and Policy Journal* 23:67-80.

Scott, Franklin Daniel. (1968). (Ed.), *World Migration in Modern Times*. Englewood, N.J.: Prentice Hall.

Seidman, I. (1998). *Interviewing as Qualitative Research.* New York: Teachers College Press.

Shaw, Stanford J.. (1991). *The Jews of the Ottoman Empire and the Turkish Republic*. Macmillan, London, and New York University Press.

Shaw, Stanford J.. (1992). *Turkey and the Holocaust: Turkey's Role in Rescuing Turkish and European Jewry from Nazi Persecution, 1933-1945*. Macmillan, London and New York University Press.

Shilling, Chris. (1993). *The Body and Social Theory.* London: Sage.

Shilling, Chris. (1997). "The Underscocialised Conception of the Embodied Agent in Modern Sociology." *Sociology* 31 (4):737-54.

Shilling, Chris, and P. A. Mellor. (1996). "Embodiment, Structuration Theory and Modernity: Mind/Body Dualism and the Repression of Sensuality." *Body and Society* 2, (14):1-15.

Sklair, Leslie. (2002). The Transnational Capitalist Class and Global Politics. Deconstructing the Corporate-State Connection. *International Political Science Review* 23, (2):159-74.

Sodeur, Wolfgang. (1974). *Empirische Verfahren zur Klassifikation*. Stuttgart: Teubner.

Soysal, Yasemin Nuhoğlu. (1994). *Limits of citizenship: Migrants and Postnational Membership in Europe*. Chicago: University of Chicago.

Strauss, Anselm L.. (1970). Discovering New Theory from Previous Theory. In Tamotsu Shibutani. (Ed.), *Human Nature and Collective Behavior: Papers in Honor of Herbert Blumer*. Englewood Cliffs: Prentice Hall.

Strauss, Anselm L.. (1987). *Qualitative Analysis for Social Scientists*. Cambridge and New York: Cambridge University Press.

Strauss, Anselm L.. (1990). *Creating Sociological Awareness*. New Brunswick: Transaction Publication.

Stürmer, Michael. (2000). *The German Empire: 1870–1918*. New York: Random House.

Sunata, Ulaş. (2002). *Not a "Flight" from Home, But 'Potential Brain Drain'*. Ankara: METU.

Tansel, Aysit, and Nil Demet Güngör. (2003). ‚Brain Drain' from Turkey: Survey Evidence of Student Non-Return. *Career Development International* 8 (2): 52-69.

Tapper, Richard and Nancy Tapper. (1991). Religion, Education and Continuity in a Provincial Town. In Richard Tapper. (Ed.), *Islam in Modern Turkey: Religion, Politics and Literature in a Secular State*. London and New York: I.B. Tauris and Co Ltd., 1991.

Taylor, Frederick W.. (1911). *The Principles of Scientific Management*. New York: Harper Bros..

The International Bank for Reconstruction and Development, The World Bank. (2005). Report No. 32450-TU, *Turkey—Education Sector Study: Sustainable Pathways to an Effective, Equitable, and Efficient Education System for Preschool through Secondary School Education*. Washington: World Bank.

The New York Times. (1911). "For Emancipation of Moslem Grils: War and Stamboul Fires Delay Lyceum Project of Chamber's New President. Admires European System." Constantinpole, November 7, 1911. published on November 19, 1911.

The World Bank, (2005). How Much Does Turkey Spend on Education? Development of National Education Accounts to Measure and Evaluate Education Expenditures.

Tilly, Charles, Brown, Harald. (1967). On Uprooting, Kinship, and the Auspices of Migration. *International Journal of Comparative Sociology* 8:139-164.

TNCE. (1961). *The Report of the Turkish National Commission on Education*. Istanbul: American Board Publication Department, 1961.

UK Home Office, Immigration and Nationality Directorate. (2004). *Country Report*. October 2004.

UN Report, Report of the Secretary General of the United Nations. (1968). "Outflows of Trained Personnel from Developing Countries." General Assembly Document No. A/7294. November, 1968.

UNESCO. (2006). *Global Education Digest 2006: Comparing Education Statistics Across the World*. UNESCO Institute for Statistics, Montreal, Quebec, Canada.

Üstel, Füsun. (2004). *"Makbul Vatandaş"ın Peşinde: II. Meşrutiyet'ten Bugüne Türkiye'de Vatandaş Eğitimi*. Istanbul: İletişim Yayınları.

Uysal, Şefik. (1973). *Yurt Dışında Yetişen İhtisas Gücü: 1416 Sayılı Kanunun Resmi Öğrencilerle İlgili Uygulamasına Ait Bir Araştırma* (High-Level Manpower Trained Abroad: A Study of Public Law No. 1416 as Applied to Government-Sponsored Students). Ankara, TUBITAK.

Vaknin, Sam. (2002). Analysis: Migration and Brain Drain-1. Skopje: United Press International. http://samvak.tripod.com /pp118.html.

Venema, Mathias. (2004). *Green Card für ausländische IT-Fachkräfte. Forschungsbericht im Auftrag des Bundesministeriums für Wirtschaft und Arbeit*. Offenbach: Marplan.

Vertovec, Steven. (1999). Conceiving and Researching Transnationalism. *Ethnic and Racial Studies* 22:447-77.

Vertovec, Steven. (2002). Transnational Networks and Skilled Labour Migration. *WPTC-02-02*, 2002.

Volkan, Vamik D., and Norman Itzkowitz. (1994). *Turks and Greeks: Neighbours in Conflict*. Cambridgeshire: Eothen Press.

Wallace, C. (2003). *Work Flexibility in Eight European Countries: A Cross-National Comparison*. Sociological Series 60. Vienna: Institute for Advanced Studies.

Weber, Max. (1904/05). *Die protestantische Ethik und der „Geist" des Kapitalismus*.

Weber, Max. (1972). *Wirtschaft und Gesellschaft. Grundriß der verstehenden Soziologie*. revised by Johannes Winckelmann. Tübingen: Mohr, 1921.

Weber, Max. (2003/1904). *The Protestant Ethic and the Spirit of Capitalism*. Trans. by Talcott Parsons. Courier Dover Publications.

Weiss, Anja. (2006). Comparative Research on Highly Skilled Migrants: Can Qualitative Interviews Be Used in order to Reconstruct a Class Position? *Forum: Qualitative Social Research* 7 (3), Art.2.

Yalçınkaya, Alper. (1999). *Training the Saviours: Educational Transformation and Elitism in the Ottoman Empire 1876-1918*. Unpublished Master thesis. Ankara: METU, December 1999.

Yıldız, Ahmet. (2001). *"Ne Mutlu Türküm Diyebilene": Türk Ulusal Kimliğinin Etno-Seküler Sınırları (1919-1938)*. Istanbul: İletişim Yayınları.

Zengin-Arslan, Berna. (2002). Women in Engineering Education in Turkey: Understanding the Gendered Distribution. *International Journal of Engineering Education* 18, (4):400-408.

Zilotnik, Hania. (1992). Empirical Identification of International Migration Systems. In Kritz, Mary M., Lin Lean Lim and

Hania Zilotnik. (Eds.), *International Migration Systems: A Global Approach*. Oxford: Clarendon Press.

Zimmermann, Klaus F., and Thomas K. Bauer. (1999). Assessment of Possible Migration Pressure and its Labour Market Impact Following EU Enlargement to Central and Estern Europe. *IZA Research Report*. No. 3.

Zürcher, Erik-Jan. (1984). *The Unionist Factor. The Role of the Committee of Union and Progress in the Turkish National Movement (1905-1926)*. Leiden : Brill.

Zürcher, Erik-Jan. (1993). *Turkey: a Modern History*. London: I.B. Tauris.

Zweig, David. (1997). To Return and Not to Return? Politics vs. Economics in China's Brain Drain. *Studies in Comparative International Development* 32: 92-126.